A Wild and Precious Life

A Wild and Precious Life

A MEMOIR

Edie Windsor

with Joshua Lyon

St. Martin's Press
New York

*This book is dedicated to my mother, Cele, for teaching
her children that they could do no wrong;*

To my glorious Thea and our love that changed history;

To my beautiful Judith for a second gift of love and joy;

*And to LGBTQ+ people everywhere for your courage, strength,
and endless inspiration.*

Don't postpone joy!

Edith S. Windsor (Edee)

Preface

Edie Windsor and I met for the first time when she was interviewing different writers to help her craft a memoir. It happened to be the eighth anniversary of the day I'd met my husband, so I went in with the attitude that even if I didn't get hired, I was lucky to get a chance to thank the woman who made our marriage possible, in person, on such an important day in our personal history; a cool little footnote to add to our story.

She took appointments in her apartment at 2 Fifth Avenue, just above the arch at Washington Square Park. When I got off the elevator on her floor, she was already striding toward me down the hallway, beaming with arms outstretched, her door open behind her. The light spilling out created a sort of background halo effect, and with her body-hugging black suit, silver nails, bright pink lipstick, and perfectly styled blond hair, I felt for a moment that I'd fallen into the opening number of an old Hollywood musical and that she was about to break out in song.

Instead, she placed her hands on my cheeks, gave me a kiss, and began talking.

When I left three and a half hours later, I walked down to the park and sat on a bench, more than a little dazed. It was early springtime and warm, the sun was shining, and my mind was racing with ideas about how to best help tell her story.

I'd known the CliffsNotes going in—her Supreme Court case that overturned Section Three of the Defense of Marriage Act, a forty-four-year love affair and how the second half of that relationship had been spent helping care for her partner, Thea, who'd been diagnosed with MS. In fact, I'd heard the narrative so many times that before our meeting I wasn't even sure I wanted to rewrite something that I thought had already been heard a thousand times.

But the stories she told . . . they were full of family intrigue, wild sex, a jungle rescue, and heartbreak, all set against huge cornerstones in American history. I was overjoyed when I learned she chose me to work with her, and I spent the next several months collecting hours and hours of audio and filling notebooks, poring over old slides and boxes of love letters.

One of the first lessons Edie unintentionally taught me was to check an ageist stereotype I hadn't realized I had. During our first official interview, I started off with a question, and her answer was about a completely different subject. Senility, I thought nervously. She was eighty-seven at the time, hard of hearing, and starting to forget words, much to her fury. "Goddamn it to hell," she'd swear. "I should have started this fucking thing years ago."

I realized that while her answer didn't initially reflect my question, it was because she wanted to provide context first, and twenty minutes later, she'd loop back to the subject at hand, her answer so much richer for it. She'd also given me thirty new questions to ask based on everything else she'd spoken about. This was a woman with so much history and such a deep memory that there was no simple answer to anything. She might not have been readily able to conjure up words like website or annulment, but she could recall with perfect clarity conversations that had taken place in 1949.

Once I put together an initial outline and some chapters for her, I also discovered she was both a phenomenal and intimidating editor, with an eagle eye for detail. Horse manure, she wrote and underlined in one margin, when I'd accidentally transposed the name of a '70s disco song with a '60s mambo. In another instance, she'd told me about a dinner party she attended where she smoked pot for the first time and how it had radically intensified the flavor of everything she ate. She couldn't remember precisely what the meal was, though, and as is standard when ghostwriting a memoir, I used creative license to make it Indian food, thinking that the spices would have been especially wild for someone who'd never gotten stoned before.

"Nobody in the Hamptons was making Indian food back then," she said when I turned the pages in, crossing everything out. After digging through Thea's old cookbook collection, I realized that of course everyone was obsessed with French cuisine at the time. This had been the era of Julia Child, and when I reminded her of this, the memory snapped back in place.

That's how we worked, and after every session, she'd grasp my cheeks in her hands, kiss me, and say, "You and me, we're good." When we sold the partially completed book in August of 2017, we planned to spend the fall embedded in her apartment and her house in Southampton to finish. We had an interview scheduled for just after Labor Day, but she canceled because she'd gotten ill and had to be hospitalized. Since she already knew her discharge date, we rescheduled for the following week. She died on the twelfth of September.

Our aim had always been for me to interview friends and members of her family to help fill in holes or jar more memories. "They'll know the details," she'd tell me, and I had a running list of everyone she wanted me to speak to. In the wake of her death, though, I didn't know how to proceed. Edie was so particular, I felt there was no way I could continue writing in her voice without her there to sign off. Since we'd gotten so far in the process, her spouse and closest friends insisted she would have wanted me to finish it. I wanted to keep working on the book as well, but it was a paralyzing prospect.

As it turned out, she had left me a gift. I knew she had hundreds of files that we hadn't looked at yet. "We'll get to those," she'd tell me. "There's all sorts of good stuff we can use." Once the shock of losing her began to settle, I started to sort through them. I found individual files on all of her family members and friends, filled with letters and photographs. There were stories she'd written for a creative nonfiction class she took in the early 2000s, old term papers from the 1960s with her musings on analysis, stacks of dreams she'd written down, family member obituaries, and *meticulously detailed day calendars that dated back to 1953, which included everything from playbills of Broadway shows she'd seen to lists of specific pieces of furniture she'd bought and how much they cost. I could now accurately trace her every move through life down to the exact address and had all the tiny details that bring a story to life.*

I began interviewing many of her surviving confidants and people who'd known her at different stages. I traveled to Philadelphia to wander the neighborhoods where she'd grown up, visiting the former sites of her favorite haunts. I spent months hanging out with octogenarian lesbians more than my own friends, and I'm a better person for it.

Despite the wealth of information at my disposal, there were still many stories that I didn't feel right telling in her voice. Plus I liked the idea of having the people who loved her get a chance to provide their own memories of her. I began experimenting with making the book something of a memoir / biography hybrid and ended up with what you're holding in your hands now.

If you're looking to read about Edie's Supreme Court case, put this down and instead get the book written by Edie's lawyer, Roberta Kaplan, with Lisa Dickey, Then Comes Marriage: United States v. Windsor and the Defeat of DOMA. *They ingeniously took all the intricate details of a legal court case and turned that experience into a page-turner for posterity.*

This book, however, is a more intimate look at Edie's life. She once said that she wanted it to show "warts and all." There are no warts, though, just the messy and complicated stuff that comes with anyone's existence—the search for identity, a longing for community, mistakes in love, and navigating a world that wants to hold you back—all relatable experiences that will resonate with anyone, regardless of how they identify. While being white, feminine, and beautiful certainly afforded her privileges many closeted gay people didn't have access to in the 1950s and '60s, it was her brain and her heart that made her an indelible figure. She used both to build a career and life that provided her with economic stability, because prior to meeting Thea, she had nothing to fall back on. (Thea herself never depended on her family's wealth and instead worked hard to become a celebrated clinical psychologist.) Edie went on to devote her time and energy to helping those not as fortunate, both financially and by vocally championing equal rights for all.

What follows is taken from Edie's words, files, and direct recollections, as well as many stories from those closest to her. I've filled in timeline details where necessary, changed some names and physical characteristics both per her request and to protect certain identities, and added historical context in places to illustrate how the gay rights movement was evolving at each stage in her life.

No one book can ever sum up a person's entirety, and for every memory and story here, there are countless others that didn't make it to the page. I doubt this will be the only book about Edie Windsor. In fact, I'm hoping it isn't.

—Joshua Lyon

One

In 1932, a polio epidemic swept through Philadelphia, with 728 reported cases that resulted in eighty-four deaths. The virus found its way inside me, and my older brother, Blackie, caught it soon after. We were hospitalized for weeks in an infectious disease ward, and despite rules that strictly forbade parental presence, our mother stayed with us every single night. I'm not sure how she convinced the nurses to let her, but I know she was there.

I was three years old, and this is my earliest memory. Stuck behind the metal bars of an industrial crib, acutely aware of the fear in the air, with my mother's constant fretting and doctors hurrying by our ward's open door, grim looks on their faces.

None of this bothered me one bit.

I turned the parade of doctors into a game. I'd stand in my bed, steadied by the rails, and wave at each white coat in an attempt to see how many I could get to wave back. My track record was strong.

My mother's name was Celia, but everyone called her Cele, pronounced like the animal. She slept on a small cot by our hospital beds, and our father would relieve her every other day so she could return home to freshen up. She'd be back within a matter of hours.

This level of devotion to her children continued throughout her life. She refused to speak much about her past, but as I grew older, I gathered bits and pieces of it together through stories told by my aunts and learned that she'd accepted the responsibility of ensuring the future of her entire family at a very a young age.

Born in Korostyshiv, a Jewish slum roughly seventy miles west of Kiev, she immigrated alone to Philadelphia in 1907, when she was just thirteen. Her older brother had already left for America several years earlier to try to establish a new life, but he hadn't succeeded in building a foundation that could support the rest of the family.

Cele was considered the smartest and most beautiful of her four sisters, and my grandparents decided she had the best chance of finding a husband in America. The financial stability of a good marriage would pave the way for the rest of the family to join her and leave poverty behind—a heavy responsibility for anyone, much more so for a girl barely a teenager.

My grandfather took her to Lisbon and booked passage on a ship in the lowest class. She made herself useful among the other Jews journeying to America by caring for their young children, but she began to worry after some of the passengers learned just how young she was.

"They'll turn you away," she was told. "You have to be sixteen to get into the country alone unless there's a special circumstance, like your whole family has been killed."

When the boat arrived and Cele exited the plank, she spotted her older brother through the crowd, waiting from behind a large gate, jumping and waving.

"Welcome! Welcome!" he shouted. "How is the family?"

"Dead!" she yelled as loud as she could, making sure everyone could hear. "They're all dead!"

By the time she made it through processing and got to the other side of the gate, her brother was weeping inconsolably, and he grabbed Cele, hugging her tightly.

"Everyone's fine," she whispered. "But keep it up."

Cele didn't find a husband right away, but she and her brother got settled enough with new jobs and the rental of a small one-bedroom flat that they were able to send for the rest of their sisters and my grandmother. The six of them lived squished into an apartment in South Philadelphia, an area deeply concentrated with other Jewish immigrants. My mother and aunts found part-time jobs while attending an all-girls high school and wore whatever hand-me-down clothes they could scrounge from charities, including boys' coats in the winter.

Teased relentlessly in the streets, taunted by calls of "greenies," a catch-all slur for anyone new to the county, they kept their heads down and worked hard, and each graduated and found jobs as secretaries or in child-care.

Cele eventually met and fell in love with a man named Jack Schlain, who had a younger brother who was sweet on Cele's youngest sister, my aunt Naomi. The two brothers married the two sisters, and our already large family quickly began to multiply and expand, as my other aunts married as well and everyone began having children.

In my immediate family, my sister, Delphina (she was quickly nicknamed Dolly), eleven years my senior, came first. She was feminine from the start, known for her beauty and love of fashion. Social and outgoing, she always had a close circle of girlfriends.

Dolly was followed by my beloved brother and sometimes tormenter, Edmond, who we all called Blackie due to his inky hair and dark eyes that sparkled like onyx. That trickster gleam perfectly matched his personality: independent, outspoken, and utterly charming. Four years later, I came along.

I was an accident. Later in life, I used this phrase while talking to a psychiatrist, who was quick to point out that even if I were, I must have been a welcome one because it meant my parents were still making love after being together for so long. I thought this was a very good point—and an important lesson. If they hadn't kept things hot, I might never have existed.

Blackie and I were both released from the polio ward unscathed, with no lasting effects except for the massive hospital bills that hit my family. My father had to borrow a lot of money from some cousins, and to help pay off the debt, he began working for them selling wholesale stationery and toys to department stores.

We lived on top of a small store that my mother operated on the busy corner of Fifty-first and Baltimore Avenue, close to the trolley tracks. We had a soda and ice cream counter and loads of candy, and we were the only members of our entire extended family with a telephone. My sister and brother and I were constantly running from house to house to deliver messages or fetch someone who had a call. A bell over the front door rang out anytime someone entered, and if it was only a family member there to use the phone, he or she would shout "Never mind!" to let Cele know that a paying customer hadn't walked in.

Between having a father with constant access to the latest toys before they hit the shelves and a mother who ran a sweets shop, I was in child heaven. The store was my playground. A boy from my kindergarten class visited one day with his mother, and he scrambled up on a stool and insisted I be the one to pour his drink from behind the counter. I had to use a stepstool to reach the syrup pumps. My cousins would come by and invent their own soda flavors, like cherry-vanilla root beer.

Dolly and Blackie were both responsible for watching over me, but Blackie more so when it came to keeping me entertained because we were closer in age. I have him to thank for my love of movies, since his method of childcare was to drag me along with him to either of our two neighborhood theaters.

They were close to our house: three blocks away was the Sherwood, with a large screen housed inside a gothic building. A few blocks beyond that was the Ambassador Theatre, which had an enormous light-up marquee and could seat up to one thousand people. When I began accompanying him to the movies while I was in first grade, he was mortified at the thought of anyone seeing him walk down the street alone with a little girl. Many of our neighbors weren't particularly fond of Jews; he had a hard enough time getting anywhere on his own without being teased for being a sissy babysitter. He'd force me to run ahead of him so no one would suspect we were together. Just before I'd reach each curb and the stream of oncoming traffic, he'd shout "Heel!"

Initially, I loved the game and would pretend I was his puppy. It didn't take long, though, for me to realize he was literally treating me like a dog, so I put a firm end to it and instead walked three steps behind him to keep him happy.

Weekend matinees were double features with cartoons, a serial, and newsreels. Blackie loved the twenty-minute adventures of *The Lost Jungle* and *Flash Gordon*. I was mesmerized by Walt Disney's Silly Symphonies like *The Goddess of Spring,* the story of beautiful, floppy-armed Persephone, who's kidnapped by Hades to be his bride and dragged to his underworld lair, causing ice to spread across the land. She's only allowed to return to the world above if she agrees to spend half the year back in hell with him for eternity.

It was the feature-length musicals that imprinted on me the deepest and kicked off a lifelong love of musicals and theater. I was so enthralled with Shirley Temple in films like *Poor Little Rich Girl* and *Captain January* that I thought nothing of bringing my harmonica to the theater and playing along with her songs. It never occurred to me that others might not want to hear it, and after several evictions from the Ambassador, I was banned for a week. Blackie worked around this by making me kneel down and shuffle through the door ahead of him, below the sight line of the woman in the windowed box office.

I earned a tiny allowance from helping out around the store and spent it all on going to the movies. If I ran out of coins, I'd swipe pennies off the stacks of newspapers that lined the little stands around our neighborhood, wrap them in silver foil from inside my father's cigarette boxes, and try to pass the counterfeits off as dimes. My con never worked, and an exasperated Blackie would avoid eye contact with the fed-up ticket taker as he paid my way in.

Because I was constantly surrounded by so many treats, it was lost on me that our family was barely scraping by. A seemingly never-ending stream of dolls from my father's work and unlimited sweets from the store made effective blinders. Little clues escaped me, like having to watch over the cash register one Thanksgiving with Dolly, waiting until it filled up with enough money so that we could run down the street to buy a pot that our mother needed to finish cooking the holiday dinner.

We lost the store the summer before I was supposed to enter the fourth grade. Taxes were owed that were too steep to cover, and the business was sold, along with the building it was housed in—our home.

Despite the fact that we were nonpracticing Jews, it was extremely important to Cele that we move to a solidly upper-middle-class Jewish enclave on the west side of town. Essentially, Cele wanted us to live somewhere Dolly and I could find good husbands. Marriage was crucial to her. Just like she had been taught, she thought it was the only chance my sister and I had for future economic security. Being Jewish, however, had everything to do with the culture around family, not God or the Torah. Cele knew Yiddish but didn't speak it very often—mostly with her mother-in-law and sometimes with her sister if they were talking *about* her mother-in-law in the presence of others. She also liked to place her hands on family members' cheeks and say *shayna punim*—"beautiful face."

In the right company, Cele would loudly proclaim that religion was nothing but a bunch of hocus-pocus and told all of us children that if anyone ever asked our religion, we should reply "Atheist."

Deciding where to move resulted in the one and only fight I ever heard my parents have. (Jack had a temper and often yelled at us kids, but he was never allowed to hit any of us—Cele forbade it.) I'd never heard the two of them raise their voices at each other, and Blackie and I were terrified; we huddled in the living room as Cele and Jack screamed in the kitchen. Jack didn't want to spend too much on rent, but Cele insisted on a better neighborhood. Cele won, and I don't know how they managed to do it—I suspect my father borrowed more money from his cousins—but we ended up in a very nice rental house on Sixty-second and Washington Avenue, in the exact area my mother wanted. Not long after, we moved four blocks north to an even better place, on Sixty-second and Christian Street.

Our new neighborhood was made up of block after block of tree-lined streets with three-story, two-family homes, each side a mirror image of the other. The structures all had slight architectural differences, a bay window here or enclosed front porch there, to keep the area from looking dull and too uniform. It was much quieter without the constant din of traffic and the trolley shuttling back and forth, but the sounds of children playing in the street made up for it. I was shy around others my age and preferred to spend my time with Blackie. He still took me to the movies; we rode our bikes together back to the theaters in our old neighborhood.

While we were first getting settled, everyone pitched in to help make money. Dolly and Blackie each had jobs, and my mother found all sorts of little ways to make ends meet while figuring out her next career move. My favorite, and the one I was old enough to help with, came during springtime. Since my mother hadn't been able to get enough people to come to the candy store to support it, she decided to bring candy to the people. Every Easter, she'd make chocolate eggs with a hinged mold that could produce eight at a time. These weren't feather-light little Cadbury eggs— each one was solid and about the size of my two fists pressed together. We'd pipe bright pink and yellow icing onto the surfaces once they cooled and hardened, decorating them with flowers and vines, and then we'd drive to the predominantly Protestant and Catholic neighborhoods and sell them door-to-door. Our eggs were a hit, and we began receiving custom orders—lists of names to add in swirly, candy cursive writing. Eventually, a few stores began to place wholesale orders as well.

I loved the time spent with Cele preparing these confections, the smell of chocolate wafting through the kitchen, and dabbing my pinkie onto the end of the piping bag for a tiny sugar rush.

I could do no wrong in my mother's eyes—none of her children could. I know now that I was spoiled, but it wasn't the material sort of spoiled. The gifts I was showered with and held on to were self-esteem and a belief that I could do anything. I think it could have gone disastrously wrong if I hadn't also been book smart in a way that backed up Cele's constant praise. There's nothing worse than a know-it-all that doesn't really know a thing. She also kept us in place with gentle teasing—anytime we drove by the zoo, she'd yell "Duck!" so the zookeepers wouldn't come after us and lock us in with the rest of the monkeys.

We were in a new school district, and when I'd first enrolled, the administration discovered that I was far more advanced in reading and math than the other children, so I skipped the fourth grade. On the one hand, it made me feel special, but on the other, it meant I was a year younger then everyone in my new classroom, which didn't do much to encourage socializing.

My only real friend was my cousin Sonya, whose nickname was Sunnie. She was only fourteen months younger than I was, but everyone referred to her as Sunnie Baby, because she was extremely asthmatic and therefore raised to be rather timid, discouraged from doing anything too exciting that might trigger an attack.

Every summer, Sunnie's parents rented a small one-bedroom apartment in nearby Atlantic City. Say what you will about the place now, but in the 1930s, it was *the* East Coast vacation destination and well earned its self-appointed nickname of "the World's Playground." I'd go on to discover its hedonism as I grew older, but as a child, it was all innocence and magic. Cousins, aunts, and uncles would come and go from the apartment, and the kids would crash on the floor and take turns sleeping in the bathtub.

Sunnie and I built our share of sandcastles on the beach, and when the sun grew too hot, we'd stake out a cool, shady spot under the boardwalk and spy on the never-ending parade of feet crossing the slats above us, popcorn and saltwater taffy wrappers raining down like parade confetti. At night, we'd stay outside on our own until 9:00 or 10:00 p.m., our skin lit up by the flashing lights of marquees and billboards. We'd watch enviously as teenagers and adults emerged from fancy hotels in evening wear, out for a night of dinner and dancing at any number of jazz clubs.

My parents and siblings didn't join me on these extended summer trips with Sunnie; they were too busy working to pay the rent on our new home. Little by little, my father began making a name selling stationery. At the time, every department store had a stationery department on the ground floor along with the perfume counter, so there was a constant market. Luckily for me, he also maintained his contacts with toy wholesalers and often brought home board games and dolls that had yet to be released.

All of this childhood bliss initially made it easy to block out the start of World War II, after I turned ten. I remember picking up on bits and pieces from newspaper headlines and hushed conversations between my parents and siblings, but it was really nothing more than a sense that something bad was happening to other people somewhere far away.

I had more important things to focus my attention on—my first real friend outside the family, a girl from school named Frances. She'd come to the house and we'd play with dolls or go to the movies, where we'd talk over the newsreels, unable to absorb the horror of marching soldiers and bomb smoke. We were riveted instead by *The Wizard of Oz* and *Babes in Arms,* released within a month of each other in 1939 and starring my new favorite matinee idol, Judy Garland. Her voice and eyes hypnotized me, and they'd stay burned in my mind for days any time I saw her on-screen.

At school, I was doing so well in math class that one of my aunts on my father's side hired me to handle the payroll for her window-washing company. It was a successful enterprise, and I enjoyed the work. She employed over fifty men, but even as a child, I found it easy to keep the books balanced; the numbers easily fell into place for me.

In 1941, Japan bombed Pearl Harbor and America entered the war, but I was too distracted by a much smaller scale of bloodshed to grasp the significance: I got my first period.

I was at school when I felt it happen. Cele was working, so the nurse allowed Frances to take me home to her mother, who walked me though all the necessary steps. Frances had already been menstruating for about a year, so despite the discomfort, I was proud to have finally caught up to her. It meant I was a woman, which meant I'd soon be able to go on dates, a prospect that excited me, but only because it was what was done. It meant I was on the right track in life.

I liked boys, I really did. I found them interesting to look at and fun to be around, and I certainly liked the attention they paid me, but I was much more obsessed with spending time with Frances. It's clear looking back now that I had a crush on her, but I had no understanding of how the deep affection I felt could mean anything but true friendship.

I planned to model my forthcoming dating life after Dolly. She was elegant, obsessed with her hair, and left a trail of the latest perfume in her wake whenever she walked by. She was a student at Temple University by then and could have had any boy, but she only had eyes for one—a handsome, intelligent gentleman named Rick, who came from a nice Jewish family.

Cele approved of the match. Rick was exactly the type of man she thought her daughters should marry. Dashing, ambitious, sociable, and to boot, he was also a big fan of Cele's cooking, particularly her meat cakes, an artery-clogging specialty that was really nothing more than a flattened, fried meatball.

As the war escalated, Rick began spending more and more time at our house, until he eventually moved in, which seemed somewhat scandalous until I realized why—they'd secretly gotten married.

———————◦◦———————

Edie's cousin Sunnie still lives in Philadelphia, in an immaculate apartment in a downtown high-rise just around the corner from Rittenhouse Square. She's eighty-seven years old, and talking about Edie is enough to move her to tears, even when recalling some of their sillier childhood adventures.

"We did devilish things," she says. "I'd threaten people all the time if they did something mean. 'I'm going to get my big cousin after you!'"

She remembers the two of them playing pranks on both sets of parents, like short-sheeting their beds. "She even taught me how to curse," she says. "It was a chant, and it went, 'Highty Tighty, Christ Almighty, Ra Ra Shit!'"

When they were children, Sunnie's mother would host all of her siblings and their families at her house for the Jewish high holidays, but none of the kids had any idea that the occasions held a religious significance, and it seems that the source of the family's ambivalence about their religion stemmed from a collective reaction to their grandfather's faith.

He was the last to arrive in America after his children and wife got set up in Philadelphia, and while they lived in a Jewish neighborhood connected by tradition and heritage, his family members were no longer practicing, which he viewed as a crisis.

Back in Korostyshiv, he had been a very respected man, known in the family as what Sunnie calls a "hereditary rabbi," but it's unclear if that meant he was the actual son of a rabbi or if the word was just used as a title of respect, meaning he was considered to have valuable knowledge on spiritual matters and people sought his counsel. Whichever the case, there's no questioning the devotion he inspired back home—his grandchildren were often told a story of how whenever he was ill, the villagers would carry him in a chair to the synagogue.

When he arrived in Philadelphia and saw that his wife and children weren't properly observing the holidays and hadn't even joined a temple, he took it upon himself to get the family back in order, but they weren't having it. "It was shoved down their throats, and they wanted nothing to do with it," Sunnie says.

Their grandfather attempted to involve himself in the community but found that his former revered status held no value in America. He was eligible to become a mashgiach, someone who supervises food to make sure it's kosher, but it was hands-on work in a slaughterhouse, and he was greatly offended by the job offer. There are vague suggestions from some surviving family members that he began to drink heavily, and the only thing Edie ever said about him was that Cele once told her she felt bad for her mother, because she once admitted to Cele that she had "misread the man I married."

His spiritual leanings did benefit them all in the end, though. Even if there were no religious attachments, strong familial bonds formed because of the tradition of gathering for holidays, and they all remained close.

In the summers, when not in Atlantic City, the extended families would gather on weekends for long days in Philadelphia's Fairmount Park. The mothers supervised enormous picnic spreads and took turns reading serial romances in a single copy of a magazine shared between all. The men played cards, mostly pinochle, while the kids rode bikes and played baseball.

Their regular meeting spot in the park fell in the shadow of the Belmont Mansion, built in 1745 and located on a high plateau with spectacular views of the city. The grand house was once a frequently used stop on the Underground Railroad, but in the 1930s, the home was abandoned and falling into ruin, the pillars on its wraparound porch buckling and threatening to crumble. Today, the house has been restored to all its Palladian architectural glory and operates as a museum dedicated to its historical significance, but when Edie spent time there, the house was locked up tightly to discourage vandals; however, the home's large, empty horse stables were easy to sneak into and investigate.

Sunnie remembers being terrified whenever Edie dragged her along to poke around the ruins, pestering her older cousin with squeaks of "I'm scared!" and "Watch out for ghosts!"

Edie would tell her to be brave, assuring her there were no ghosts there, and besides, there were no such things to begin with. Still, Edie insisted on inspecting every hidden corner and door, unknowingly roaming through a pivotal, but at the time forgotten, location crucial to the dawn of the fight for civil rights in America. More than seventy years later, Sunnie again found herself looking up to her older cousin for her bravery. "Whenever I'd see her on TV or in the papers, I'd tell everyone, 'That's my cousin!' I was so proud of her."

Two

I wish I knew the exact details of why my sister and Rick had to marry in secret, but the reasons are lost to time. I can speculate that perhaps Rick's parents didn't initially approve of the pairing or they thought the kids were too young. All I do know is that my mother was thrilled, and Rick quickly became just as much a part of the family as Blackie, who formed a fast friendship with his new brother-in-law.

With so many of Dolly and Rick's friends cycling in and out of active duty, the neighborhood always seemed to be celebrating a soldier's safe return from the war. Each serviceman would make the rounds to the houses of his friends' parents to pay his regards, and he'd be welcomed with open arms. Families took turns hosting parties and late-night card games, but our place was the central hub. There was always a crowd of young men sitting around the dining room table, the air layered with cigarette smoke, empty beer bottles littering every surface, and laughter loud enough to hear from the street.

Our family nicknamed these boys Rick's Crew, and they were local heroes. Cele always made a fuss over them, cooking up a storm for their visits. One young man brought me a photograph of himself at an air force base, dressed in a smart, fleece-lined bomber jacket, standing and grinning in front of a small fighter plane and pointing to the words *My Edie* painted on the side. I loved that he'd thought of me all the way from . . . well, wherever he'd been. The war still wasn't quite real to me; it all seemed like a grand adventure happening on another world.

The visits from Rick's Crew and the consequent outpouring of community love for the servicemen felt like one big ongoing party, until one of the boys didn't return. I came home from school to find Dolly crying in Rick's arms as he struggled to hold back his own tears. It was only then that the reality of the war sank in for me. It created a sense of urgency to the get-togethers at our house—they became even livelier, more raucous, because there was a growing feeling that whenever the boys got together, it might be for the last time.

The prayers that were being said by students at my school for all of these soldiers got me interested in the idea of God. Since my own family didn't practice, I wanted to see what all the fuss was about because he seemed to mean so much to my peers. When I told Cele I wanted to learn about our religion, she was incensed and tried to talk me out of it, but I stubbornly held fast. She refused to attend temple with me, as did everyone else in the family, but she finally told me I could go to a synagogue located a few blocks away.

I was bored out of my mind after the first ten minutes, but I didn't want to give my family the satisfaction of being right, so I continued to pretend to go every Saturday for the next several weeks, until Blackie was out walking and found me sitting on a park bench, all dressed up in my finest, waiting for the service to be over so I could finally return home.

My body began to develop quickly, and I suddenly started to look more and more like Dolly. I'd always wanted a body like hers, full of curves. I was frustrated with my own flatness, and then seemingly overnight, I developed large breasts. I quickly learned that they hindered direct eye contact with men on the street.

Despite my growth spurt, I straddled the line between girlhood and adolescence. I still liked to play outdoors with Sunnie—we'd secretly dig up vegetables from the victory gardens that both of our families planted to help supplement their food rations, and I developed a taste for cabbage-and-mayonnaise sandwiches. I was mad for Frank Sinatra—the entire country was—and I'd invite Sunnie and Frances over to listen to his records, crooning along with him.

Once I turned thirteen, afternoon playtime with Sunnie and Frances gave way to studying and homework, because the evenings now belonged to boys. From that age on, I was rarely without a suitor, since both Dolly and Cele had been telling me since I was around eleven that once I reached high school, I'd be allowed to date.

Academically, I felt prepared for ninth grade because I'd tested so well that I skipped yet another grade. Blackie had just graduated, and I studied his yearbooks religiously, familiarizing myself with all the teachers. He warned me about one in particular who had hated him for reasons unknown, and on my first day in his class, I realized I'd inherited the man's hatred by default. The teacher was downright nasty to me and would make snide remarks that I'd made a lucky guess when he'd call on me and I got the answer right. After the third time this happened, I called him a son of a bitch under my breath, but he heard me.

"What was that, Miss Schlain?" he asked.

I looked him right in the eyes and thought, *This is for you, Blackie,* before I repeated quite loudly, "I said, you're a son of a bitch."

He called Cele in after school to report my behavior, but she refused to indulge any of his attacks on my character. "If I understand this correctly," she said, "you told my daughter that she had a lucky guess just because she got the answer correct?" Her voice grew louder, and I tried to hide my smile.

"I'd say that you're the one who started this. Are you scared that my daughter is smarter than you?" Her face turned red, and then she really started to yell. "She probably is! She should be the one teaching this class! Come on, Edie, let's go." He left me alone after that, and I got my deservedly earned A at the end of the semester.

Dating in high school soon proved as effortless as schoolwork. My father let it be known that no boy would have a chance of escorting me off our front porch unless he was dressed in a jacket and tie. Which was just fine with me. I had high standards after growing up watching so many dashing leading men in movies.

My own sense of fashion was growing into a personal style, and Dolly often took me shopping with her. She was an ace at sniffing out sales, and since Cele didn't have much of a fashion sense, she was happy to let Dolly take over this portion of my upbringing. Not that I needed much help when it came to clothes. I instinctually knew what types would flatter my body, while still ensuring that I appeared respectable. I wasn't a fan of the loose sweaters and cardigans popular with most girls in my school—I preferred blouses and two-piece suits in neutral colors, tailored to accentuate the chest and hips. I always wore black loafers or saddle shoes with white socks that bunched just so, right above the ankle. Any kind of pattern, plaid in particular (it was all the rage), was far too busy for me. Accessories were usually limited to one standout piece per outfit—a wide belt with a paste jewel buckle, or a single strand of pearls. I believed that when it came to first impressions, one's personality should make the initial impact.

My new appearance didn't go unremarked on in the house. I noticed members of Rick's Crew eyeing me appreciatively, much to the consternation of Blackie. One day, one of them even told him, "Blackie, Edie used to be your little sister. Now you're just her older brother." He didn't much like that, but the attention secretly thrilled me.

I especially liked the shy looks I received from a friend of Blackie's who'd begun showing up regularly to play cards with the crew, a young man named Saul Wiener. He was a full head taller than I was, and that head seemed almost twice the size of a normal man's, but not in an off-putting way. He was solidly built with quarterback shoulders, full lips, and dark eyes that followed me around the room, but never menacingly. He wasn't tongue-tied around me like some of the other members of Rick's Crew, and our conversations were easy and natural—we chatted about the weather, made up jokes, compared what sorts of foods we liked. If there was any real flirting going on, it was innocent and went completely over my head.

I wish the same could be said for all the young men who passed through our door.

I never felt unsafe, but there were times when I'd find myself alone at the dining table with one of the soldiers on leave, and the comments about my new mature looks crossed a line. One evening when Dolly, Rick, and Blackie were all in the kitchen preparing snacks and restocking beers, a friend of theirs asked me outright if I'd lost my virginity yet.

"No, of course not," I said. I refused to look at him and felt my face flush. I wanted to say something smart and snappy, something that would put him in his place, but I didn't know how to put my feelings into words. All I understood was that what he was asking me was very wrong. "Not that it's any of your business" was all I could muster.

"Well," he said, tipping back in his chair and leering at my chest. "You look just as good as your sister does. Maybe better. Come find me after you've had intercourse for the first time. I'd love to take a turn, but I don't want the responsibility of being your first."

Intercourse. It was such a clinical word for something that he made sound so dirty. He might as well have just said *fuck.*

This same man made a more aggressive pass at me several weeks later. I was leaving the house one evening after dark and hadn't noticed him on our front porch. He grabbed my shoulder and tried to turn me toward him. I wrenched away and ran down the street, too frightened and confused by the experience to tell anyone. This same man had once treated me like a little sister; now he felt as though my body belonged to him and he could do anything he wanted with it. I don't know why he assumed I wouldn't tell my father or Blackie, but the fact that I didn't proved he was correct. His power, just by virtue of being male and older, somehow made me feel like I was the one who'd done something wrong.

His actions also threatened to undo the pride I felt in my new body. Rather than being something to celebrate, I became deeply embarrassed about my curves for a time, and my rising hormones were suddenly stunted by the idea that losing my virginity would be an act of hostility against me.

Luckily, the boys I went out with were much safer and far too scared of my father and Blackie to cross any lines, and I soon put my fears to rest. I became a serial dater and a bit of a heartbreaker. My crushes were real, but never too intense. Nobody ever tried anything too serious aside from kissing me good night, and sometimes I was the aggressor. I was curious about sex but remained firmly in the "good girls don't" camp.

I enjoyed dating because I liked the attention, but nothing exciting or romantic ever really happened. Dates themselves followed a script, starting with a boy arriving at the house to meet my parents. I'd wait upstairs for a few minutes, not because I wasn't ready (although that was always the excuse) but because I liked spying on my family's reaction to whomever showed up at the door. My father's was always the same—a firm handshake, a stern command to have me home by curfew, and then he'd leave the room.

Cele would bustle around and offer water and snacks, keeping up a steady stream of chatter, gushing about how handsome my date looked. Like I said, I had high standards. They were *all* handsome. She'd then start up with questions that sounded like small talk, but to anyone familiar with her tactics, it was obvious she was sussing out whether the boy was marriage material.

Queries like "Where do you live?" and "What are your favorite classes?" really meant "Do you come from money?" and "Are you smart enough for my daughter?"

Blackie loved playing the role of the intimidating older brother at first, glowering and staying silent in a corner, a cigarette dangling from his lips, but he'd always soften before we left, and he'd give the boy a good-natured cuff on the shoulder and echo my father's sentiment about getting me home on time.

The nights out were formulaic: a movie, followed by dinner at a fast-food joint. There'd be hot dogs, milk shakes, and gossip about any other kids from our high school that we'd see out together. If my date had a car, we'd park somewhere near Cobbs Creek, not far from my home and surrounded by dark woods, the closest thing we had to Lover's Lane. Kissing was fine, and I'd allow a hand over the bra if I really liked him, but nothing more.

Not that I wasn't interested. Being touched felt good, but it was suddenly becoming overshadowed by an almost scholarly detachment. *Someone is feeling me up. How wonderful and strange that feels.* I think that during all those early fumbles in the front seats of cars, I enjoyed being wanted more than the actual touching.

I wasn't aware of any sexual desire for women yet. Not even dreams at night offered me that truth. Exploring my body was about personal pleasure, discovering what felt good to me, rather than fantasies of another person. I knew that I much preferred the company of female friends, particularly Frances, whom I remained close with all through high school, but I understood my intense feelings about her—my need to have her at my side whenever possible—to mean that I adored her as my best friend. The thought of kissing or touching her never entered my mind; it was an unknowable possibility. The idea that anything physically intimate with a girl could happen simply did not exist.

It's strange to think of now and difficult to reason how I remained so ignorant. The easy excuse is to blame it on the time period and my relatively sheltered life, but I was intuitively smart about so many other things that I find it odd this one facet of my core eluded me.

One night after returning from a date, I found Blackie, Saul, and several other members of Rick's Crew staring at me as I entered the front door. Blackie let out a whoop and slapped his hands on his thighs, and I noticed Saul smiling at me. The rest of the men began grumbling and throwing coins into a pile onto the table.

"What's going on?" I asked.

"We saw the car pull up," Blackie said, reaching out and gathering the money toward him. "These clowns all thought you were going to stand out there on the porch and neck. I told them that you're better than that and that you'd come inside immediately. And I was right."

"Then it's actually my win," I fumed. "That money should be mine." I glared at the rest of the men before storming up the stairs.

I smiled, though, when I heard Saul call out after me.

"I bet on you, too, Edie!"

My mother's wish for me to find a Rick of my own—someone respectable to marry—came true with Benjamin. At eighteen, he was three years older than I was, a member of a very wealthy and prominent family, and had a smile as wide and wicked as Sinatra's, which is what drew me to him in the first place.

When he asked me to go out with him, I promptly broke things off with the poor boy I'd been currently seeing, and Ben and I became a serious item. He took me out several nights a week and elevated the entire dating experience. Instead of casual diners, he took me to real restaurants, and we went to the theater much more often than the movies.

As his senior year drew to a close, he proposed. I laughed at first—I thought he was teasing, but then I saw the hurt in his eyes. I told him I'd consider it, though I had no intention of doing any such thing. I knew I was far too young to settle for anyone, regardless of what a catch he was.

Cele felt very differently. We were in the kitchen when I mentioned offhandedly that he'd asked me to marry him, and from the way she screamed, you'd have thought I'd won the lottery. Which, I suppose, in her mind she thought I had, and she couldn't understand why I hadn't said yes immediately. With Dolly married and newly pregnant, Cele's mission to set up respectable and secure lives for her daughters was nearly complete.

"I have two more years left of high school!" I protested. "It's absurd he even asked!"

"What's absurd is that you aren't out shopping for a ring with him right now."

I thought she was joking, but one look at her face told me she was dead serious and expecting a response.

"That's not going to happen," I said.

Blackie supported me, and between the two of us, we got her to back down. Benjamin broke up with me shortly after.

The same year that I received my first marriage proposal, I added a new accessory to my look, one that would take decades to let go of—cigarettes.

Blackie was the one who taught me how to smoke. It was inevitable, really. Everyone around me did. My indoctrination happened late one night after the last of Rick's Crew had left. Dolly and Rick had announced earlier that evening that they were moving to an air force base in Texas so that Rick could train to become a bombardier. I was upset by the news and fiddling with an empty pack of Chesterfields that one of the fellows had left behind, and I discovered one last stick tucked away inside a crease. As I pulled it out and inspected it, I heard a scratching sound and caught a whiff of sulfur in the air as Blackie extended his arm, his dark eyes barely visible above and beyond the flame.

I wasn't nervous. I'd seen it done thousands of times before, both in my house and on movie screens. My first inhale was small, but I still coughed, and Blackie laughed. I tried again and coughed a whole lot more.

"Hold it in," Blackie instructed. "Force yourself to not let it out, no matter how much it hurts." I obeyed on the third inhale and managed to keep the smoke in my lungs for close to five seconds before it all came sputtering out, but a delicious little buzz ran through me. I finished exhaling and tapped my ash into the blue glass, scalloped-edge ashtray Blackie scooted across the table toward me with his knuckles.

"I suppose I'm a smoker now," I said. I bent my elbow and wrist back, holding the cigarette above my shoulder and parallel to my ear, trying to make my voice low and gravelly like the film vixens we both adored.

"Welcome to the club," Blackie replied.

I hid my new habit from everyone at first, except Blackie. Nice kids didn't smoke in our high school, and I ran with the smart set. I was still a whiz at math, and the subject only seemed to be getting easier for me. I was one of the few girls in the honors class, but I was friendlier with boys anyway. I think all of them would have been shocked to know that in between classes I was sneaking out back behind the building to smoke. I kept my cigarettes hidden away inside a wooden pencil box with a tiny chalkboard on the lid. If anyone in class was struggling with a particularly tough math problem that I'd already solved, I'd scribble the answer on top and angle it just so, where it was visible to anyone who needed it.

By my junior year, Rick, Dolly, and their son, Jeremy (continuing our family tradition of nicknames, we called him Rem), were all living on the base in Texas. I missed them terribly, so it was a great shock when Blackie decided to enlist and join them.

"It's not like I'm doing much else hanging around here," he said when I asked why he was leaving me. Which was true. Dolly and Rick had both graduated from college, but Blackie didn't seem to have much interest in anything aside from playing cards, dating, and going to the movies. But like me, he was also a voracious reader. He'd dive into anything he could get his hands on, and his bedroom was stacked with everything from trashy pulp paperbacks to philosophy. He sought adventures in those pages, and joining the military must have seemed an easy way to find them in real life.

With my siblings and nephew gone, the house was eerily silent. Cele purchased a small secondhand piano, and I started lessons, both to pass the time and to help add some much-needed sounds to the rooms. Saul and the rest of Rick's Crew stopped coming by. My father was working harder than ever and often took overnight business trips to nearby cities. Cele was busy managing a small general goods store downtown, so we'd miss each other after school let out, but she'd wait up at night to hear about my dates, and we all anxiously awaited phone calls or letters from Rick, Dolly, and Blackie.

It turned out that they weren't having an easy time fitting in down in Texas. They didn't quite blend in with the state's proud natives. As Blackie put it in one letter, "I think you should know that there's a rumor floating around Houston to the effect that Texas, with the help of the Continental United States, is winning the war."

They also experienced anti-Semitism, something none of us had dealt with since we'd lived in our old neighborhood as kids.

Dolly called one day, terribly upset. She'd taken to watching her neighbor's child during the day along with Rem, and one afternoon when the mother arrived to pick her kid up, she made an off-color remark about Jews.

"But I'm Jewish," Dolly told her.

"No, you're not," the woman scoffed. "I know what Jews look like." She then proceeded to make little horn motions with her fingers above her head. Dolly was too shocked to say anything.

The prejudice Rick experienced was much more terrifying. He'd be up in a small airplane and get taunted by the pilots, their verbal slurs evolving into sudden drops in altitude designed to scare him.

As hard as it was to hear about this happening, we were still grateful that they were stationed on a base safely inside the United States and not off at war. News of more deaths of the young men that made up Rick's Crew arrived as the months wore on, and their passing made me sad, but none ever stopped me in my tracks. The ease with which I was able to shrug off these losses after an initial brief period of mourning can be blamed on the blissful ignorance of youth, the invincibility of being a teenager, even when faced with the loss of local boys and the constant grainy battle footage from the newsreels in movie theaters.

The dire economics of war were everywhere—there were food rations, signs about water conservation, my father's own victory garden. But at home, money was no longer a big worry for us, at least that I was aware of. I didn't witness poverty around me—Philadelphia had an ammunitions plant and a naval base, both of which helped boost local employment. We were comfortable, and it's disconcerting to look back on that feeling of security coupled with the parade of death happening around us.

———◇◇———

Edie was hardly the only American teenager who felt emotionally shielded from World War II, despite the ever-present reminders. This was the period of history that birthed the concept of the American teenager as we now know it. Seventeen magazine launched in 1944 and provided businesses with insight to an untapped market. Adolescent girls were bombarded with advertisements for clothes and makeup. Articles breathlessly informed them of dating tips. Death was everywhere if you went looking for it, but if you were a girl who was young enough to be surrounded by boys not quite old enough for the draft, life for white, middle-class, teenage America was all about having the most fun in the present while perfecting the skills to cement the right future.

Mainstream culture frothed over the same message Cele had been giving Dolly and Edie all along—land the right man, and you'll have it made.

It's safe to say that the older members of Edie's family were having a more difficult time processing the war. It was about the murder of their people, and it touched their lives on a much deeper level than what Edie experienced or at least remembers experiencing. Dolly's firstborn son, Rem, can recall Cele passionately protesting in later years when George Lincoln Rockwell, the leader of the American Nazi Party, came to Philadelphia to speak. "She really wanted a piece of him," he says.

And on the other side of the world, the war had a profound effect on a young Jewish girl named Thea Spyer, whose father packed her up in the night and fled Amsterdam just before the Nazis invaded the Netherlands.

Three

Cele continued to dip in and out of various small business ventures, and so it had fallen to Dolly to take care of basic life tasks for me like driving lessons and making sure I got to doctor appointments on time. By the time my sister left with Rick for Texas, I was certainly old enough to handle those responsibilities for myself, but for whatever reason, it somehow failed to occur to me that to get accepted into college, I needed to *apply* to college and file a lot of paperwork well in advance of graduation. By the time my friends began getting accepted to their top choices of universities, I'd missed all the application deadlines.

However, by then, the war had been over for most of the school year. My siblings returned home to Philadelphia, as did thousands of soldiers who'd made it back alive, including Saul. The city was suddenly packed with people who needed either a job or schooling. The signing of the GI Bill by President Roosevelt provided funds for vets to get an education, and a large market for higher learning suddenly opened up, since most colleges weren't equipped to handle the sudden influx of new prospective students.

Luckily for me, the unimaginatively titled Pennsylvania Area College opened a branch called Rittenhouse College that held courses in the evenings and accepted my very late application for admittance. The down-side was that it was located at my high school, so the excitement about entering a new phase of my life felt a bit diluted. Although I was pleased with how my senior yearbook photo turned out: Next to a list of my various academic accomplishments and social activities, the editors had written, "In her spare time she does Trig problems and breaks hearts."

Both activities would continue for several decades.

The summer before college, I remained committed to dating boys, but my enthusiasm waned considerably. I chalked it up to the fact that Dolly, Rick, Blackie, and Rem were living with us again, and while things didn't quite reach the levels of boisterousness that we'd had when Rick's Crew was coming around, the house was once more full of life. I had plenty to distract me from going out.

When September rolled around, I still wasn't particularly thrilled about returning to school. Since I'd skipped two grades, I'd be younger than everyone else, only seventeen, and nothing seemed to be changing—I was still living at home and going back to the same building where I'd spent the past four years, only this time in the evening instead of morning. There would be no dorm room, no roommate to befriend or loathe, no quad filled with new people to meet. Just the same old bricks and the same old lockers, and I didn't even have access to those anymore.

To keep myself busy and active, I signed up for the school paper as well as a physical education course in tennis. I'd never been interested in sports, but I knew the exercise would be good for me and would put me in a social atmosphere where I could meet new people outside the class-room. I appreciated that it was an activity that allowed me to choose my own outfit, so long as it included a short skirt. It also meant that for one hour each day, I couldn't turn my head in any direction without seeing a pair of bare female legs.

I'd like to say that's the reason I was so awful at tennis; that I was simply distracted by how strangely interested I suddenly was in all those prancing limbs around me. That was probably a part of it, but really, I was just bad at the sport.

We practiced on the roof in the late afternoon, after all the high school extracurricular activities let out. The area was lined with a tall, curved chain-link fence around the perimeter to keep errant balls from flying over the side. Good thing, considering how many of mine whizzed past their intended target and bounced off the barrier; I can't imagine how many people below I would have clocked on the head had it not been there.

There was another girl in class just as bad as I was. Her name was Renee (pronounced *Ree-nee*) Kaplan, and she was always stationed right next to me. She was a tall, beautiful brunette, and we were constantly in each other's way. I'd dive to hit a ball but end up colliding directly into her side, or she'd overestimate the breadth of her serve and knock me on the elbow with her racket.

Instead of getting angry with each other, we'd laugh it off, and over those first few weeks, the physical contact between us began to seem more and more intentional. Instead of getting better the more we practiced, we got worse. I found myself missing serves on purpose as an excuse to stumble and cause our arms to forcefully brush against each other. Each brief bit of skin contact filled me with a rush of energy that I'd use to fuel my next collision with her. I knew it couldn't be my imagination that she seemed to be doing the exact thing with me.

As I grew more aware of this real physical attraction, I also started to pay closer attention to my fellow students in the hallways and outside the school. The vets for whom Rittenhouse College mainly existed were easy to spot. They looked older, and many seemed slightly haunted. There were a few men on crutches because one of their legs had been amputated due to a war injury. Many of the female students still wore their Women's Army Corps uniforms.

Among them was a pair of Women's Army Corps vets who were glued at the hip, and they always wore slacks. The two of them fascinated me—it was obvious by their body language that they were a couple, and while I only had the faintest idea at that point what the word *lesbian* meant, I knew that's what they were.

It's difficult to explain how a brain and body can know what it's attracted to sexually but still prevent you from knowing that those feelings help define who you are. My physical attraction to Renee was obvious to me, as was my curiosity about the women in slacks, but it never occurred to me that I might be a lesbian. I intuited that Renee felt the same attraction toward me, but I never thought of her as a lesbian either. That word was so large and impossible to fathom, I only knew it meant a type of person that I was convinced at the time I was not. I was following a path of hormones and curiosity, not looking for an identity. I felt secure with who I was, confident and intelligent, and somehow wise enough to know that if you want something to happen in your life, it's absurd to sit around and wait. You have to make it happen yourself.

With that in mind, one afternoon when Renee knocked me particularly hard on the elbow and flashed her customary apologetic-yet-flirty grin, I leaned in and said under my breath, "Do that again, and I'll kiss you on the mouth."

She looked startled and a little shocked, but after class, she came up to me and asked, "Did you mean it?"

"Yes," I said, feeling impossibly bold.

"Where can we do that?"

It was a very practical question and one I hadn't considered at all. "Your house?" I suggested, knowing that mine was always filled with too many people coming and going. She looked horrified.

"Absolutely not."

We were standing on the school's front lawn by that point, and I saw the two women in slacks walking away from the building. "I have an idea," I said. "Stay here."

I ran up behind them and called out, "Excuse me!"

They turned around in unison and looked me over. The taller and slightly gruffer one answered, "Yes?"

Rather than feeling my confidence waver, I only felt bolder. It was even more obvious up close that there was a connection between these women that went beyond friendship. They even looked alike, with their cropped-short hair and square jawlines.

"I was wondering if you might know of a place where two girls could go to be alone."

Equal looks of horror swept over their faces. The shorter one swiveled her head in all directions to make sure no one had overheard me and then fixed her eyes on me with a near-murderous gaze.

"What do you mean?" she asked.

"I mean that I'd like to spend some time with my friend over there, and I would also like to make sure that we will be left alone. I thought you might be able to help us."

The shorter one was still aghast, but the taller relaxed and smiled; I clearly wasn't trying to expose them. There was an odd look in her eyes, a mix of envy and sadness. "We have a studio a few blocks away," she said. "We could rent it out to you for a few hours in the afternoons."

"Have you lost your mind?" the other muttered, but I could tell which one of them called the shots and knew that I'd found a way for Renee and me to be together.

Over the next several weeks, we explored every inch of each other's bodies. Kissing her was so different from kissing a boy; equal parts soft and firm, and no whiskers tearing at my skin. Timid at first, we grew bolder the more time we spent together. Though I was curious about what life was like for the older female couple whose home we'd taken over, we never had time to poke around the studio because every minute was spent in the bed.

We had our own key and designated hours, and when we were finished, we'd go out to dinner or a movie or simply take long walks. I began to bring her over to my house and introduced her to the family as my new friend. I didn't dare try to sneak in a kiss, though, even when we were in my bedroom with the door shut. I didn't have a curfew, but she still did, and I always made sure to get her home on time.

I can't say that I was in love with Renee. I was fascinated with her—or perhaps I was fascinated with what our bodies could do together, but aside from a deep affection, I think I knew even then that we were temporary.

Her stronger feelings for me were what caused our trysts to end. Renee's mother discovered a diary she'd been keeping, and while she never wrote in explicit detail about what we were doing, there was enough flowery prose to give probable cause.

Rather than accuse us herself, her mother paid a visit to Rittenhouse's dean, who then phoned my house with the intention of summoning my mother and me to his office. Renee, utterly hysterical and sobbing, managed to beat him to the punch and warn me, so I was able to intercept his call, but I still had to bring a guardian with me to see him. I enlisted Dolly, figuring that I might be able to more easily fool her than Cele.

"I have no idea what the meeting is about," I told her. "I think he might just be a bit worried about that friend of mine, Renee. She's been rather down lately."

When we arrived at the dean's office and sat across from him, he was visibly squirming. After a few pleasantries with Dolly, he looked at me, took a deep breath, and said, "Renee Kaplan's mother paid me a visit recently, and she's very concerned about the two of you."

"What on earth for?" I asked, keeping my voice calm.

"She found a diary that alludes to an unnatural relationship between the two of you. Her mother seems to think that the two of you . . ." He paused to clear his throat and looked at the ceiling as he polished his glasses with a small handkerchief. "That the two of you are engaging in homosexual relations."

Dolly looked aghast, and I snapped, "That's absurd. She's a good friend I met at tennis practice." I sat up straight and narrowed my eyes at him. I'd known what was coming but was still shaken inside to hear it said out loud. I also silently cursed Renee for being so careless as to keep a diary about us. "My friendship with her is nothing but platonic. How could I have any idea what sorts of things she writes about me in her diary?"

I cringed at the betrayal but knew I had to keep up the act. Dolly was looking at me strangely.

"Apparently, this is not the first time this has happened with Renee," the dean said.

I tried to hide my surprise. This was new information to me; I'd thought we were each other's firsts. "She must have misunderstood something Renee wrote," I said. "We're close friends and nothing more."

"Her mother has asked me to tell you to stay away from her, and while I appreciate that you've come today, Dolly, I do think we should inform your mother about the situation."

"Call her," I scoffed, ignoring Dolly's petrified look. She'd yet to say a single word and seemed relieved that I'd taken over the situation. "I've done nothing wrong."

His threat held no weight for me. The longer I sat in that office, the more I'd begun to wish that I *had* brought Cele instead of Dolly. I recalled the time she'd berated the teacher I'd called a son of a bitch, and I knew I could use that same fiery defense on my side right about then.

My mother's children could do no wrong, and I regretted not believing enough in that aspect of her personality in the case of this meeting. It might have even been amusing to see how she'd react to the situation, what sorts of insults she'd hurl at the dean, although I knew any satisfaction I'd get out of watching her tear the man down would be fleeting. She'd be fighting in my defense when in fact I was guilty.

"I think we can leave our mother out of this," Dolly said, finally becoming the adult and standing up. "I'll ensure that Edie and Renee stop spending time together, although I'm sure this is nothing more than a misunderstanding. Edie should be focusing on her education anyway, so I'm sure it's all for the best."

He relented, and I kept my cool, despite wanting to kick over my chair and sweep everything off his desk. Dolly and I both lit up cigarettes as soon as we got outside. We marched down the front steps in unison, side by side, near mirror images of each other with our heads held high.

"None of that's true, I presume?" Dolly asked.

"Of course not."

"Good. Then we'll keep Cele out of it."

I was furious, and the more I puffed, the angrier I became. My emotions had nothing to do with being accused of being with a girl or even Dolly's obvious suspicion.

It was that I was being told what to do. Period.

My fling with Renee ended abruptly after that day. She wouldn't make eye contact with me at tennis practice and moved to a different court so that she was no longer next to me.

So that's that, I thought.

I walked to the studio and left the keys on the table with a note, thanking the women for the rental, and I left them an extra week's rent to make up for the short notice. I paused before I left, to try to understand the life that was lived there when it wasn't being used as my illicit crash pad. There was no art on the walls, and the furniture was dull. There was nothing that made it feel like someone's home, much less one belonging to a couple in love. I left feeling much more depressed about that than about the end of my friendship with Renee.

———— ◆◆ ————

The end of World War II was a pivotal moment in gay history, and the couple from the Women's Army Corps who rented out their studio to Edie are likely an example of how the army brought gay people together and created relationships and communities that continued after the war was over.

In his seminal, rigorously detailed book Coming Out Under Fire: The History of Gay Men and Women in World War II, *Allan Bérubé describes how prior to the war, it was the act of sodomy that was the crime that got you court-martialed from the military. Before America entered the war, the U.S. military was rather anemic, but a surge in patriotism sent millions to enlist, which allowed recruiters the freedom to be picky and discriminate on the basis that certain types of people, including gays, made for poor soldiers.*

Different parameters were set up to help weed out gays, everything from observations on physical appearance to a frank question of "Are you a homosexual?" Some doctors and psychiatrists didn't see the harm, though, and let many slip through (out of eighteen million who were examined, fewer than five thousand were officially rejected for being gay). As for women, World War II was the first time they were allowed to serve in official military roles other than nursing, and any masculine traits that were typically assumed as markers of homosexuality were often ignored. Butch leanings were sometimes even considered a good thing when noted in the enlistment process, since it was assumed the lady in question would be able to work like a man. As one woman recalls in Bérubé's book, "They would say, 'Have you been in love with a woman?' You would say, 'Of course not!' sitting there in your pinstriped suit."

The military almost served as a sort of precursor to the internet when it came to finding new friends. Lonely young gay men and women from different towns and cities all over the country were thrown together for basic training, and it was suddenly much easier to find like-minded people. Your social circle geographically opened up in ways not possible before. Add to this the inherently queer segregation of the sexes in barracks and you have an environment much like prison, where even straight men and women search out companionship. Fluidity is nothing new; there just wasn't a common language yet with which to talk about it. Romances flourished, and once the war ended, new gay couples returned along with everyone else to set up homes and lives for themselves.

Four

At the end of the school year, I needed to find a summer job, so I did what many college students from our area did—I headed to Atlantic City for work. I'd made a few casual friends in my classes after I stopped spending all my time with Renee, and a group of us rented a tiny apartment several blocks away from the boardwalk. There were six of us total in a two-bedroom flat, but since some of us worked days and others nights, it never seemed quite as crowded as it should have.

During the war, our family trips to Atlantic City had ceased. The destination had become a base for training and recruitment, and the threat of German submarines lurking off the coast caused nightly curfews that required all the city's lights be turned off so no enemies at sea could view it as a target. Many of the larger hotels had been transformed into makeshift hospitals for wounded soldiers. All in all, it wasn't a particularly enticing spot for vacationers.

After the war, however, the city came back to life in all its salty, sticky, garishly lit glory. I was thrilled to have my playground back, but there were signs of the war everywhere. The hotels were still getting back on their hospitality feet, and the boardwalk felt, at least to me, as though it had a bit more of an edge to it. I felt a constant sexual charge in the air, likely a combination of all the soldiers who'd stuck around, the businesses and women that catered to them, as well as my own late-adolescent hormones. I began to date boys again, with the same gusto and consistency that I'd maintained in high school, moving from one to the next, trading up and breaking hearts.

My first job that summer was as a valet at a hotel, which I enjoyed because I loved cars, but nobody seemed to think I was a particularly good driver. I couldn't understand why, although I admit the tires on one side of any vehicle I drove often met the curb when I made turns, and I was easily distracted by interesting-looking people on the sidewalks. When I was let go after a few too many close calls, one of my roommates found me a job as a waitress at a restaurant located next to the Bellwyn Hotel, just off the boardwalk and close to all the action.

Restaurant might be too generous a title. It was little more than a diner, heavy on the fried seafood. I wore a crisp white uniform that I went to great lengths to keep from getting covered in stains, never to much success. After work, a dip in the salty waves of the ocean did more than any shower could to slough off the sweat and grease that layered on my skin throughout the day.

That summer was one of the first times that I really began to think hard about what I could do for a career. I was leaning toward childhood education in classes at Rittenhouse, but mainly because it was what so many other women did. After the summer ended and I resumed school, I got straight to work applying to Temple University, where Dolly had gone. It was a respected university and local, so I knew I'd be able to save money by continuing to live at home.

Even though I was dating boys, my experience with Renee was never far from my mind, and I began surrounding myself with girlfriends. I'd grow close and develop bonds, but there were never signs from any of them that they might be willing to experiment with me, and I soon gave up my cautious attempts at flirting.

I was accepted to Temple, majoring in liberal arts with a focus on psychology. I knew there was something different about the way my brain worked, and I thought that if I could understand the reasons *why* I was having feelings for girls, then perhaps I could stop them. I spent another summer in Atlantic City before classes began and then dove right into my studies, eagerly trying to discover as much as I could about homosexuality.

Unfortunately, most of my classes didn't touch the subject, and I didn't want to draw attention to myself by always raising my hand and asking what each psychologist we learned about thought of it. I wrote a paper on the first Kinsey Report, *Sexual Behavior in the Human Male* (their report on women wouldn't come out until 1953), and while I knew that Kinsey intended for the book to be only a progress report, and that his initial survey samples were likely skewed since they were largely made up of prison populations, I latched onto his theory that 10 percent of the population was homosexual and that a much larger number fell somewhere in between. This idea, that humans held different degrees of same-sex attraction, felt correct and natural to me, especially considering how many boys I'd dated in life—they weren't *all* bad.

One night during my first semester, I was home smoking on the front porch and thinking about all of this, when I heard the door open behind me. It was Saul, on his way home after a night of playing cards with Blackie. He sat down beside me on the top step, asked if he could have one of my cigarettes, and inquired how school was going. We chatted for a bit, his arm brushing mine every now and then.

"Did you know that I just about worshipped you when I was a little girl?" I said. "You must have known. I'd dress up special, just for you."

"Would you like to again sometime?" he asked. "It would be my honor to take you to dinner."

I considered his offer. He was handsome and smart and practically a member of the family. But therein lay the problem. If things didn't work out, I didn't want it to affect his friendship with Blackie or hinder the door-is-always-open status he held in our home. I told him as much.

"Edie, nothing could keep me away from this house," he said solemnly. "And I promise that if you break my heart, I will continue to come around for Blackie. I'll probably be too devastated to say much to him, and I'll sulk in a corner and stare at you whenever you walk through the room, but I won't bother you."

"All right, then," I said, followed by a short laugh. "I'll hold you to that."

We became an item, and my family couldn't have been happier. Even Blackie didn't mind that his friend was dating his sister.

Many of our early dates involved some very heavy drinking at bars. I'd never gotten too deep into alcohol; I loved a cocktail or beer here and there, but almost always followed it immediately with coffee. Saul enjoyed the bar scene, the smoky, loud rooms and people shouting above the music. He was a jazz fiend and close with a group of talented musicians, including a trumpet player who would go on to play in Pupi Campo's orchestra. These men were pretty wild, and for a brief time, I joined in the partying. I had no interest in their drugs, but I did have Saul order me whiskey because I thought it set me apart from the rest of the girls in the crowd.

After one particularly boozy night, he drove me home, swerving more than just a little on the road. He pulled up outside the house, and we began to kiss passionately in the front seat when I felt my stomach roll over.

"I have to go," I said, pulling away from him. I opened the passenger-side door but somehow instead of standing as I exited the car, I rolled out onto my side so I was sprawled on the sidewalk. Saul came running around and helped me up and inside the house, where I promptly fell asleep on the downstairs couch.

My headache the next morning was a throbbing splinter through my brain, and that was the last time I ever got truly out-of-control drunk. Tipsy was fun. Getting that sloppy simply wasn't worth the pain or embarrassment, and Blackie teased me mercilessly about my fall for weeks. I also didn't like the disapproving look in Cele's eyes. She never would have chastised me, but I remembered whispered stories about my grandfather's drinking.

That night also marked the beginning of the end for Saul and me. The school year was drawing to a close, and I was looking forward to getting back to the freedom of Atlantic City. The work was exhausting, but the time in between shifts was glorious. I couldn't wait to bake in the sun with a good book, bare skin on display everywhere you looked. Saul and I hadn't gone all the way—I was still a virgin when it came to men—but although I just wanted it to be done with, the idea of sleeping with him felt extremely strange. He was too much like family. I began to distance myself and make excuses as to why I couldn't go out with him. There was always a test the next day or a big paper I needed to write. Apparently, I wasn't getting the message across strongly enough, because after my last day of classes, he proposed.

"Oh, Saul," was all I could say in response, but it was enough. He heard the *no* in my voice, saw the sad way I looked at him.

"It doesn't have to be right away," he said quickly. "It's not as though I even have a ring yet." Which was true. We were sitting in the front seat of his car outside a restaurant we'd just eaten at and he'd blurted the question out, almost as if it had been a spontaneous decision.

"Any girl would be lucky to have you," I said. "But I'm not ready. I've got the whole summer ahead of me and the rest of college after that. I need to learn more about myself before I can commit to anyone."

He took the breakup like a gentleman and kept his promise about not letting it affect his friendship with Blackie or his presence in our house. The first time I ran into him afterward, I felt awkward, but he acted so natural that he put me at ease. I played cards and smoked with him and my brother and affectionately gave him a small kiss on the top of his head on my way up to bed at the end of the night.

Back in Atlantic City, I felt my body come alive. The heat, the crowds, the sheer fast pace of it all thrilled me. Days at the restaurant were so busy that they flew by, and my shift ended early enough for me to catch several hours of good sun on the beach.

Two of the girls I was living with had a schedule similar to mine, and we had a designated beach spot where we'd meet and set up, close to the Claridge Hotel. It was a hangout spot for people around our age, and it somehow had more of a festive vibe than other parts of the beach. (What I didn't know at the time is that the area was notorious for attracting homosexual men—apparently the phallic nature of the tower that still sits atop the Claridge served as a turgid beacon.)

There was another clique of young adults around our age who seemed to be on the same work schedule as we were, since they were always on the beach when we arrived, spread out with towels, metal coolers, and magazines. The core of the group revolved around a couple named Marty and Ellen and their friend Caroline.

Marty was tall, somewhere around six foot three, and when he fixed his green eyes on me for the first time, I was struck by his dashing, movie star face.

Marty's girlfriend, Ellen, was the envy of the beach for being the one on his arm. For some reason, she never wore a swimsuit or got in the water. Instead, she'd wear white, loose, short-sleeved dresses, but when she'd stand up, the wind coming off the ocean pressed the material to her skin. The outline of her slim body and small breasts beneath all that fabric was more erotic to me than any bikini.

Marty had no such modesty. His bathing suits were always an inch or two shorter than the ones other men wore on the beach, and when he'd stretch out on his back in the sand, I'd sometimes catch him inching them up even farther with his fingers, revealing bands of pale skin above his tan.

Their friend Caroline had a bit of a witchy quality. She often dressed in black, on and off the beach, and had thick black hair with blunt bangs. When I caught my first glimpse of Bettie Page in a magazine a few years later, I instantly thought of Caroline.

The four of us became fast friends, and I began to spend more time with them than my girlfriends from the apartment. Marty, Ellen, and Caroline were clever and worldly. They were all from Philadelphia, and they had gone to school on the Main Line, a much wealthier area than where I was from, but they weren't snobs about it.

It turned out that Caroline attended Temple as well, but I'd never seen her on campus. From the very start, I felt the same kind of magnetic pull toward her that I had with Renee, but this time, it had a much richer and deeper hold on me. Renee had been a childlike curiosity, schoolgirls fooling around, all giggles and bumping knees. Caroline was a whole different level. Lying on my back on the beach, she'd use my flat stomach as a table for her magazine, and when her fingers would graze my skin as she flipped each page, my entire body quivered enough for her to comment on it.

"So ticklish," she'd say, sounding almost bored, her eyes never leaving the print.

I thought she had to know how I felt, had to have sensed that I longed for her. I got away with causally touching her as much as I did because everyone on the beach touched one another. We all tanned naturally and nobody used sunscreen, but backs and necks often required oil or lotion slathered on in hard-to-reach spots. Before going out for the evening, makeup needed applying, and my hand on Caroline's cheek steadied her head as I helped shade her brows, our faces close enough to kiss while I tried to avoid flushing whenever our eyes met.

Nothing happened that summer, though, and soon we all returned to Philadelphia. Marty and Ellen went back off to college, and Caroline and I promised we'd see each other on campus, but that school year proved to be quite busy, and we didn't truly reconnect until the following summer.

We'd already agreed that we'd rent an apartment together in Atlantic City, and we found a two-bedroom, with Marty and Ellen in one, Caroline and me in the other. It was quite an upgrade from the places I'd been sharing before, closer to the beach with new furniture and silk flowers in vases on the side tables. They must have agreed ahead of time to lower my portion of the rent. The three of them had jobs as well, but didn't work nearly the same number of hours as I did, and I got the sense that the jobs were more for show, an agreement with their parents so it didn't seem as though they were simply goofing off all summer long.

Caroline and I both arrived with similar news—we each had a boyfriend. Hers was named Michael, a childhood friend with a prematurely receding hairline, whom she'd recently reconnected with. Mine was named Alan, and I'd met him during my first semester in a history class. I'd latched onto him because he was a bit older and was quite well built, with broad shoulders and biceps straining against his sleeves. The attraction to his muscles was less physical and more nostalgic—he reminded me of the long-gone boys from Rick's Crew, the ones who'd always been around the house when I was a little girl, trying to tousle my hair and then teasing me when I got angry about it. The ones who'd all disappeared one by one during the war.

Michael and Alan both had summer jobs in Philadelphia, but would drive out to see us in Atlantic City any chance they could, and the four of us began to double-date often, since Ellen and Marty were getting more serious and spent much of their time off alone together.

Alan was obsessed with me, and very possessive, I think because he was onto my true nature. I wasn't aware of it at first, but he watched the way Caroline and I spoke, the way we interacted. Hell, the way we flirted, quite openly, now that I look back on it.

"You two sure are close," he'd say as we'd stroll along the boardwalk after a dinner in which Caroline and I dominated the conversation and neglected to include our dates.

"Inseparable," I'd hear him comment to Michael as we'd stand and brush sand off our legs as we prepared to wander down the beach alone, looking for shells.

"What the hell were you two doing in there?" he'd ask when we'd return from a particularly long trip to the ladies' room.

"Just talking."

Unfortunately, that was true. The pull between us was growing stronger, but neither of us made a move, and the tension was becoming unbearable. I was always tired from staying up late into the night talking with her in the dark, her twin bed on the other side of the room, impossibly far away from my own.

One afternoon, Caroline told me that she wanted to take me to a party back in Philadelphia that a friend of hers was throwing.

"Someone a little older," she mentioned, and so I took care to dress in a slightly more grown-up look, with a modest high-necked black dress, but tight enough to still show off my chest.

The bash was held in a row house not far from Rittenhouse Square, and as we approached the door, I wondered if I'd know anyone there, but it quickly became apparent that I definitely would not. It was indeed a slightly older crowd, which I'd expected, but much more sophisticated than I'd anticipated. The pieces of furniture were all high-quality antiques, the brand of champagne poured by servers an expensive one.

I decided that I wanted something a bit stiffer to help me relax, so Caroline led me to the kitchen in the back of the house, where she introduced me to her friend the hostess, a woman named Nancy who had short brown hair. I wouldn't have immediately pegged her as the home's owner by the way she was dressed, in a casual skirt and blouse. But her background and breeding revealed itself once she began talking. Her elocution was perfect, and her posture was straight out of a New England private school—her head didn't move a centimeter as she shook a cocktail shaker back and forth.

"I want to know everything about you," she said as she poured chilled vodka into a martini glass for me. I thought she was stationed there mixing drinks for everyone in an effort to be sociable, but she picked up her own half-finished glass and maneuvered me up against a wall and began a rapid-fire string of questions about my family, where I was from, what school I went to, what I was studying, and how I knew Caroline, who'd disappeared as soon as she'd deposited me in the kitchen.

I kept my answers vague but honest, perhaps elevating my family's financial status a tiny bit.

"Caroline's just lovely, isn't she?"

"Beautiful," I agreed. "She's become a dear friend. How did the two of you meet?"

"Here and there. I can't exactly remember. It feels as though I've known her my whole life." Nancy set her glass down and leaned in a bit.

"Tell me," she said. "Do you ever have homosexual relations?"

I kept my face utterly still, shocked by the question but also strangely pleased. This was considered casual cocktail conversation? The last time I'd heard that exact phrase—*homosexual relations*—had been in the dean's office back at my starter college. It had been used as an accusation, not with this easy curiosity and the possibility of a future finally opening if I answered correctly.

I gathered myself up so my own posture matched the perfection of hers.

"On occasion," I said.

She smiled and opened her mouth to respond just as a short bespectacled man in a tweed suit appeared next to her, lobbing a pair of air kisses at her face like tiny bombs shattering the bubble of our conversation.

"Darling, hello!" Nancy cried out. I excused myself to search for Caroline.

I found her in the small backyard, leaning against a tree and smoking.

"Did Nancy give you the third degree?" she asked.

"She did."

That's all that was said. We didn't stay at the party much longer, but I saw Caroline and Nancy huddled in a corner later, glancing furtively in my direction from time to time. I could tell they were talking about me.

We rode back to Atlantic City mostly in silence, my excitement building. I knew we'd be arriving to a very different bedroom situation from the one we'd left.

Caroline was my first great love, and I made sure that she knew it. We both confessed how deeply we'd felt about each other and made up for lost time. We were able to hide in plain sight: we were roommates with devoted boyfriends, and our constant double dates deflected any suspicion. Even Alan eased up on his grumbling about our friendship. Marty and Ellen were still in their own world, but their increasing arguments seemed to portend a breakup. They weren't paying any attention to us, but we still had to stay silent whenever we had sex

while they were home at night, a nearly impossible task that we somehow still accomplished.

In order to keep our cover, we also had to spend plenty of alone time
with our boyfriends so they wouldn't suspect anything was amiss, and
after Caroline confessed that she and Michael had already slept together, I
decided it was finally time to lose that side of virginity myself.

It was not a momentous occasion, though Alan thought otherwise. He
booked a fancy hotel room, and I tried to enjoy his body, I really did. I
recalled my girlhood crush on Frank Sinatra, hoping that would stimulate
some sort of mental response, to no avail. To make things worse, Alan had
no idea what he was doing. He stumbled his way around all the things
Caroline had known instinctively to do to me on our very first night together.

He stared at me adoringly when he'd finished, believing that I was feeling the same endorphin rush he was. "I'm going to marry you someday,
Edie Schlain," he murmured.

I gave him a terse smile before rolling over and lighting a cigarette,
wondering what Caroline was doing at that moment.

It didn't take long for the double dates to become torturous. Having
to feign affection for someone else in the presence of the person I really
wanted to be with was frustrating enough when we were on the beach
half-naked, but it became excruciating when we all went to the movies,
where I'd have to make a show of holding hands with Alan on one side
while I kept my thigh and foot pressed against Caroline's on the other.

We'd discuss the situation at night, naked with the windows open because of the heat, but with the curtains drawn due to my fear of being
caught, even though I knew there was no way anyone could possibly see
in. I'd even purchased a rubber wedge that I shoved underneath the door
whenever we closed it to help secure the room, despite there being a lock
in place.

"There's really nothing to be done about it," Caroline would say. "We
have an ideal situation with the boys and shouldn't do anything to rock the
boat. My god, what would your family think if they found out?"

I couldn't imagine their reaction. It would confirm Dolly's suspicions, and I wasn't sure if Cele even knew that women slept with other women. Based on Blackie's love of pulp fiction, I assumed that he was intimately aware it happened, but I wasn't about to fess up to it myself.

None of that stopped me from arguing with Caroline and ranting about our situation. At times, my temper flared up enough that I'd have to leave the apartment. I knew that having to stay hidden wasn't her fault, but she was the only target I had to lash out at. There was no one for me to talk to about my feelings, no friends to confide in or turn to for advice, no gay public figures I could look to for inspiration or courage. I carried the weight of our secret alone.

After calming down, I'd return to the apartment to find Caroline smoking by the window, sulking at first, but quick to forgive my outbursts.

Before I knew it, the summer was over, and I cursed myself for not making a move on Caroline earlier in the season. All those wasted nights, awake and pining, when she'd been right there alongside me aching with the same feelings. After spending the day cleaning the apartment and returning the keys to the building's owner, we rented a room for one last night at the Brighton, a glamorous old hotel on the boardwalk that was famous for a signature cocktail called Brighton Punch, a concoction of bourbon, brandy, Benedictine, and various citrus that was far too sweet for my taste, but that Caroline adored.

In the middle of the night, as we lay naked in bed, smoking and listening to the surf, she turned to me and said, "I loved you today. I'll have you know that's a very great compliment. I don't always love you."

I could tell by her tone that she was teasing. I took the bait.

"And why's that?"

"You're too many different people for me to love all the time. There's Edie the impossibly smart scholar. There's Alan's devoted girlfriend, Edie. There's the Edie who can sometimes fly into a rage for no reason whatsoever."

I swatted her leg.

"Today, though," she continued, "you were the Edie I loved best. Today, you were my girl." She sat up and took the cigarette from my hands and stubbed it out before climbing on top of me. She bent down at the waist so her hair brushed my cheeks as she looked in my eyes. "We're headed back to school, into the cold fall," she said. "But you will always be my spring."

I held her, kissed her. Morning came too soon.

Alan was over the moon to have me back in Philadelphia, but I threw my-self into my schoolwork, making any excuse I could to break dates with him and be with Caroline instead. We decided to rent a small, inexpensive room near campus where we could be together for trysts, similar to my situation with Renee. I took a part-time job as a salesgirl at Gimbels down-town, rarely giving in to the temptation to use my paycheck to purchase clothes. I'd put the money aside for the rent on our love nest instead and socked the rest away. I'd have sex with Alan when we saw each other to keep up the ruse, eventually teaching myself—and him—to get what little I could out of it.

Whenever Michael was in town during holidays or school breaks, we'd double-date, but it was cruel torture. With our boyfriends always by our side whenever we went out, there were few opportunities for us to be alone. Even making eye contact with Caroline was painful. When we'd all walk anywhere together, she and I would drift behind, arms entwined, the very picture of two close friends chatting, but look closely enough and you'd see the difference. Our linked elbows brushing up underneath each other's breasts, our shoulders pressed a bit too tight, and whispers that went on too long.

Alan's suspicions soon flared up again.

He started with teasing. "You sure you like me as much as you like Caroline?" he'd ask when we were alone in his car, me feigning interest as his hand repetitively bumbled around inside my shirt like a sneaker in a dryer.

I laughed his comments off the first few times, but I knew I was in trouble after one night at the movies with the boys when I couldn't help myself from holding on to her longer than what anyone would have deemed normal as we hugged goodbye. Alan was silent as we walked back toward his car, his jaw clenched. He suddenly stopped.

"Edie, are you queer?"

"Why on earth would you say that?" I asked. I tried to keep my voice normal, but then quickly realized my reply wasn't a denial. "Of course not."

"I wonder about you sometimes."

"Well, you shouldn't."

On top of my uncertain future with Caroline, I still had no idea what to explore as a career path. I continued to lean toward the idea that I could be a teacher. Psychology still fascinated me, but I didn't see myself doing anything with it professionally since I couldn't even sort out my own mind.

Despite the intensity of my love for Caroline, it had so far remained easy for me to classify what was happening between us as ongoing "homosexual relations" and not fully acknowledge or embrace the word *lesbian*. I held no fantasies about running away together. I knew that eventually I'd marry a man and have children. I wasn't happy about it, but there was simply no other choice, no other available reality. The one thing I did know with certainty was that I did not want to be married to Alan and that despite his accusation about me being queer, it was clear he was steering us down a path toward marriage. Not in spite of the fact that he thought I was gay but because of it. He wanted to lock me down.

By this point, Dolly already had a second child on the way, and she and Rick had moved to a nice-size starter home in the suburbs. I could feel Cele's eyes on me whenever they visited our house or we visited theirs.

"When is Alan going to propose?" she'd ask at least once a week. I'd shrug and leave the room.

"Leave the kid alone," Blackie would tell her. He still lived at home, because he didn't see much point in looking for a bedroom elsewhere. He wasn't freeloading; he worked odd jobs, mostly in carpentry, and contributed to the expenses. Cele didn't seem to be in as much of a hurry for him to settle down, probably because she never liked any of his girlfriends, of which there were many. And since my father had started traveling more and more for work, she enjoyed having her son around for the company.

Blackie's continued presence in the house meant Saul was still around too, and he gently made it clear that his feelings for me hadn't changed. He'd join Blackie in coming to my defense whenever he overheard Cele grumbling about my unengaged status.

"She's just waiting to fall back in love with me," he'd say. And the more he said it, the more sense it began to make.

I broke up with Alan and Caroline the same week, within days of each other. Both of them cried, but I only cried with her.

I thought Alan might fly into a rage when I told him that I didn't see a future with us together. His face turned red and he trembled, but he got himself under control fairly fast and grew cold.

"I hope you find what you're looking for," he said.

All those words meant to me at the time was finding a way to safely navigate the world, which was how I explained it to Caroline when I told her that I wouldn't be going to Atlantic City with her that summer and that we had to end our affair.

She was furious, which I'd anticipated, so I'd chosen a public place to break the news, a bench in Fairmont Park, rather than our rented room. In part to prevent a scene, but also so I wouldn't be tempted to touch her and lose my resolve. I knew that if we had a door that closed and locked, I wouldn't be able to go through with it.

"Why are you denying yourself what you want?" she demanded.

"I don't want a life of sneaking around."

"It's not hurting anyone."

"It is, though, that's just it. It hurts me. And your boyfriend has no idea who he's really with. We'd always be deceiving everyone around us, and that's no way to live. There's no*where* for us to live, without always hiding. And I can't do that anymore."

We were both quietly crying by then. It was a beautiful day, cloudless, and families and young couples kept passing by us, too lost in their own happiness to notice the misery on the side of the path.

"So that's it, then," she said, not meeting my eye.

"I suppose it is. Will you stay with Michael?"

"Of course I'll stay with Michael," she spat. "What choice do I have?"

"That's exactly my point," I told her.

I went straight from my dual relationships with Alan and Caroline back into Saul's arms. It didn't take long for him to propose to me again, and this time I accepted.

———◆◆———

Anyone who knew Edie understood that once she made up her mind to do something, nothing could stop her. Throughout history (and still), so many homosexuals chose to hide behind a heterosexual marriage and satisfy their desires in secret, but this was not the case with Edie. She decided to treat her gayness as a switch she could simply turn off, and she took her new commitment to leading a heterosexual life with absolute seriousness. She had no doubt that her marriage to Saul would last forever, that her feelings for and experiences with women would remain nothing more than a painful part of growing up. She was ready to put all of it behind her and consign herself fully to her husband.

The one thing she couldn't commit to, however, was Saul's surname. There was no way in hell that she was going to become Mrs. Edie Wiener.

Many Jewish people have changed telltale surnames for something more, say, Connecticut WASP. Betty Perske became Lauren Bacall, Bernard Schwartz became

Tony Curtis, Ralph Lifshitz marketed preppy chic to the masses by becoming Ralph Lauren. The list is long.

Nothing in Edie's history suggests she ever had any shame about her last name. (Though she did once admit that when she was younger she worried that an overtly Jewish last name might hurt her chances at a career, an ingrained fear left over from witnessing the anti-Semitism in World War II.) Her family may not have been religious, but being Jewish was a huge part of their identity from a cultural and emotional standpoint. But a woman getting married in 1951 took her husband's last name, without question. Knowing how particular Edie was about presentation, Wiener had to have been a bit much; it simply wasn't the right name for her. So she tweaked it—after they married, she convinced Saul to change his last name to Windsor.

Edie Windsor sounds distinguished, and she knew it. It's a name that enters the room before the person it belongs to; it announces someone important. She accepted her new life but knew she'd be playing a role. And every lasting character requires a standout name.

Five

Iburied all my feelings for women. I truly thought I was done with acting on that part of myself. It was time to get serious, to look to the future. Finding stability and creating a family was the only way forward. Working helped too. I had no intention of becoming a housewife; I knew that would have driven me crazy. I was too interested in the world, and Saul was supportive of this. It's one of the things that endeared him to me. He was willing to let me be the person I wanted to be. At least, the person I told him I wanted to be.

After leaving the air force, Rick had set up a very clever business with a friend in Baltimore that was growing faster than they could handle alone. He'd noticed that neighborhoods with dense populations of immigrants had their own newspapers in the native language of its majority residents. Rick and his partner began looking at advertisements in the main paper and then reaching out to those businesses to see if they'd like to run translated advertisements in these other papers so they could reach a whole new demographic. Many wanted in on it, so Rick needed extra help. He hired Saul as a salesman, and I became the bookkeeper.

It felt good to have a plan after the nuptials. There was no honeymoon, just a move to Baltimore so we could get right on with our lives. Since

Saul and I had already consummated our relationship, it was also a relief to not have the pressure of pretending to be a naïve blushing bride on our wedding night.

The ceremony had been small and held at our house. The guests were my immediate family along with Saul's parents, his sister, and her husband and daughter. I didn't want to wear a typical dress. I expected Cele to protest this decision, but she was happy enough that I was finally getting married, and to someone she already considered family, no less. Saul was also fine with my decision not to wear a flouncy gown, so I bought a pearlescent white skirt suit with a peplum top at Gimbels, and I paired it with a birdcage veil that I had to remind myself not to accidentally set on fire with the lit cigarette I kept in my hand during most of the wedding.

Saul's family was more faithfully Jewish than ours, so we set up a chuppah in the kitchen and did the whole bit with the smashing of the glass. We rented a bigger place for the reception afterward, played jazz and danced, drank champagne, cut the cake. Altogether, it was a lovely little wedding, if somewhat unremarkable. It was a day meant for big emotions, and I felt them. I really did. I thought that Saul was forever. I knew I would be able to make it work with him, because as I constantly told myself, any woman would be lucky to have him.

Which was exactly what I told him when I asked for a divorce just six months later.

Our marriage started out wonderfully, but maybe it had more to do with the excitement of so many things happening at once. Living in a new city, a new apartment, starting a new job, plus getting to spend time with Dolly and Rick and my nephews again.

Moving in with Saul didn't require much adjusting since he'd practically lived at our house since I was a child anyway. He made big breakfasts of toast and eggs every morning and brewed the best coffee I'd ever had, which he'd deliver to me in bed at the start of each day.

Work kept us busy. We all sat in one large room together in a rented warehouse, the salesmen making cold calls, with copies of newspapers spread out on every surface, covered in large red circles around ads they wanted to pursue. If there happened to be a slow day, Rick would grab a phone and say, "Let me show you how it's done." He'd dial a number and spin out a rapid-fire speech full of charisma that always ended in a successful sale. He'd hang up the phone and say, "*That's* how you do it." Everyone would applaud, including myself, even though as the company bookkeeper in charge of tracking incoming billable clients, I soon realized these were staged calls—there was never anyone on the other end of the line.

We made new friends from work, and then that circle expanded outward, so we kept up an active social life. One new acquaintance that we often dined out with, a pharmacist named Gerald, was obviously attracted to me but managed to hide it well from Saul. To be honest, I didn't mind the secret attention, because it served as a distraction from my own marital bed, which was fairly lackluster, but not through any fault of Saul's. For a time, rather than blame my own sexuality, I thought our growing lack of physical chemistry might be due to the very thing that had brought me back to him in the first place—he was already family. Not much of a turn-on.

I remained committed to making the marriage work, though, even when put to a near impossible test: Caroline and Michael were planning to pass through town and wanted to see us. When Saul found out, he invited them to stay overnight at our house.

"I thought you'd be excited!" he said when I was quite obviously not after hearing the news. "How long has it been since the two of you saw each other?"

"A while."

"Did you and Caroline have a falling-out that you didn't tell me about?"

"Of course not. It will be lovely to see her. Michael too. It just requires some extra cleaning I wasn't anticipating."

I had about seven days to steel myself before their arrival. They'd be getting in after dinner and planned to leave in the morning, so it would be a quick visit, but when the doorbell rang that night, my heart still raced.

Caroline seemed to have matured when she strode into our living room ahead of Saul and Michael, who were still shaking hands and clapping each other on the back in the hallway. Her bangs weren't as severely cut as she used to keep them, in the manner that had always made her look like she was about to dare you to do something you oughtn't. She still dressed all in black, though, and when she embraced me, we both felt the electricity. I pulled away quickly.

She slipped out of her long coat and handed it to me as she glanced around and took in our small apartment.

"Are you putting us on the couch?" she asked.

"Of course not. We have a second bedroom upstairs," I said.

She arched an eyebrow.

The men came stomping in, talking loudly. I sighed with relief and turned my attention to them, playing hostess and fixing drinks. I kept sneaking glances at Caroline, curled up on the couch with her feet tucked under her legs, watching me with a bemused expression that made me angrier and angrier as the night went on.

The men got louder as more alcohol was consumed, but Caroline and I both nursed a single cocktail each. When Michael yawned and suggested they go to bed, Caroline told the two of them to go on upstairs.

"Let Edie and I catch up for a bit on our own," she purred.

She patted the space next to her once they left, but I sat on the opposite end of the couch, as far away from her as I could get.

"I'm not going to bite," she said. "This time, anyway."

"Don't be crass. How are you? Really?"

She shrugged. "Perfectly fine. I've been making love to an adorable girl; she works behind the counter at a soda shop and wears a little white apron like the one you used to have when you worked at that diner. I think you'd like her."

"Shhh," I hissed. "Keep it down. And no, I wouldn't."

"They've probably already passed out," she said, rolling her eyes at the ceiling and lighting a cigarette.

I snatched my own pack and did the same.

"Come on, Edie," she said, exhaling. "You can't tell me you're happy here, in *Baltimore*. Though I admit, nicely played on the switch to *Windsor*. Very aristocratic."

"Still cheating on Michael, I see," I shot back. "Why bother stringing him along? You should just leave the poor man."

She shrugged. "He's a sweetheart. He takes care of me."

"What would he do if he found out?"

"I don't know," she said. "Part of me thinks he suspects. For all I know, he's got someone on the side too."

"A man?" I asked, shocked.

"God, no." She laughed. "Although wouldn't that be funny? I really don't know what to tell you. What we have works. Is it working for you and Saul?"

"Yes," I said. "Wonderfully."

"And how is the sex?"

"That's none of your business, but it's wonderful."

"You keep using that same word. Got any other adjectives?"

I fumed silently but also couldn't help myself—she was turning me on, and unfortunately, she could tell. We'd spent enough time together to recognize the signs.

"Come on," she said, stubbing out her cigarette. She turned toward me and leaned across the couch, placed her hand on my thigh. "They won't hear a thing. No one will get hurt. You must have thought about it."

Of course I had. It's probably what gave me the strength to push her hand away and stand up. She fell back a bit into the cushions, losing some of her grace.

"No," I said. "That's not part of the plan."

"The plan? What plan?"

I looked away.

"You mean the plan someone else dreamed up? The big plan that everyone's marching along blindly to even though no one signed up for it? Dates, marriage, kids, death?"

That was the one, all right. But I couldn't think of a clever reply.

"You forgot work," I finally said, already halfway up the stairs.

Even though I stayed faithful to Saul, Caroline's visit was the beginning of the end, probably because it was the first time in ages I'd spoken about homosexuality out loud. The last time had been with her on the bench, almost two years earlier. I'd buried the feelings for so long. But being face-to-face with Caroline, a woman whose naked body I'd held in my arms, whose very presence in a room made me flush, pushed the words to the front of my mind. Once they were there, there was no packing them back away.

I'm a lesbian.

It started as a whisper, but it kept getting louder. I began to allow my eyes to linger on beautiful women on the street for longer than I'd ever dared before, drinking them in. The shining hair, the full lips, curves everywhere that promised to reveal secrets and heat.

I'm a lesbian.

At night, when Saul would make love to me, I found myself less and less able to react, unable to even pretend to go through the motions. "Should we talk to someone?" he finally asked. "A professional?"

No. I'm a lesbian.

I began going to the movies by myself to lose myself again in the fantasy world of musicals—*Annie Get Your Gun, The Toast of New Orleans, Tea for Two,* and *Summer Stock,* starring my beloved Judy Garland, but it was impossible to follow her chipper "Get Happy" advice from the film. Especially since by that point everyone knew she'd tried to commit suicide at least once.

Guess what, Judy? I'm a lesbian.

I thought about the party Caroline had taken me to several summers earlier, when I was so proud of myself for telling Nancy that I experienced homosexual relations "on occasion." I'd boxed myself into a life where that answer could never apply again, and even if I hadn't been married, I knew that I didn't want those dalliances to be *on occasion*. I wanted them every night, and preferably with as many different women as possible.

I could no longer keep up the charade. The core of my identity, my natural biological instinct, wasn't going to change. And once I arrived at that conclusion, I experienced the same gratifying sense of precision that I felt whenever I solved a math equation. All the sums of my parts slipped into place and gave me an answer I couldn't deny as the absolute truth.

But I'd only finished one problem out of a much bigger test.

I knew honesty was the only way to go with Saul, and I hoped that my confession would soothe his worry about our sex life and reassure him that our problems had nothing do with his masculinity or prowess.

I finally told him late at night while we were in bed, after I'd rebuffed yet another one of his gallant attempts at pleasing me.

"I think you're the most attractive man in the world," I said after he gave up. "But I'm attracted to women."

I braced myself. I had no idea how he'd take it. I didn't expect anger or yelling; that wasn't his style. Maybe there'd be sadness. Instead, he was stoic. He didn't ask a lot of questions, and he didn't try to change my mind. He knew me as everyone did—headstrong and logical. If I was telling him something this wildly socially unacceptable, that I wanted to embark on a journey into a life where I risked complete ostracism at every turn, then he knew I wasn't taking my confession lightly or that my feelings were a passing whim.

"Honey, you're so kind, any woman would be lucky to have you," I said. I stared into his eyes and held his cheeks in my hands, the way my mother always did when she wanted to show her most extreme love and affection. "But you deserve more, and I need something else."

Two days later, I quit my job at Rick's business and left Baltimore to move back in with my parents. I could tell that Cele was devastated, even as she tried to show her support for me. "What happened?" she kept asking, and I kept giving her the same generic answer.

"It just wasn't working out." It was my stock response for anyone who asked, and my tone strongly hinted, *Don't ask for details.*

Dolly called every day to try to get me to talk about the separation. She told me that Saul was acting very quiet at work and that no one was pressing him for more information. The rest of the family and our neighbors were walking on eggshells around me as well. Whenever someone asked if I was all right, I always said that I was.

After I'd been home for about a week, trying to figure out my next move, I was sitting at the kitchen table with Cele, smoking, when she leaned in and said, "How was the sex?"

I was shocked. I'd never heard her say that word before; all my education on the subject had come from health class and Dolly.

"Not great," I answered truthfully.

"Well, then, there's no need to wait to get a divorce." She seemed suddenly content to leave it at that.

Gerald, the pharmacist friend from Baltimore who I was pretty sure had the hots for me, arrived in town on business one weekend and rang up the house, asking me out to dinner to catch up. I agreed to meet him because I was concerned about Saul. We were in touch about the divorce proceedings, but he wasn't opening up to me about his feelings, and I hoped that maybe he was talking to friends who weren't his future ex in-laws.

I met Gerald at a popular place downtown near his hotel, and he quickly assured me that Saul was doing just fine, that he didn't seem depressed. "You kids gave it a go, and it didn't work out," he said. "It happens." He didn't press me for information, and nothing in his demeanor suggested that Saul had told him the truth about why we'd separated. With every glass of wine he drank, his hand would linger a bit longer on mine whenever he leaned in to emphasize a point, and his true intention for asking me to dinner became clear. On some level, I must have half suspected from the start.

I wasn't questioning my decision to figure out what life would be like living as a lesbian, but I realized his overtures presented an opportunity.

Maybe I should give it one last try with a man, I thought. *Just to be absolutely sure before I take the leap.* He was certainly handsome, and he had more of an animal charge to him, very different from Saul's gentle good nature. So when the check arrived and he invited me back to his hotel for a nightcap, I accepted. I think he was surprised.

Sex with him was very, very different. It was the most grown-up type of sex I'd ever had with a man; he was rougher and a bit kinkier than anyone I'd been with at that point. Or maybe it all came from me, from a place that knew it might be my very last time with a guy, so I'd better make it count.

Afterward, I smoked in bed, watching him sleep. I thought about how easy sex had been with him and for a moment had a wavering thought that perhaps I was bisexual. Then he grunted and rolled over, tugging all the sheets with him, which left me naked on the mattress. I looked down at my own body, imagined a woman curled up beside me, keeping me warm.

He was snoring loudly as I dressed and quietly closed the door behind me.

I knew that Greenwich Village in New York was the place to go. I'd read enough news articles about how the neighborhood was supposedly littered not just with gays and lesbians but poets.

I'd always been drawn to poetry and thought of it the same way William Wordsworth did, as "the spontaneous overflow of powerful feelings: it takes its origin from emotion recollected in tranquility." I found solace in it and used it almost like therapy, as a tool to help me look inward. And outward as well—I remember gasping out loud while reading a poem by one of my favorites, W. H. Auden, and realizing that coded in his words was the revelation that, like me, he was gay.

The emerging beat poets added a whole new level of adventure to the written form, and there was an excitement that crackled through every breathless account of the Village's bohemian atmosphere. Even if the writer of an article was clearly biased against the whole scene, and preached how immoral it was, all I saw in their words was an underlying fascination about that world that matched my own.

Another source of information about the Village came from the trashy pulp fiction paperbacks Blackie loved. He bought them all, and when he wasn't home, I'd sneak into his bedroom and search under his bed through the standard smutty men's adventures for the really good stuff—anything that featured more than one woman on the cover. Women in various states of removing their army uniforms, standing suggestively close together, or anything with two women together on or near a mattress. I'd devour the cheap paperbacks or lurid magazine tales in my bedroom and commit the crucial scenes to memory for later enjoyment, and then rush to return them to Blackie's room before he arrived home from whatever odd job he happened to be working at the time.

Despite the good parts, they were miserable fables—everyone seemed to go insane, die, or end up with a husband by the end. Still, I looked at these stories' existence as proof that there were larger worlds than the one in which I lived and that I wasn't alone. I remember reading a line in one in which a woman said something like, "Ah, I'm in New York now, where I can kiss a woman!"

"Where?!" I shouted out loud. The books were proof that community was possible, not just secret affairs I could never share with anyone. I wanted more than just multiple lovers; I wanted a group of friends that I could have intellectual conversations with, people I could talk to about my own adventures.

I was shopping downtown near Rittenhouse Square one afternoon when I ran into Caroline's friend Nancy. She seemed delighted to see me. It was a fortuitous meeting because I'd already been contemplating searching her out for advice, since she'd seemed so worldly about "homosexual relations" when we'd met at her party. I'd even gone so far as to consider reaching out to Caroline for her phone number, but I was still angry with her for trying to seduce me in my married home.

I wasted no time spilling everything to Nancy right there on the sidewalk, and she quickly ushered me into a little diner, where we slipped into a booth near the back, ordered coffee, and continued talking in hushed tones.

"You're absolutely right. Greenwich Village is where you need to be," she said. "And I know just the woman to introduce you to. Her name is Janet. Her family is quite wealthy, and she grew up on the Upper West Side, but every time I see her, all she talks about is the downtown scene. I'm positive she'll help you find an apartment."

I regret not asking Nancy more about her own life. She was clearly some sort of doyenne of Philadelphia's upper-class gay clique, but I knew that the city of my childhood wasn't the place for me to grow into the adult I wanted to become. I'd be living in fear, constantly looking over my shoulder. I needed someplace new, where I wouldn't risk exposing my family to who I really was. I couldn't fathom the humiliation Cele would have felt. I'd never heard her say anything disparaging about homosexuality, and so I continued to suspect that the concept wasn't within her realm of understanding. If she could barely bring herself to discuss heterosexual sex, there didn't seem to be much hope for her comprehending two women together.

"Janet works at the shipyard," Nancy continued. "She's the head of some department that keeps track of what equipment goes where, I'm not sure exactly." She waved her cigarette in a way that indicated she couldn't be bothered with the details. "She doesn't need the money, but she sure enjoys the company." She winked. "She's got quite the staff of women working under her. I'll set up an introduction."

I'm not sure what I was expecting out of Janet, but it certainly wasn't what I got. The plan was for me to meet up with her and some friends for a picnic at a park outside of the city. It was late fall, and I arrived early at the designated spot and unfurled a large white tablecloth as a blanket after clearing away the red, orange, and brown leaves scattered on the ground. I was busy unwrapping a few sandwiches I'd brought when I heard an engine rumbling down the road and voices singing. I stood and saw a convertible packed with women, and two alert Dalmatians poking their noses out the sides. I recognized the song they were chanting, "Come On-A My House" by Rosemary Clooney. They were making it sound positively raunchy. I was entranced.

I'm gonna give you candy, I'm gonna give you everything.

The car screeched to a halt, and they all stumbled out, laughing and chatting, and I suddenly felt nervous. These swaggering women were clearly much more experienced and at ease with who they were. There was uniformity to their look: they all had dark hair, cut short and either wavy or curly. Each of them wore pants, some rolled up at the cuffs, with short-sleeved button-down shirts.

I recognized Janet from Nancy's description; she was the driver and obviously the leader of this little pack. She was a bit bigger than the rest, and her face was a bit severer. She had on a wide-brimmed hat tied with a sash to keep it from blowing off when she drove.

As the small group neared me, I tossed my hair back and took a casual puff of my cigarette, the very picture of confidence. The feeling quickly became real when I noticed the looks I got from the girls. Janet held back a moment and untied her hat, tossing it onto the front seat before striding toward me, flanked by her two dogs.

"Pleasure to finally meet you, Edie Windsor," she said. "I've heard all about you."

Several of the girls laughed, but I wasn't embarrassed. In fact, I was quite pleased to learn that I was being discussed.

I spent the afternoon getting to know Janet and her friends. I quickly learned who was sleeping with whom and which ones had had their hearts broken by another. I was fascinated that they all somehow remained close throughout it all.

Nancy had been right: Janet was the person for me to know. We became fast friends from the start, and she soon found me a studio apartment in Greenwich Village at 7 Cornelia Street. I took it sight unseen, forwarding a check for the first month's rent plus the security deposit to the landlord, along with the signed copy of the lease. The only problem was that it wouldn't be vacant for several more months, so Janet also helped secure me a temporary place several blocks away on West Eleventh Street. I couldn't wait that long to get to New York.

I spent the next couple of weeks palling around with Janet in Philadelphia while getting ready for the move. We developed a bit of a flirtation, but nothing happened—I was attracted to her charisma, but that was about it. I asked her endless questions about what life was like in New York, but she never gave me anything solid to work with. "It's different for everyone," she told me. "You'll find your own way."

"I need to know more about the women's bars," I asked her one evening. "Tell me everything."

"You've never been to one?" She seemed shocked. "I thought you lived in Atlantic City every summer. You never went to Snake Alley?"

She laughed at my blank stare and shook her head.

"Sunday morning. Don't make any plans, and be ready bright and early; I'm picking you up at 8:00 a.m., and we're driving to the shore."

"Snake Alley" did not sound like my kind of place at all, but it turned out to be an area in Atlantic City, not a specific bar. A nickname for a winding side street called Westminster that I'd passed a hundred times during my summers there. I'd never walked down it because the area had a reputation for being seedy. It hadn't occurred to me that *seedy* might be a code that included *gay*.

That Sunday, we arrived around 11:00 a.m. and parked the car. Janet led me down New York Avenue to the turnoff, and I immediately felt a difference in the atmosphere. There was a heavy sense of expectation in the air, fed mostly by the many well-dressed men eyeing more effeminate-looking ones who leaned up against the sides of buildings, hands on hips. I was dumbfounded—how had I never noticed this before?

I could have stood there all day and watched the pickup dance, but Janet took me by the arm as we walked farther down the road and around a corner to what looked like someone's house. She rapped on the door, and it swung open immediately. We were ushered inside by a fashionably dressed but rather stern-looking older woman who led us through a small vestibule, past a large black curtain that she held aside as we walked into what must have formerly been a parlor but had been converted to a bar, with many small two- and four-top tables scattered against one wall. Sunlight streamed in through a set of large windows in the back, and though it was quite noisy, all eyes swept our way as soon as we entered.

At first glance, the room seemed to be filled with heterosexual couples, but I quickly realized that there wasn't a single man anywhere.

There were plenty of women dressed in suits and men's caps, though. Almost every single feminine woman was paired with a butch counterpart. I caught a stunning brunette with a haircut similar to Caroline's looking at me, and so I smiled at her, but she was jostled as the woman sitting next to her shot a protective arm around her shoulders and proceeded to glare at me like a panther guarding a fresh kill.

"Careful," Janet said, steering me toward the bar. "They can be a bit proprietary."

"Then how on earth are you supposed to meet anyone?" I asked. I was rattled by the animosity the woman had thrown my way. I'd been expecting open arms everywhere I looked, a crowd of women thrilled to have another like them in their midst. I snuck a glance back over to their table only to be met with a look of pure hatred by the butch. I nervously lit a cigarette.

"Best forget that one," Janet said. "What'll it be?"

"Just a coffee." It was far too early in the day for a drink, though that didn't seem to stop anyone else, including Janet, who ordered a whiskey sour.

Our bartender was pretty and not much older than I was, with shapely hips and a blue kerchief covered in little white anchors around her neck, but she was too busy to strike up any kind of real conversation with. When our drinks arrived, Janet and I surveyed the room once more. I'd feel a rush of excitement anytime a woman glanced my way with what looked like interest, followed by a flash of anger whenever her partner inevitably snarled at me. After one cup of coffee, I'd had enough and asked Janet to drive me home.

"Are they all like that?" I asked as we exited. My excitement about moving to New York was quickly evaporating.

"Sometimes," she admitted. "But New York will be much different. There will be more single women. I imagine most of the ladies here are on vacation together, so they're coupled up already."

"They don't have to be so rude about it."

"Oh, come off it. You'd feel the same way."

I hated that I couldn't tell her one way or another if I would, simply because I'd never experienced a remotely similar situation. If a woman had ever made eyes at a man I'd dated, or at Saul while we were married, I'd been oblivious to it. And I'd like to think the man I was with would have been as well. He'd have been with me, after all.

———◦◦———

*D*espite only being home for about two months in between the time she left Saul and when she moved to New York, this was a vastly important period in Edie's life. She made her first lesbian friends and experienced her first gay bar. (It's unclear if the place in Snake Alley was specifically a women's bar—based on the area's history of catering to males, it's likely that it was a gay men's establishment with dedicated times set aside just for lesbians.) Edie began to set her plans in motion to start living an entirely new existence. She also booked several sessions with a psychologist for the first time. When her father expressed concern about it, asking her if anything was the matter, she told him, "Think of it as me going to graduate school, and the subject is myself."

As for Saul, Edie remained fiercely protective of him for the rest of her life. Initially, she wanted to give him a pseudonym in this book since we were going into such specific detail about their marriage, until I reminded her that his real name was already on the record due to her Supreme Court case.

Whenever she spoke about him, it was with a deep and evident fondness. She seemed to carry a lot of guilt over their marriage, and her stories about him were always accompanied by a small shake of her head, a decades-old disappointment in *herself for getting him wrapped up in her own confusion in sorting out the person she would become.*

Since Edie held concerns about revealing intimate matters of their relationship and attributing them to his true name, I reached out to Saul's widow, Muriel, to get her thoughts about it after Edie died.

"You have my blessing," she said. "And in fact, I'm pleased. Saul really loved Edie's entire family, her mother especially. They were all so different from his own family—they weren't very educated or sophisticated, and he wanted a bigger world, which he got with the Schlains. He loved the arts, classical music, things like that. And I imagine that side of him must have attracted Edie."

Saul was still was living in Baltimore and working with Dolly and Rick when he met Muriel in 1956, four years after his divorce from Edie was finalized on paper. (He'd promptly changed his surname back to Wiener.) "He worshipped them, but I don't think he stayed friends with Blackie," she said.

This might have something to do with the fact that Blackie had been the one person in Edie's life at the time who intuited their relationship was doomed from the start. Dolly's son Rem remembers a family story about his uncle Blackie visiting Dolly one night and scoffing, "That marriage won't last six months." Dolly was so livid that she threw him out of the house.

Saul and Muriel were together for fifty-one years and raised a family of two children and four grandchildren before he died of complications from dementia in 2007. When he first realized that his mind was slipping, he wrote down everything he'd experienced in World War II for his family to read. It turns out that Saul had fought in the Battle of the Bulge and was awarded a Bronze Star for bravery, but he never spoke of it.

Edie didn't learn any of the details about his new family until much later. She and Saul lost contact almost immediately after the divorce, and aside from a brief phone call she received from him on her seventieth birthday, she knew little of what had happened to him until Muriel herself reached out to Edie once she saw her start popping up in the news during her fight for marriage equality. She told Edie that Saul had always spoken only kind things about her.

Six

I made the move to New York City in November of 1951. Blackie and Rick drove me, the car packed with several suitcases of clothes, my makeup, my record player and collection of show tunes, and a folding director's chair. The only furniture was a twin mattress and box spring strapped to the roof of the car. I wanted all new furnishings to symbolize my new life.

When we arrived in Greenwich Village, the sidewalks overflowed with young people. It was a sunny fall day, and boys lounged on stoops in short sleeves, with cigarettes dangling from their mouths, and every other girl wore slacks. There was a hum in the air, an electric current like a shock directly to the center of my brain that made me feel instantly alive and awake. I knew this was where I was supposed to be.

When we turned onto West Eleventh Street, the sun dipped behind the buildings, and the Village suddenly seemed dark and quiet, ominous, almost. But I refused to let that deter my excitement. We found parking right in front of the building, and they all followed me as I unlocked the front door and began the three-story climb to my new apartment.

"Here we go," I said, twisting the key in the lock and swinging the door wide open. I strode right in, even though there really wasn't very far for me to walk. Blackie and Rick held back doubtfully.

"It's perfect," I called out to them, still lingering in the hallway. I was lying through my teeth. The place was a wreck, with peeling, water-stained wallpaper and a bathtub in the kitchen. "Come in!"

"I don't know, kid," Blackie said. He shuffled inside and cupped his hands over his face, trying to peer through the gloom on the other side of the room's only window, which faced a dismal air shaft. "I feel like I'm in a Sylvia Sidney movie."

"It's temporary, and it's great," I snapped, annoyed that he'd evoked a tragic noir film star, widely regarded as having the saddest eyes in Hollywood. "Please help me get my things."

We moved it all up the stairs, and Blackie promised to return by himself in February to help me move into my real apartment on Cornelia Street before I sent them on their way.

I'd transferred all my savings to a bank near Times Square, and while I easily had enough to live on for several months without having to worry about a job, that was neither my style nor my work ethic. I was excited to start exploring the neighborhood, but my first priority was finding employment.

My salesgirl experience at Gimbels landed me a job selling cosmetics at Whelan's Drug Store in the heart of Times Square. The customer base included everyone from frenzied backstage makeup artists who'd just realized they were out of cake mascara, to women dressed in their finest for an evening at the theater who needed a large mirror to touch up their lipstick. It provided me with the perfect opportunity to successfully sell them a new color.

I loved seeing all my matinee idols on billboards seven stories tall, and the lights at night sparkled brighter than Atlantic City and completely blocked out the night sky. After my discovery of Snake Alley, my eyes had become much more attuned to the hidden gay sexual energy in crowds around me. Times Square was nowhere near as sordid as it would become in later years, but I learned to keep an alert eye on the men and women loitering near the narrow novelty stores that sold kinky books in the back. It was now obvious to me that these people were on the hunt for sex.

They weren't the only ones, but I still wasn't ready to go looking for myself just yet. I didn't have a proper space to bring anyone home to, so I counted the days until my real apartment became available in February.

As promised, Blackie drove back up to help me move, and in the ultimate sign that I'd made the right decision by coming to New York, I noticed that one of the names listed next to the door of my new place was W. H. Auden! My hero poet had lived in the same building at one time, and the tenants had kept his name there out of respect.

When we opened the door to the new place, I think Blackie and I both sighed internally with relief. It was tiny like my other studio, but much nicer. The single room was long, narrow, and rectangular, with a bathroom through a door on the right and a small kitchenette along the wall opposite the door. The window caught a bit of daylight that streamed in. The walls were a hideous brown, but a wide fireplace had been painted white, which helped brighten up the space.

After trudging the rest of my belongings upstairs, I showed Blackie around the neighborhood since I was now familiar with it, and we got slices of pizza for lunch. He approved of the area, particularly all the beautiful women. I felt the same and hated that I still felt like I had to live vicariously through his impish grins and friendly nods at each girl that we passed. Even here, in my new bohemian paradise, I still didn't feel safe enough to tell him that I was gay. It was simply that ingrained in me to keep it secret.

When we returned, he helped me move the mattress around to different corners of the apartment until I finally settled on an area where it could double as a sofa during the day, but also feel separate enough from the rest of the space to sleep in.

"Your fireplace doesn't work," Blackie said. He'd bent down to peer up inside the chimney, and his voice was muffled. "It's all sealed up." He stood and dusted his hands off on his pants. "Just as well. You don't want any rats getting in."

He caught the irritated look on my face and backpedaled quickly. "It's still a great detail. It looks a little empty in there without logs, but I've got just the thing. Hang on."

He ran down the stairs and a few minutes later came bounding back up, carrying a beautiful piece of sculptural driftwood, bleached by sun and salt water into the color of pale honey. He placed it lengthwise inside the fireplace alcove, and it fit perfectly. "I found it on the beach in Atlantic City ages ago," he said. "It's been sitting in the trunk of my car, just waiting for a home. Look at that—reborn as a piece of fancy art."

He was teasing, but I felt a rush of affection and hugged him.

"You're going to be just fine," he said into my hair before kissing the top of my head.

"I know," I said. "Now get out of here. I've got work to do."

After being in apartment limbo for so long—I'd never even unpacked my suitcases on West Eleventh Street—I got to work setting up the studio as a real home. I lightened the walls with several coats of a neutral pale gray and freshened up the white paint on the fireplace to make it really pop. I wanted minimalist clean lines around me, to contrast with the craziness of the city outside. My one exception was a colorful abstract painting that I hung above the mantel.

I kept my record player on the floor by my bed within easy reach, and for furniture, I decided to dip into my savings and splurge. I went to the famous W & J Sloane on Fifth Avenue, a furniture-and-rug store known for once decorating the White House and popular with the upper class. I splurged on several Paul McCobb side tables and a cabinet, and a simple diamond-pattern rug to place on the floor of the "bedroom" portion of my studio, to help enhance my sleeping nook as a separate area.

I positioned my director's chair in front of the fireplace and placed a large crystal ashtray on the smallest of the tables in front of it. The final touch was a large black telephone with a cord long enough for me to carry it to any corner of the apartment, including the bathtub.

Before I knew it, I'd been a New Yorker for four whole months. It was suddenly almost spring and getting warmer. Jackets came off the women in the neighborhood. I couldn't take my eyes off the parade of breasts pressed high against the thin cotton of warmer-weather blouses, and each flash of sunlight on the back of a bare neck was a beacon telling me that it was time.

Janet still worked down in the shipyard in Philadelphia, but planned to return to New York to live with her parents at the end of the summer.

"What am I going to do until then?" I asked her on the phone.

"Go exploring! You don't need a chaperone."

"I've poked around a bit, but I've only found places for men."

"Elitists, all of them," she scoffed. "You don't want to be in one of their bars. They hate lesbians. Go to the Laurels." She gave me the address, on Vandam Street off Varick, a bit farther south than I'd traveled since I'd arrived.

"Are the women going to be rude?" I asked, remembering the nasty looks thrown my way in Snake Alley.

"The crowd should be younger and a bit more sophisticated," she said. "Just don't go for anyone who's obviously taken. And if you're nearing it and see a police car drive by, turn around and head in the other direction."

"Let's hope for a more auspicious start. Wish me luck."

I hung up the phone and turned on the bathwater for a pre-evening soak. While I waited for the tub to fill, I scanned my closet, trying to decide between wearing a skirt or slacks and decided on the former. I wasn't interested in trying out any sort of femme/butch dynamic yet. I just wanted to meet some women, and I knew what kind of clothes looked good on me. There was no need to alter myself so I could play to a crowd of strangers.

After I bathed and dressed, I brewed coffee and sat in front of the fireplace, smoking cigarette after cigarette. I wasn't nervous, at least not that I can recall. I just wanted to arrive at the right time, which I'd decided was 9:30 p.m.

The bar was only about a ten-minute walk away, and as I rounded the corner, I could make out a small sign that read *The Laurels* hanging next to a stoop and above several recessed steps. The street was deserted until

I saw the door open and two women exit, strolling away in the opposite direction, deep in conversation.

It didn't occur to me until I was through the door that I'd never once been to a bar by myself before. Hell, I'd never even ordered my own drink before. But the sudden wave of nerves disappeared as soon as I began to absorb the sights and sounds around me.

This was nothing like the surly crowd from Snake Alley. Everywhere I looked, women were laughing and talking in small groups. The air was thick with smoke, and upbeat jazz poured from a jukebox in the back corner. The song ended and a show tune came on, one I couldn't immediately place, but every woman there seemed to be familiar and sang along.

Some wore suits and hats, but they didn't exude aggression, and I perked up even more as I noticed several women looking me over appreciatively.

I wasn't quite ready to enter the crowd yet, so I made a beeline for the end of the bar closest to the door, where a woman who looked to be in her midforties, with curly blond hair, thick glasses, and rolled-up shirtsleeves, approached me from behind the counter.

"What can I get for you this evening?" She flashed a warm smile, and I smiled back.

"Whiskey sour," I said, feeling incredibly proud about my first independent drink order. I took a seat on the barstool and tipped her generously when she brought me the cocktail. I casually turned in my seat so that I faced the room and surveyed the crowd, unable to keep the enormous grin off my face.

This was what I'd been waiting for. Laughter, friendship, dancing, smoking, and best of all, the promise of sex everywhere. You could see it in every flirty glance or prolonged stare, every arm slung tight around a shoulder. I heard it in every joyous off-tune singing voice and could even smell it through the cigarette smoke, all the bodies packed in tightly together, mixing into a heady scent that I inhaled deeply.

I finished my drink faster than I'd meant to but shook my head at the bartender's offer of another. I wanted a clear mind as I scanned the room again, trying to find just the right woman to approach. It didn't take me long to find her.

Her hair was dark and about the same length as mine, cut just below the ears. She dressed like me as well, casual, without spilling too far into either side of the butch/femme divide. She looked firmly in the middle. Not to sound close-minded, but she looked *normal,* and that was important for me at the time.

Normal doesn't negate beauty, though. She had large, gorgeous eyes, and we'd been exchanging glances for some time, so I finally stood and strode across the room toward her. Her friends seemed to understand they should suddenly make themselves scarce, and by the time I arrived in front of the woman, it was just the two of us facing each other. I stretched out my hand and flashed my winningest smile.

"Tell me your name," I said. "I'm Edie Windsor, and I'm new here."

———◇———

*E*die was still using that same line on women several months later when she met *Shirlee Hirschberg, who recalls her introduction to Edie at the Laurels with almost perfect clarity: Edie walked right up to her with her hand outstretched and a huge smile on her face.*

"She was sophisticated," Shirlee says. "And she knew herself." She recalls their first conversation as low-key and easy, mostly pleasantries and a basic data exchange. Edie was impressed that Shirlee had grown up in Queens and told her that it meant she was a true New Yorker, but Shirlee was equally impressed that Edie lived alone in the Village.

"I still lived with my parents, and I would have done anything to get out," she says. "I'd have to ride the bus to get downtown, and it always took forever. There was one time when I rode all the way down only to see a police car out front of the bar, so I turned right around and rode all the way back home."

More than police raids, Shirlee was scared of the Mafia. "We were convinced that they would just come in one day and wipe us all out," she says.

The gay bars of the period were run by the Mafia but not out of any sort of love for the community. They were used as drug dens and to launder money, and aside from a few long-term moneymakers, most were known as "bust out" joints: places meant to only exist as a short-term money grab. In Phillip Crawford Jr.'s book The Mafia and the Gays, *he describes the spots as "an operation in which mobsters targeted a fledgling bar to become a gay joint with the understanding that eventually it would be shut down as a disorderly premise." The idea was to turn a quick profit, close up shop, and move on to the next.*

The bars that caught on and did well financially remained open longer because the mob paid off the cops. Appearances needed to be kept up, though, so when community pressure got too hot, oftentimes the police would give whoever was greasing their palms a heads-up that a raid was on the table. In exchange for the warning, the police were given a specific time to show up, usually in the afternoon when business was slow, so the majority of the customer base wouldn't be affected. The bars also served as a sort of underground tourist attraction, with straight people wandering in off the street to gawk. Edie's own father, who never found out she was gay, told her once that he'd gone to one on a work trip with some associates. "Bunch of boy girls," he'd grumbled to her.

Aside from Shirlee's fear of the mob, she describes the Laurels as a warm and welcoming little dive bar, where she'd developed a strong community. "There were no men," she recalls. "It was a wonderful atmosphere. The women were all thrilled to find one another. I'd usually get there late on a Friday or Saturday, around 10:00 or 11:00. We danced, and we drank, and it was fabulous."

The night Shirlee met Edie, she let slip that her twenty-first birthday was coming up the following week, and without batting an eye, Edie offered to throw her a birthday party at her studio. "She was aggressive," Shirlee says. "A private birthday party in the Village? Okay, then, why not?"

They exchanged numbers, and the following week, Shirlee and several friends arrived at the apartment. Edie had laid out white napkins on all of her new tables to protect them from water damage. In addition to cocktails, Edie offered up a spread of what Shirlee remembers as "hand food," and in pictures, it appears to be a cheese ball covered in almond slices. She also served Shirlee a birthday cake covered in white frosting surrounded on all sides by twenty-one tall candles, like thin spires on a crown.

"I'd brought her a thank-you gift, a stupid one," Shirlee says. "Since we were both smokers, I got her a cigarette box and ashtray. From Hallmark! It was so outré. I mean, nobody did that. I should have gone to the Village ahead of time and gotten something Village-y. She graciously accepted it, but it was a very dopey present."

It's safe to assume that even if Edie had been secretly appalled, she never would have shown it.

Shirlee brought six friends with her, including a woman named Doris. "She was my very good friend, my lover, I guess," she says. While they weren't officially dating, at least according to Shirlee, they'd been sleeping together long enough that there was no reason for Doris to imagine that they wouldn't be leaving together after the party. But not long after they arrived at the studio, Shirlee secretly began to develop a different plan.

Edie blended in quickly with Shirlee's friends. "She was forthcoming and inviting and gracious." The group played records, ate, drank, lit the cake candles, and sang "Happy Birthday," but all the while, Shirlee's eyes were continually drawn to one thing—Edie's bed in the corner, sitting out in the open like an invitation.

"So I crawled into it," she says. "And waited for everyone to get the hint and leave. I was so blown away by Edie that I didn't care what anyone thought."

Things got awkward fast, and all of Shirlee's friends, including Doris, whom Shirlee describes as being somewhat in shock, quickly left the building.

Doris was indeed in shock, and not just for the reason Shirlee thought: "At that party, Edie made sure that I developed a crush on her too!" she remembers. "She was very seductive with me as well!"

Edie joined Shirlee in bed, where they then continued to meet regularly several times a week for the next couple of months.

"She blew me away from the very beginning," Shirlee says. "She was very sexual, a great lover, and we started dating exclusively after the party."

Their dates consisted of meeting up two or three times a week at the Laurels for a drink, followed by a meal, and then directly to bed. "It was a short hop," Shirlee says. "We didn't go to the movies after dinner, that's for sure."

She remembers Edie telling her that she had been married briefly, but other than that, she didn't talk about her family or her past. "She was very career driven," Shirlee says. "But she was at odds. She'd just moved from Philadelphia, had very *little money, and not many ideas regarding a career." It was clear to Shirlee that financial security was extremely important to Edie and that she was willing to work as hard as possible to get it, and she even revealed a career path Edie had once explored but never mentioned—stewardess.*

"I drove her to LaGuardia and waited while she went inside and had an interview with one of the airlines," she says. "She came out upset beyond belief, because she was half an inch too short."

It's not hard to imagine Edie's sputtering indignation at the unfairness of it all.

Seven

I left my job at Whelan's not long after I arrived in the city and hopped around from one bookkeeping job to the next. I took more classes on early childhood education at Hunter College, since I'd continued to knock around the idea of becoming a teacher, the safe backup plan for a woman in the early 1950s. I scoured the newspaper classifieds, which were divided into "Help Wanted—Men" and "Help Wanted—Women" sections, until I finally got my first real job as the confidential secretary to the assistant general manager of the Associated Press. My starting salary was seventy dollars a week, and the position involved lots of dictation, travel arrangements, and long lunches with my boss and various global reporters as they stopped through New York.

My employer had been the man responsible for expanding the AP into broadcasting, and while it was fascinating to witness the inner mechanisms of the media cycle as well as the business behind it, there were so many subjective and emotional variables at play in any given situation— remember, these were the days of the three-martini lunch—that I longed for the rational sense of math and numbers, work problems that had solutions I knew I could solve with logic. I also didn't enjoy being at the beck and call of anyone. Frankly, it took quite a bit of personality adjustment for me to settle in.

I ended things with Shirlee after a few months so I could date around a bit. I had my share of affairs, and I can't tell you how exhausting it was in those pre–cell phone days to have to run all over the city from bar to bar trying to find a person if plans got mixed up, or if I was trying to locate a particular conquest I hoped to make.

I had a brief fling with a woman named Dev, who would go on to become one of my closest friends after we amicably broke up. We met at one of the women's bars, where I was perched in my standard spot—at the end of the bar close to the front door so I could keep an eye on everyone who came in and out. I usually had a book or the newspaper with me and drank coffee instead of alcohol. The night we met, she approached me and complimented me on my literary taste. I was reading from my favorite book of Auden poetry, and when I wasn't looking, she scribbled her name and number on the inside cover with a green pen. I called her but never forgave her for desecrating the book.

One night while we were still dating, she rang me up and said, "I'm taking you to a party at a gay man's house."

That sounded just fine to me, and when we arrived at the party, it was filled with well-dressed young people. It reminded me a bit of Nancy's party so long ago, a similar mix of sophisticated professionals and artists.

We placed our coats in a bedroom and made our way to the living room for cocktails. Dev scanned the sea of people through the cloud of cigarette smoke and pointed to the back of a tall man's head. "There's our host," she said. "Let me introduce you. Marty! Hey, Marty! Over here!"

The man's arm was slung comfortably around the shoulder of another fellow, and he was mid-laugh as he turned to face us. The smile on his face disappeared as soon as I felt my own began to spread as I recognized my old friend and roommate from the apartment I'd shared with Caroline in Atlantic City.

"*Marty?*" I called. "Marty! Marty, it's me! It's Edie!" I began jumping up and down and waving, but he turned the other way and shoved through the crowd in the opposite direction.

"You two know each other?" I heard Dev say, but I was already halfway across the room, chasing him down. I saw him duck into a door at the end of a hallway and close it. I ran after him and tried the knob, but it was locked. "Marty! Open up! It's me!"

There was a long pause before I heard the lock click and the door opened. He was handsome as ever, but he looked furious.

"What the hell are you doing here?" he snapped.

"Aren't you happy to see me?" I asked, confused by his animosity.

"Not particularly. How did you find me?"

"I was told I was going to a party at a gay man's house."

His look shifted from angry to distant and cold. "Well, now you know."

I couldn't figure out why he was being so cruel when I was overjoyed to find him, but then it dawned on me. "Marty, I'm gay too! That's why I'm here! Dev is my friend—she brought me!"

I laughed as his expression relaxed into a smile. "You're joking. Last I heard, you got married and made the poor guy change his name."

"I'm Edie Windsor now, and that's all you need to know about that." I briefly considered telling him all about Caroline and what we'd really been doing in the bedroom while we all lived together, but decided against it. Better to leave the past in the past.

"Did you know?" I asked instead. "About yourself, I mean. Back when we were friends."

He nodded.

"Are you still in touch with Ellen? Does she know you're gay?"

He shook his head and seemed momentarily troubled before shrugging it off. "Well, then, this is a fortuitous meeting," he said. "Let's drink to old friends with new lives."

We embraced, and then he held me at arm's length and gave me a sweeping up-and-down stare. "Funny. You don't look like a lesbian."

"We come in all shapes. Now, introduce me to absolutely everyone."

We stopped in the kitchen for drinks, and then he took me to a far corner of the living room, where six tall, strikingly handsome men stood together smoking.

They were dressed almost identically in white dress shirts, slacks, and ties. They all had dark hair, and I assumed even before hearing their last names that most were Jewish. As the introductions were made—Lee, Gerald, Walter, Leo, Paul, and Bernie—and we shook hands, it became clear what they had in common aside from their wardrobes. With their deep, masculine voices and clean-cut good looks, they all passed for straight.

It went unspoken, but with my feminine appearance and respectable job, I think they recognized me as someone who passed as well, and from that night on, they became my core group of friends.

Each of them had fascinating careers that overlapped with the creative. One was an artist in advertising, and another ran a gallery. Lee worked for DC Comics as a writer for *Wonder Woman* and *Green Lantern*.

I don't recall any of them ever coming to a women's bar with me, but I did accompany them to the men's bars from time to time, where even though I was usually the only female there, I felt welcome. I loved dancing with the boys, and though the occasion never arose, I knew I could provide a cover to protect at least one reputation should there ever be a police raid, by posing as one-half of a curious straight couple.

On weekends during the summer, we'd drive out to Jacob Riis beach in the Rockaways and walk down to the farthest edge of the public swimming area, where the gays congregated. The scene was friendly; you could walk up to anyone and start a conversation. Opinions on almost any topic were strong and loud (there was a stretch of wall you had to walk by to get to the gay area on which someone had proclaimed their disdain for the poet and critic Dame Edith Sitwell, writing in very large letters that she "eats shit"). In later years, the area earned the nickname Screech Beach due to the higher-pitched affectations of some of the more effeminate men.

I mostly kept to myself and enjoyed watching everyone else. I'd bring a clipboard along, place it upright in the sand, and lean against it, creating a makeshift beach chair. I'd read and sunbathe while my boys strutted around in tiny, revealing swimsuits, pairing off with strangers and disappearing to god knows where for long periods of time.

There were lesbians at the beach as well, but they tended to huddle in their own smaller section, still close to the men. On weekends when none of my friends were available to go with me, I'd take the subway and then a bus by myself to get there. At the beach stop, you could always count on a very butch woman nicknamed Uncle Sandy waiting to escort women to the lesbian area. She had a car, and if I felt too tired to handle the long public transportation journey back to the city at the end of the day, I'd accept her offer of a ride home and join several other women she'd picked up and packed tight into the backseat.

Between work and friends, life was full, but I made sure to keep in close touch with my family. I called the house several times a week to catch up with Cele and Blackie, and I spoke regularly with Dolly about her growing family—she'd given birth to another boy by that point, for a total of three nephews. Both Cele and Dolly had been worried about me when I first arrived in New York, but as I grew more settled, they seemed to relax.

Dolly never asked about my dating life, preferring not to know anything about it, and I took this to mean that she'd figured out and accepted the score. Blackie, being Blackie, minded his own business, but not a single conversation with Cele passed without her asking if I'd met anyone. My standard line was that I was focused on my career, but she could hear the growing unhappiness in my voice whenever I spoke about my job at the AP.

"Why don't you reach out to Aunt Tilly?" she asked one night. "If you want to go back to accounting so badly, I'm sure she knows some business owners in New York who could use the help."

It had been ages since I'd spoken to my aunt, who'd employed me as her bookkeeper back when I was in elementary school, but I rang her up, and my mother was right—she knew an accountant who oversaw several small businesses, and he had an opening. He needed someone who could work on-site for him at one of the companies, a place that sourced various accessories to department stores across the country. I resigned from the Associated Press, not realizing that I was leaving a company that reported on crime to start perpetrating it myself.

Cooking the books started out innocently enough. I didn't even realize I was doing anything illegal the first time the company's owner asked me to write a check against an invoice that hadn't come in yet. "It will be here next week," he said. "But we need to pay this other bill now. It will balance itself out." He handed me a second ledger. "Just keep a record of it in here so we remember to correct the other."

Filling the columns of the second ledger and keeping track of the original quickly became the main focus of my daily routine. In the beginning, the two books did indeed balance themselves out within a week or two. But as the months went on, the second ledger became the de facto one used to represent the company, and the further the numbers grew from each other, the more panicked I became. I was terrified to tell the head accountant that we were getting in serious trouble. Every time I tried to warn the owner that we were drowning, he'd scoff and tell me everything would be fine, that more money would come in soon, but before long, the ledger was inflated beyond repair. "This isn't sustainable," I'd insist. "We're never going to catch up." I just knew that the IRS was going to bust down our door any moment and haul us off to prison.

Lee, my friend who worked in comics, and his partner at the time had a house in Barnegat Light, New Jersey, and they'd often invite me out to visit for the weekend. It was there one Sunday that I met a lawyer friend of theirs and confessed about the dodgy bookkeeping situation I'd found myself in. His advice was "Leave, immediately," and he warned that my actions could put Aunt Tilly's accountant friend out of business for good. I resigned the next day and called my boss to confess everything and tell him where he could find his client's secret ledger with the real company numbers.

With no income and no immediate job prospects, I needed to take a much harder look at my life and what my options were for creating a real career. I needed a job that could support me both financially and intellectually. I knew that I had value as an employee; I was a dedicated worker with excellent references. But I knew I'd never have a real career without higher education.

At the time, if you worked for New York University, you could get free tuition, so I set out to find a job there. I knew that I wanted to study math, and I approached that department's main offices for work. They had an opening for a secretarial job, but when I went in for the interview, the woman in charge of hiring for the position took one look at my résumé and told me that I was overqualified.

"You wouldn't be happy," she said, despite my protesting otherwise. "I'm sorry."

I went home furious. How could this person have any idea what would make me happy? I stayed up late, chain-smoking and trying to figure out another way in, or some other way to raise money for tuition, and I decided that the only real chance I had was to try to plead my case once more.

I showed up at the office again the next day unannounced. "Please, just give me five minutes," I begged.

The woman agreed and brought me back to her office, where I laid all my cards on the table. "I'm desperate," I said. "I'll be honest—I really need this. I only applied because I want to enroll in a master's program and I can't afford it on my own. If you hire me, I promise I will love the job. I'll be grateful for it, and I'll be great at it."

The woman leaned back and looked me over, almost as if she were seeing me for the first time. I held my breath until she said, "All right, then. The job is yours. And lucky for you, the admissions office is just across the street."

By the following year, I was enrolled at NYU, studying all the different kinds of mathematics that I adored—like theorems and number systems. I'd also moved out of my studio in the Village. I hopped around a bit from apartment to apartment before landing on East Thirty-fourth Street close to FDR Drive, in a two-bedroom that I moved into with a woman named Abby.

I'd met Abby at Provincetown Landing, a women's bar on Bleecker and Thompson. She'd just broken up with a boyfriend and claimed to me that night that she wasn't a lesbian. She continued to insist on this for the next couple of years that we lived together. We were on again and off again, sometimes lovers and sometimes roommates. I'm positive that she had an affair with Blackie during one of his visits. I'm not sure how to define our relationship aside from "being unmarried in our twenties."

School provided a solid distraction from the drama at our apartment. I studied hard, made excellent grades, and was desperate to get my hands on the university's UNIVAC, on loan from the United States Atomic Energy Commission. It was the first computer meant for commercial use and had a memory of one thousand words and could do five hundred operations a second. These are laughably minuscule specs by today's standards, but mind-boggling at the time.

I knew that any student granted permission to work on it needed to obtain security clearance first, due to whom the machine belonged to. I didn't think much of it, imagining the checkup only meant the government needed to confirm my place of residence and make sure I'd never been arrested. (One night in the drunk tank as an undergrad was all it took for one of my fellow students to be denied access.) My record was clean, but I soon became terrified they might somehow discover I was a lesbian. There was a massive witch hunt happening in the government at the time called the Lavender Scare, and scores of homosexuals were getting fired because it was illegal to be gay and work for them. Or study computing using their property, apparently.

I pushed the thought out of my head. No one in my department suspected a thing. I'd barely had time to visit with any of my gay male friends since school had started. Abby and I didn't go out on the town all that much; I was sure that if I'd been spotted by anyone, I would have known.

Several weeks after putting in my request, I received an expected but still nerve-racking letter on official letterhead from the Atomic Energy Commission.

> Dear Miss Windsor,
>   It is necessary that you be interviewed informally by a member of my staff regarding your security clearance.

The word *informally* did nothing to ease my anxiety. I was convinced they'd found out. I had no intention of lying about my sexuality if they asked me outright, and so I steeled myself for forced exposure.

Still, on the day of the interview, I dressed in a voluminous crinoline skirt and high heels. I wore a much cheerier red lipstick than my preferred darker shade and pushed my chest out as I entered the commission's security office on Columbus Avenue.

My interrogator's name was Mr. Girtin. He was polite but no-nonsense, and he launched into his questions right away. We covered the basics of my background, my siblings, my parents, and where I went to high school. I kept waiting for the timeline to reach my move to New York, but Mr. Girtin began reading through a list of all my high school teachers' names, asking me to confirm that I'd studied under each one.

"What about Sidney Fox?" he asked.

The name sounded familiar, but he wasn't one of mine, and I told him so, but he asked me to think harder.

"Perhaps he was my sister's teacher?" I asked. "English, maybe? It rings a bell, but I really don't remember."

The questions continued, but he kept circling back to Mr. Fox, and I continued to truthfully deny any knowledge of him.

"What about your sister, then? You say he was her teacher. Do you remember if they ever spent any time together outside of the classroom?"

"I should think not."

"And what are your thoughts on communism?"

I involuntarily breathed a sigh of relief. This wasn't a case of the Lavender Scare; it was the *Red* Scare.

"I'm a proud American who believes in the democratic process," I told him.

"Have you ever studied communism? How familiar are you with it?"

"I've studied it in school, yes. And I firmly believe in the importance of the freedom to grow and to find opportunities for self-fulfillment."

The words came out automatically, taken from a book by the philosopher Erich Fromm, but I remembered too late that he was also a democratic socialist. We wrapped up soon, but not before Mr. Girtin asked one final time if I could remember anything else about Mr. Fox.

After I left the security office, I went straight to the nearest pay phone and called Dolly.

"Who the hell is this guy?" I asked after filling her in on what I'd just gone through. I listened to her answer, hung up, and went home to type a letter.

Dear Mr. Girtin,

I should like to add the following information to the record of our interview this morning.

Upon leaving your office, I telephoned my sister, and asked her who Sidney Fox was. She related the following. When she attended Shaw Jr. High School in Philadelphia, Mr. Sidney Fox was a music teacher. Mr. Fox's claim to mention among my sister and her friends was that he was extremely young and extremely handsome. They were teen-agers, whose greatest enthusiasm was teachers young and handsome. She subsequently (many years later) was introduced to him, told him that she had been a student of his. In the course of conversation he took her phone number and later contacted her to ask if she would be interested in doing some work for a "worthy" organization. She asked the nature of the organization and of the work, and upon learning, expressed her disinterest and so ended her brief encounter. She never in any way heard from him again.

In the course of conversation, she clarified and strengthened for me my impression that she strongly disapproves of communism in theory and in fact.

I received my UNIVAC clearance two weeks later.

———◆———

The mysterious Mr. Fox was likely recruiting youths for the Communist Party. His name appears in a 1954 transcript of a hearing before the House of Representatives' Committee on Un-American Activities, in which a witness claims that he and his wife held Communist meetings in his house and that he resigned from the school system and fled the city the night before he was required to take an oath of loyalty under Pennsylvania law as part of his job requirement.

He was hardly the only one living a secret life at the time, though. The last living member of Edie's group of male friends from this time period—Lee Goldsmith, the comic book writer—is now in his late nineties and living with his husband in a Florida retirement community. (Fun fact: Lee was engaged to a pre-fame Estelle Getty before he enlisted in World War II.)

He remembers his time with Edie fondly but describes a large element of stealth in their lives. "Like all gay people, Edie and I moved very carefully in public," he recalls. "Walking down the street holding hands with someone you were involved with was asking to be put in jail immediately."

It seems only natural that gay men and women would have banded together to help each other pass as heterosexual, but for the most part, that wasn't the case. "In those days, gay men and women did not mix at all," he says. "There was kind of an unspoken arrangement. If you knew a gay woman, you'd say, 'Hi, how you doing,' maybe have dinner occasionally, but that's it. It was very divided, so my friendship with Edie was unusual."

He never discussed gay issues with Edie when they were together. They were bonded in friendship by their homosexuality but rarely addressed that part of their lives with each other. In fact, they actively avoided it. Lee remembers a stroll down Third Avenue with Edie looking for a place to eat and finally agreeing on a restaurant.

"When we walked in, there was a huge dinner party going on," he says. Several smaller tables had been pushed together to form one large one, and he and Edie quickly deduced by the crowd's flamboyant behavior that they'd walked in on a group of gay people loudly celebrating a birthday.

"We turned right around and walked out," he says. "We didn't have the nerve to stay."

Even in New York City, cosmopolitan capital of the world, the fear and paranoia of exposure ran deep. He and Edie were also spooked to stare too long at a small diorama set up in the display window of a men's tailor shop around Christmastime. "The owner had a little display, like a map of New York, all miniature buildings, that pointed out where all the gay bars were that we frequented, and there were little stuffed birds flying above it all." Those were a coded reference to the Bird Circuit, a nickname given to a handful of gay bars spread up and down Third Avenue, between Forty-fifth and Fifty-second Streets, places with names like the Swan, the Yellow Cockatoo, and the Golden Cockerel.

"It was very elaborate and beautiful," Lee remembers of the display, but it only lasted about two weeks. "Everyone knew about it, and it took guts to put that up. The business could have been closed on the spot if word got out to the wrong crowd."

It's not surprising that the diorama appeared in the window of a tailor, because there was a different sort of circuit among some of the men who cut cloth for a living in New York. Many of them created bespoke clothes specifically for gay men. "Most were hidden away in the Village, and you could get normal pants cut to order so that they would specifically accentuate your crotch," Lee says. It was just another part of the secret world they all moved in.

Edie was impressed with Lee's storytelling talents, but she could hardly be considered a comic book junkie. "She wasn't really interested in my job," he says, but that didn't bother him. "I always had a little group of people at the bars waiting to hear about the adventures I'd come up with." When asked if he ever thought to try to hide a gay character in any of the comics he worked on, he says, "You could nibble at it, but everything was buried in subtext. Characters could have a good friend who was always very lonely and never able to find someone he or she wanted to be with. You'd make the person French, or very good-looking."

Edie always hid in plain sight quite well from her instructors and fellow classmates also working on the UNIVAC. In one of her files, I found a sheet of stiff, *yellowed computer paper, the kind with holes lining each side to help eject it from a printer, but old enough to predate perforation to remove the strips. There are two messages typed on it. The first reads:*

THIS PROGRAM WAS WRITTEN BY EDIE WINDSOR

WHO IS VERY IMPRESSED BY THE UNIVAC PRINTER

AND WHO IS ANXIOUS TO TAKE THIS OPPORTUNITY

TO PUT ON RECORD

THAT ABBY IS A BUM

The second is a quote from an Auden poem called "The Prophets."

PERHAPS I ALWAYS KNEW WHAT THEY WERE SAYING:

EVEN THOSE EARLIEST MESSENGERS WHO WALKED

INTO MY LIFE FROM BOOKS WHERE THEY WERE STAYING

She used her computer code to print out a form of personal code, and the contrast in the two messages is pure Edie. One is all pride about her work, accompanied by a mild jab at her girlfriend for some perceived slight, while the lines of poetry she selected hold a self-awareness about the gay life she was currently living.

Regarding Abby the Bum: The stories Edie told about Abby conflict with Abby's own memories. (She's still alive and a total spitfire. Her name has been changed, per her request.) A friend of Edie's once mentioned offhand that there are three sides to every story, and Edie's love life in the 1950s has at least seven times that. Many interviews with Edie's ex-lovers and friends who knew her back then tended to unravel into a midcentury version of The L Word. Much will remain secret, but the main takeaway is that Edie was quite the heartbreaker.

Take the end of her relationship with Shirlee Hirschberg: They'd made plans to meet up at the Laurels, and Shirlee arrived early and took a seat at the bar. As the place grew busier, the stools on either side of her filled up with other women, but she didn't think anything of it, imagining that these other patrons would either leave or move to a different area once Edie arrived. When Edie did finally enter the bar, though, all she saw was Shirlee surrounded by other women.

As Shirlee tells it, "She was extremely crazed that I was with other people, even though I wasn't. She came over, slapped me across the face, and said, 'You are so lucky that I didn't turn my ring around before I did that.'"

No one who knew Edie during this period doubts that the event happened; her flare-ups were well known. "People thought that she had a very violent temper," Abby says, though she doesn't recall her hitting anyone or breaking anything. "She was really unpredictable."

At any rate, Shirlee was devastated by the breakup. "I didn't know what to do," she says. "I was so shocked! I wasn't with anyone else. I should have gotten up and chased her, but I was so blown away. She just lost it." It was the last time Shirlee saw Edie for over fifty years, but she remembers hearing that Edie began dating another woman right away.

"Edie dumped everybody," Abby says. "She went through so many women. She was full of life. She was a young woman who came to New York to seek her fortune."

No shame in that game, but her reputation was fueled by the fact that she simply didn't like to be seen leaving a bar alone; she wasn't sleeping with each person she walked out the door with. On one occasion, she left with a young woman who didn't want to take a late bus back to New Jersey. Edie let her sleep over, but since she had no interest in sex with her, she insisted on a no-touching rule and huddled by the edge of her bed the entire night, facing the wall. That girl went on to become an assistant to Liz Smith, and twenty years later, when Edie met Liz for the first time at a party out in the Hamptons, the legendary gossip columnist told her, "Oh! So you're Edie Windsor. I hear you have a very lovely back."

In 2013, Shirlee Hirschberg saw Edie pop up on the news in a story about her Supreme Court case and wasn't surprised at all. "What Edie wanted, Edie got," she says. "She was very, very successful that way. She succeeded in life beyond her wildest imaginings."

Eight

E very couple of weeks, Blackie would come to stay with Abby and me
at our apartment for a weekend visit. I was sure he'd already figured
out for himself that I was gay, so I wasn't nervous when I finally told him,
and as I'd suspected, he didn't seem surprised or bothered at all by it.

"So is Abby your girlfriend?" he asked.

"Oh, who knows. Sometimes, I suppose."

"So she's available?"

"Most definitely not," I warned.

He had promised to install a set of shelves for us, and since I was deep
in my studies, I gave him his own set of keys so he could come and go.
After spending so much time writing generalized mathematical programs
for the UNIVAC, I'd been hired as a research assistant at the Atomic Commission Computing Facility (ACCF), which was operated by NYU's Institute of Mathematical Sciences. I started out writing simple and fast codes
for use with a particular class of computational algorithms, and before
long, the ACCF assigned me to the Reactor Calculation Group, where I
investigated various iterative schemes for elliptical differential equations.
I worked the night shift and regularly arrived home after midnight completely exhausted.

One night, I unlocked the door and found Blackie and Abby sitting close together on the sofa, and they scooted apart when they noticed my disapproval. Another evening, I came back to find a note explaining that they'd gone out to dinner together. My wheels began to turn, but when I confronted them with my suspicions, they both denied anything was going on, and Blackie hightailed it back to Philadelphia.

I liked returning home for brief overnight visits with Cele and my father, and I tried to get there at least every other month. I had my own car by then, and whenever I'd pull onto our street, I'd find my father pacing back and forth in front of the house, where he'd been waiting and worrying about my driving. This pacing was apparently genetic; I'd recently found myself doing it whenever I was worried or trying to puzzle out a programming issue, all while puffing on a cigarette.

Jack and Cele were doing quite well for themselves. His stationery business was succeeding far more than any of us could have expected, and my mother had opened a small stationery store to sell the wares he also peddled to larger department stores. She'd been trying to get Blackie involved, but he was miserable about the prospect. The retail world of flowery paper wasn't exactly his idea of a career path.

My parents bought a large house close to Rittenhouse Square, and I loved seeing my mother able to finally relax a bit and buy herself nice things. They earned extra income by renting out the second floor of the house as an apartment, while Blackie took up residence on the third.

They'd both met Abby and liked her very much, but neither seemed to suspect that there was anything between us. Cele always asked about my love life, and luckily, school provided the perfect cover. As far as she knew, I was too busy with my studies to be bothered with dating, and she was too proud of my straight As to press the matter, lest I got distracted and allowed my grades to slip.

IBM had a fairly constant presence at NYU. I knew that they recruited students right out of school, and I made sure that my supervisor on the

UNIVAC alerted them to my abilities and GPA. They were becoming known for being particularly open to hiring women, something downright revolutionary for both the field and time period. The year before I graduated, they appointed a woman to their board of directors for the first time and also hired their first female routing analyst, Veronica Knizikiaucis, to prepare engineering specifications for manufacturing processes. They even had recruiting brochures specifically geared toward women. The cover featured a bouquet of purple flowers tied together with an IBM tag and the words *My Fair Ladies* printed above to serve as their welcoming introduction.

In school, I was focusing on models of linear and nonlinear elasticity. My thesis, titled "Iterative Solutions of Biharmonic Difference Equations," went over tremendously with my professors, but it was my work with the UNIVAC that made me believe I was a shoo-in for IBM's system design and development department, and I was correct. They hired me right after graduation.

A month after I started my new job, my father came to stay with Abby and me while he was in town for a conference. I was distracted, trying to make a great impression at the office and establish myself. I didn't feel much like hosting, but he'd been having some health issues, and Cele insisted he stay with me and not at a hotel.

I'd moved with Abby back to the village by then, to a place on West Tenth Street. Our building had an elevator, but it was broken the day my father arrived, so I lugged his suitcase up the stairs. He was beside himself with embarrassment and kept trying to take the luggage from me, but I refused to let him help.

We went out to dinner that night, somewhere nearby and unmemorable. Later in the evening, as I gathered blankets and prepared the sofa for him to sleep on, he clutched his chest and fell to the couch.

I screamed for Abby and told her to sit with him while I called the hospital and asked for an ambulance (911 had yet to be invented), because I thought my father was having a heart attack.

"We don't have any open rooms at the moment," the woman on the other line told me, sounding distracted.

"I don't care about a goddamn room!" I shouted. "Send someone now to come and get him!"

When the ambulance arrived, I rode with him to the hospital, but once he was wheeled inside, I wasn't allowed to see him. The nurses wouldn't budge, no matter how hard I pushed.

"Come back in the morning. He's resting comfortably and out of danger."

I called Cele before bed and told her what had happened, and after she calmed down, she said that she and Blackie would be at the hospital by morning. I got only a few hours of fitful sleep and was dressed and showered before dawn. They hadn't arrived by the time I found my father sleeping in a large room with several other patients. The morning light streaming in from the windows hit his face directly, but he was dozing softly. I stood over him and watched him sleep for a few moments until his eyes flew open.

"Gray," he said, looking me up and down, assessing my light wool two-piece skirt suit. "Why do you always wear gray? Is everything okay? Are you feeling down?"

"Only about this," I said, gesturing to the room. "And gray is a very convenient color. I'll never have to worry about what I'm going to wear to work if I have a consistent uniform."

I bit my lip, realizing I'd made it clear that if everything seemed all right with him, I'd planned to go to the office rather than stay. I opened my mouth to try to save face, but he spoke first.

"Very clever of you. Go, get out of here," he said, gesturing toward the door. "You don't want to mess anything up by being late, and the nurses are taking very good care of me. Is Cele coming?"

I nodded. "And Blackie. They'll be here soon. I really think I should stay, at least until they arrive."

"No, go on. I insist. Your job is too important to miss over me. I'm completely fine."

The truth was I did want to get to work, so I agreed. I leaned over, kissed his forehead, and left. I was about to get in the elevator at the end of the hall when I heard a terrible racket behind me and turned to see several doctors and nurses running into the room I'd just left.

I ran back, but only got about a foot inside before a nurse pushed me out and slammed the door behind her, barricading the entrance. "Let them do their jobs," she said. I sank to the floor as I heard yelling from inside the room, strange thumping sounds, along with my father's choked cry.

I placed my hands over my ears, and it was all over after a few minutes. The door swung open, and the nurse motioned to one of the doctors as they all filed out. I saw her whisper to him and point to me. He knelt down.

"I'm so sorry," he said. "We did all we could. He died peacefully."

I was too shocked to berate him for lying to my face.

I couldn't sleep for days, and Abby stayed up with me every night until it was time to drive to Philadelphia for his service. It was held at a funeral home, and the room quickly filled with his friends and our huge extended family. It was lovely to catch up with my cousin Sunnie, all grown-up now and working as a buyer for a department store. She told me about the times she'd accidentally run into my father whenever he was paying a call to her particular store, and they'd go for coffee and catch up. I loved that even while I was off in New York living my own separate life, the rest of the family continued to spend time together.

My father was only in his midsixties when he passed. It seemed so stupidly young, and as the grief slowly subsided, I found that I couldn't stop thinking about my own mortality and what I wanted to accomplish with my life.

I had two main goals: career and love. I felt I was on the right path with my career, but in the weeks after the funeral, the unstable situation with Abby got to be too much. We fought constantly, and she started to see someone else.

I wanted out of the whole deal, and since I knew that IBM offered graduate school fellowships, I applied to Radcliffe for a Ph.D. in applied mathematics. (At the time, Radcliffe functioned as "Harvard for Girls." Harvard itself was all male then, and they called Radcliffe their "female coordinate institution" before the two schools finally merged in 1977.)

As soon as I was accepted, I broke up with Abby for good. I had a full summer to get through before moving to Boston, and I couldn't bear another moment with her. She did not take it well, and after moving back in with her father, she called and threatened to expose my homosexuality at work. "I know who all your managers are at IBM. You'd better be careful," she said.

"And I know how to reach your father," I replied. That was the end of that.

———⋄———

When Edie first related the story of her father's death, she rushed through it and seemed almost eager to get it out of the way. But when she got to the end, the moment when the doctor lied to her face even though she'd heard everything that was happening, her eyes widened in disbelief; the pain and bewilderment of losing him so abruptly was still there, as if it had just happened. Then the look vanished as she launched into another anecdote that skipped ahead several years in the timeline.

Jack Schlain remains somewhat of a mystery. He was only sixty-five when he passed, but as Edie's cousin Sunnie says, "The Schlain family is famous for heart attacks." Edie didn't talk about him as much as she did the rest of her immediate family, but that may have been due to the fact that the rest of them had such huge personalities that they dwarfed his own. Sunnie, Abby, and Rem all assert that Cele was by far the more dynamic of the two. To be fair, Edie was only twenty-nine when he died, and she had decades left of stories about her siblings and mother to fill her head.

Abby remembers staying up with Edie for days after Jack's death. She didn't attend the funeral in Philadelphia with Edie but says that Edie didn't linger long at home and went right back to work at IBM. It makes sense that she would have wanted to throw herself even deeper into her career after her father died; she'd often sent money home before her parents began doing well for themselves, and getting a

Ph.D. at Radcliffe would have both advanced her job opportunities and put her in a position to make more money to help out Cele in case she needed it, now that her mother was a widow.

Not surprisingly, Abby's version of their breakup differs slightly from Edie's recollection, including the precise timeline, but she readily admits, "History keeps changing the perception of what happened." She insists that she didn't have an affair with Blackie and that the woman who entered her life toward the end of her time with Edie was straight but that Edie took their friendship badly. Then again, Abby herself still identifies as straight and says she was during her entire time with Edie, even when they were sleeping together, so the label doesn't hold much weight. At any rate, the relationship was over, and Edie left for Boston.

Edie tended to gloss over her time at Radcliffe. She said that it was very cold and that she was lonely, but didn't elaborate much more. She was still in touch with Abby, though, who was able to provide a few more details. "I don't think it was much fun for her," she says. "The students were brilliant, like she was, and they all intuited where the world was heading. But Edie was also older than all of them, and she felt like it was the wrong place to be."

By then, Edie was thirty-one with two years of job experience at a cutting-edge company under her belt; it's understandable that the age difference between her and her classmates would have bothered her. Even in little ways: Abby recalls a phone conversation in which Edie lamented that she couldn't even find the right sort of makeup at the drugstores.

"Everything here is for eighteen-year-olds," she'd grumbled.

So she dropped out of school. IBM was more than happy to take her back. Before returning to New York, she found and rented a small apartment on the Upper West Side at the Normandy, on Riverside and Eighty-sixth Street. She couldn't find any gay bars in the neighborhood, so on her first night back in town, she rang up her old friend Dev and said the words that launched her into the next phase of her life: "If you know where the lesbians are, please take me!"

Nine

As anxious as I was to start dating again when I first got back to New York in 1961, I found myself working more than socializing. I'd go to the women's bars in the Village a few nights a week, order a cup of coffee, and sit at my usual spot at the end of the bar with a book or newspaper and my cigarettes. There were occasional affairs, nothing that left much of an impression. Abby and I made up as friends and met for dinner at least once a month. With the exception of Marty, my group of boys had mostly disbanded, either coupled off or moved away.

Life centered around IBM. By this point my particular branch had been moved into the Time-Life Building, which was terribly glamorous. We'd lunch on the first floor at La Fonda del Sol, full of Eames furniture and Latin American cuisine (though much of it was too spicy for me). The restaurant on the top floor was called the Hemisphere Club and members-only by day, but it transformed into the Tower Suite in the evenings, open to the public who could afford it; each table came with its own butler. Having *Life* magazine housed in the same building meant occasional celebrity sightings and beautiful photography exhibits in the lobby.

I'd been placed in a department that programmed corporate strategy and technical standards, and then the company would develop our ideas into practice if they were approved. I had a key role in the creation of the IBM 7040, a historic second-generation computer that was relatively inexpensive and used by universities in the early '60s. We were somewhat of a computer systems think tank, and a fairly small team of around ten. I was the only woman in my particular department at the time, but I never felt any sort of discrimination about my gender.

That isn't to say my gender wasn't acknowledged. My teammates constantly wanted to know about my love life, as I was an older single woman. I kept things vague, though, and even went on a few dates with men in other departments to keep everyone's curiosity placated. The fact that these fellows also worked at IBM was my easy out—I insisted that I couldn't continue to see any of them because we were professionals and needed to conduct ourselves as such.

Every few weeks, I'd take the train up to IBM's offices in Poughkeepsie for presentations or meetings and would stay for a night or two at a hotel. Much more fun were the business trips to Florida or the West Coast for conferences, where I'd bond with my coworkers over late dinners and sightseeing day trips.

I moved from the Normandy back down to the Village, to Leroy Street. The early '60s were a fantastic period for the joyful sorts of Broadway musicals that I adored, but I also made sure to stay well rounded with more intellectual shows like a revival of Eugene O'Neill's *Strange Interlude*. A Marcel Marceau performance of *Youth, Maturity, Old Age, and Death* moved me to tears, but truthfully, that doesn't take much whenever I find myself in a theater.

One evening in 1963, Dev invited me out to dinner at Portofino, a restaurant on Thompson Street just off Bleecker. It wasn't technically a gay establishment, but it attracted a very particular crowd—a mix of artists, actors, writers, as well as their patrons and other upper-class people who appreciated the vibe. Much of that had to do with the fact that it was managed by Elaine Kaufman, who, at the time I was frequenting the restaurant, was preparing to open her own place on the Upper East Side. Elaine's would go on to become a legendary hangout for authors, editors, and celebrities, but she honed her skill of curating a fascinating mix of people while working at Portofino.

Along with artsy crowds come the homosexuals, and soon, Friday nights became an unofficial lesbian night, where women would come to see and be seen. It wasn't considered a place to find a lover; it was a spot for fairly decent Italian food and neck craning.

Dev and I arrived early because we had plans to attend a party at her friend's house after, but the dining room was already full, so we sat at the bar while waiting for a table. We caught up over drinks, each occasionally peering over the other's shoulder to give the room a quick sweep, when she interrupted me right in the middle of a story about work. Admittedly, it was probably a boring one for someone not quite as passionate about the computing world as I was.

"Oh, look, there's Peggy." She began waving, and I turned to see her friend, a woman I'd met a few times out at the bars, making her way over to us. A striking woman with dark hair followed closely behind. There was something almost regal about the way she carried herself, and every person she passed, men and women alike, did a quick double take.

"Hello, darlings," Peggy said, leaning in to kiss us both on the cheek. "Do you know Thea Spyer?"

Dev apparently did, and they nodded politely at each other before Thea turned her eyes to me.

How to describe her face? Eventually, photos of her would surround me, but that first good look still stands out, forever burned in my mind. She was only a few inches taller than I was; that much I could tell even from my spot on the barstool, but she somehow seemed to tower over everyone. She had the posture of a monarch. Her hair was jet-black, and she wore it down, but swept back away from her face. Her eyes were as dark as her hair, with thick brows perfectly arced in a half oval. Her lips were wide, with a sharp little cupid's bow in the center that gave her face a slight hardness, instead of the overly cute pucker that the feature usually sculpts from one's mouth.

Despite the vague sense of masculinity she radiated, she wore a high-waist skirt made of the same lightweight gray wool that I favored, with a short-sleeved white blouse. Several of the top buttons were undone.

The attraction was immediate for both of us, I could tell. I felt my face flush as our eyes met. She seemed to truly see me, and when a warm smile broke through her rather haughty expression, her eyes lost their steely armor.

"Edie Windsor," I said, lighting a cigarette to calm my nerves. I exhaled away from her and gave my hair a slight toss when I turned back to face her. She smiled but didn't say anything. She only stared and seemed slightly amused by my attempt at flirting through body language.

"What do you girls have planned for the rest of the evening?" Dev asked.

"Well, if we ever get a damn table so we can eat, we're headed to a party at Sylvia's place later," Thea said, swinging her head to look at Dev for a moment before turning back to me. I felt as though I were being appraised, but I liked it.

"Well, perfect, that's where we're headed!" Dev exclaimed.

A server appeared to tell us that our tables were ready. Dev asked if we could all sit together, but we were told that would likely be a long wait. There were two small tables available immediately, but not near each other.

"It's fine," Dev said. "We'll meet back up here and we can walk over to the party together."

Plans in place, we separated, and the moment I sat down, I opened my mouth, but Dev stopped me before I could say a word.

"She's spoken for," she said.

"Damn it," I said, grinding my cigarette out on the ashtray and moving it closer to me. I could tell it was going to be a half-pack meal. I peered around to see where they'd been seated and finally spotted them against a far wall behind us. Any subtle eye contact was out of the question.

"What do you know about her?"

"Not much, just what Peggy's told me in passing. They dated briefly. She recently got her Ph.D. in psychology and comes from money. She's Dutch, and I believe there's some story about her escaping from Nazis as a child. She's also quite the heartbreaker. From what I've gathered, you either like her or you don't. Or perhaps it's that *she* either likes you or doesn't."

"Interesting," I said under my breath, but Dev heard.

"It's serious between her and Frederica," she warned. "Do you know her? They live together in a town house on West Twelfth."

"I don't believe so."

"Don't worry, we'll find someone for you at the party."

Throughout dinner, various people stopped by our table to say hello, women we either knew casually from the bars or brief flings that had ended amicably. After paying the check, we waited at the bar for Peggy and Thea to finish, and we all strolled to the party. I lagged behind a bit at first, pausing to light a cigarette and hoping Thea would halt and wait for me, but I ended up having to walk fast to catch up with them when she didn't fall for my little move.

The party was hot and crowded; I recognized most of the people there from either the bars or earlier in the evening at Portofino. It was difficult to make conversation with anyone above the din, and as the room grew more and more packed, Thea suggested the four of us leave and go to her place for a nightcap.

Dev gave me a warning glance when I enthusiastically agreed.

"Frederica won't mind us coming in so late?" Dev asked, and I thought I saw Thea shoot her a dark look before smiling and saying that she was out and wouldn't be home until much later.

She led us to a stately brownstone and up into the front parlor, switching on lights as she went. The furniture was antique and the art exquisite; this was a home that belonged to someone with money and taste, and I wondered if it was Thea or her girlfriend who was responsible.

Thea thumbed through a stack of records next to a player and a moment later, Jackie Wilson's sexy, soulful voice filled the room. Thea spun around and danced backward to the middle of the room, beckoning me with her fingers and mouthing the words to "Baby Workout."

Hey, you, come out here on the floor.

I kicked off my heels and obliged.

Now when you get out here, don't you have no fear.

She slipped effortlessly from one dance move to the next: the Mashed Potato, the Monkey, the Pony. Dev and Peggy joined us and tried to keep up, but they might as well have still been out on the street. Peggy in particular seemed to be trying to dance awfully close to Thea for someone who was supposed to be an ex, but Thea and I were in our own world. We'd burst out laughing every time a song ended, and she'd rush over to the stereo to put on a new 45 RPM, lest we lose momentum. In those few seconds of silence between each song, I could hear my heartbeat in my ears as I tried to catch my breath.

She played joyful, bouncy songs like "If I Had a Hammer" by Trini Lopez and "Mockingbird" by Inez and Charlie Foxx. Peggy and Dev eventually collapsed on the couches, exhausted, but Thea and I kept at it.

We were both sweating, and the room soon filled with Thea's sharp musk. I felt dizzy, and as we danced, I realized that she was leading me. I'd danced with my share of women, but none had ever been able to lead. Without even touching, she guided my body with hers into every new song and each new step.

The spell broke abruptly. One close look at the clock on the mantel above the fireplace and Thea shut down. The needle scraped across the record, and she told us we all had to leave as she opened the windows to air out the room and began to straighten the furniture.

"Until next time, then," I said as I slid my heels back on. I'd worn giant holes in the bottoms of both stockings, and the loose fabric bunched up and around the sides of my shoes. I used a finger to poke the fabric back in.

"Yes, yes," Thea said, ushering us out the door and peering nervously up and down the deserted street. "Until next time."

————— ⬥ —————

I never blamed Edie for what happened."

So says Frederica, Thea's ex-girlfriend. An extremely talented artist, she worked for the Museum of Natural History painting dioramas, mostly in the ocean life wing, and much of her original work is still on display there.

"Thea was not trustworthy at that time," she says. "I knew that." Still, she found her very attractive and intelligent, and they came from familiar socioeconomic backgrounds. As she puts it, "I didn't have the kind of money Thea did, but I was okay."

They were accustomed to a certain level of comfort in life, but both were too smart and talented to simply fall back on their family's money. They worked hard, and they enjoyed it. Despite their similarities in that regard, Edie and Thea had something stronger in common: they were both Jewish.

"My family is German, three generations back," Frederica says. "But Thea had dreams in which she thought I was a Nazi. I sure as hell am not. Most of my friends are Jewish!"

It isn't surprising that Thea had nightmares in which the threat of Nazis played a prominent role. She was two years younger than Edie, born in 1931, and raised for the first years of her life in a well-to-do area of Amsterdam. Her grandparents lived in a grand canal house and her father, Willem Spyer, made his fortune in the pickling business. It was a family endeavor—he ran the company with one of his brothers, Theo—but there was no question he was the patriarch.

Thea's mother was a milliner and therefore not of the same social class as Willem, but he fell madly in love with her, and they married. Thea was born, and when she was around eighteen months old, her mother went into septic shock after contracting a throat infection during a vacation in Switzerland and died. Willem was heartbroken, but he married a woman named Jetty not long after.

From all accounts, this was a marriage of convenience. Willem thought Thea needed a mother figure to grow up with, and Jetty came from a wealthy family. It was a good match socially and financially, but not emotionally. Many described Jetty's personality as quite cold, and her relationship with Thea was strained throughout *their entire lives. One relative remembers that a governess primarily raised Thea for the first several years of the marriage. Thea was extremely close with her, to the point that Jetty saw her as a threat and had her fired.*

Willem paid close attention to Hitler's early rise to power and saw the warning signs that something terrible was happening in Europe. The Nazis had claimed the area south of Germany with Austria, and then east within the Sudetenland in Czechoslovakia. When Germany continued their counterclockwise invasion of its bordering countries with Poland on September 1, 1939, he correctly predicted that the Netherlands would be next.

He spread the alarm throughout his family, Jewish friends, and work acquaintances, and then overnight, he packed up his family—Jetty, Thea, as well as his brother, Theo, and Theo's children—and fled to England, with an eye on America next. They left all their possessions behind, including Thea's beloved pet dog. The only thing she was allowed to bring with her aside from a small bag of clothes was a doll named Willy. Willem and Theo's other brother, Josef, stayed behind to deal with his insurance business. After being betrayed by a neighbor, he was taken by members of the Dutch Nazi party and killed in a gas chamber at Auschwitz.

Throughout her life, Thea carried guilt about her escape. She was acutely aware that her family's wealth was the only reason she survived. "We were not in any way typical of what happened to Jews in Holland," she says in the documentary Edie & Thea: A Very Long Engagement. "We had the great benefit of having had money. The percentage of Jews who survived in Holland is so small."

Willem and Jetty arrived in America and began rebuilding the pickling business, first by spending time in Canada and the South before settling in White Plains, just outside of New York City, because they heard the schools were good there. They were helped by business connections with Heinz and eventually regained their comfort and status.

Thea's education was top-notch. She was a gifted violinist and took great pride in her abilities. So much so that when she entered college to study music at Sarah Lawrence, she was always selected as concertmaster or first violin for performances. As her program progressed, she was required to form a quartet with three other classmates, but when her professor passed her up as first violin for another student, she was so infuriated that she quit the program on the spot and switched her major to psychology.

People who knew Thea well often repeat this story, and it's a revealing indicator of her personality—headstrong, talented, and unwilling to ever settle for second best. It also exposes two traits that many, even those who knew and loved her best, will readily admit to: she could sometimes be quite snobbish and jealous.

Edie only ever had to contend with the jealousy when it came to her ex-lovers, but Thea's ego, particularly when she was younger and making her way through New York's lesbian scene in the 1960s, didn't leave a favorable impression with many who crossed paths with her. Imperious, cold, vain—all are words that were used to describe her during various interviews. But even those who didn't like her all that much admitted to her brilliance. There's no doubt that she was respected, which one can gather meant much more to Thea than being liked. To those whom Thea herself liked, she was nothing but generous and warm.

It's ironic that Thea was eventually kicked out of Sarah Lawrence for being a lesbian, since the college would go on to become a hotbed of feminist and lesbian activism in the 1970s. Like most institutions in the 1950s, though, the powers that be weren't very tolerant. Thea's first affair was with a woman nine years her senior, a former Sarah Lawrence student herself. She was extremely glamorous and worldly, wore slingback heels, and drove a red convertible. Most important, she was Thea's gateway to the women's bars of the West Village.

One night, after an evening of barhopping in the city, the woman drove Thea back to campus, where they made out in the front seat of her car, unaware that a security guard was watching them. Rather than break it up, he got his eyeful and then reported what he'd seen to the dean's office. Thea was called in the following day and expelled.

Willem and Jetty were horrified and embarrassed about their daughter's scandal. They tried to control her by arranging dates with men and restricting her access to money, but Thea moved to the West Village and began commuting to classes on Long Island. She found a family friend in her cousin Dick, who was also living in the Village and working as a teacher at the Art Students League of New York. As a painter, he too had experienced his share of conservative disappointment from the family for not entering the family business.

"The only thing worse for the Spyers than being an artist is being a lesbian," he told Thea, and they formed a close bond as she continued her education in psychology and began to make a name for herself socially as a voracious dater and heartbreaker. She also picked up the violin again, but only so she wouldn't get rusty.

Frederica recalls that when they met and moved in together, Thea wore clothes that were much more ladylike than the style of dress she became known for later. "She was very feminine originally. She played the femme role. I wasn't exceptionally butch, but much more so than she was. She left her mules by my bed once when my mother came to visit, and that's how she found out I was gay."

But Thea was still developing her look and was fascinated by Frederica's more masculine clothing. One year, she gathered up several pieces from Frederica's wardrobe and had a professional photographer take pictures of her wearing them and then presented the photos to Frederica bound in a book as a birthday present.

"I was not pleased," she says. "I didn't want her dressing in my clothes and pretending. And as a gift, it had nothing to do with me! It was all about Thea."

Thea often exasperated Frederica, particularly with her flirting when they were out together or even when they had guests in the house. When asked if she recalled hearing or sensing that Thea was actually unfaithful, she just sighs. "I think common sense would have told anyone that. But I cared about Thea. I really did."

Frederica's own circle of close friends included many artists and writers, like Louise Fitzhugh, the lesbian author of Harriet the Spy, with whom she shared a painting studio. "I had to sign the lease, because Louise looked like a child," she says. Another close friend happened to be Edie's first girlfriend, Renee Kaplan, whom Frederica met right after she moved to New York. Renee had been dating Lorraine Hansberry, author of A Raisin in the Sun.

Renee is believed by some LGBTQ historians to have been Lorraine's first lesbian lover—we know for a fact that she was Edie's—and Renee was listed as an "honorary pallbearer" in Lorraine's funeral program, her name nestled in with the likes of Rita Moreno and Shelley Winters. Some friends recall Edie telling stories of roaming around the Village with Renee and Lorraine in the late '50s and how *she complained that Lorraine's husband, Robert Nemiroff, was always lurking about ominously. Edie also told people that she accompanied Renee and Lorraine down to Philadelphia for the opening of* A Raisin in the Sun *when it debuted there, and indeed, in Edie's files, there are copies of both the playbill and Lorraine's funeral program.*

Edie told me that last she'd heard, Renee had moved to Mexico and eventually committed suicide. After I repeated this to two different people who'd known Renee but hadn't heard anything about her killing herself, they both had near-identical responses: that Renee seemed the type who would have taken control of the situation in her own way if she'd discovered she was terminally ill.

"She was a close friend," Frederica says. "She had a wonderful sense of humor and a beautiful sense of design. And she had taste—I think you're born with it, and she always had it." She was unaware that Edie had even known Renee, but when she found out that she'd been Edie's first lover, she wasn't surprised.

"Well," she says, "Edie had good taste too."

Ten

I began running into Thea at parties fairly regularly. Our social circles overlapped slightly, and while I knew that she was spoken for, I didn't see the harm in maneuvering my way closer to her on makeshift living room dance floors whenever we happened to be at the same place. Her face always lit up when she saw me, but there was never a situation in which we could have a real conversation.

I dated around, nothing serious. Enough to satisfy my needs, and let's just leave it at that. Two of my favorite hangouts, the Bagatelle (an admirer I'd met there used to send me flowers addressed to the Belle of the Bagatelle!) and Provincetown Landing, had closed down by then, but there were other bars that came and went, and I even took a few trips to the actual Provincetown for some romantic interludes. One time, I returned to Manhattan with a terrible case of poison ivy in some very uncomfortable spots.

There was a woman named Jean, whom I considered to be the ringleader of all lesbian sexual activities in downtown New York. She'd slept with almost everyone I knew and always kept an eye on who was dating whom at any given moment. She fascinated me—she could vacillate between femme and butch to match the desires of any woman she happened to be dating at the time. Her hair was the perfect length, short enough that she could slick it back into a masculine pompadour if she were sleeping with a femme. If she were dating someone who leaned butch, she'd style her hair down with soft waves in it.

I'd always been curious about what it would be like to sleep with her. To me, she represented the pinnacle of sexual perfection. Despite being very comfortable with the person I was, I envied her ability to become whatever and whomever she wanted, mainly because it seemed like it would be so much fun. So I flushed with excitement when I heard from Dev that she'd been asking about me. My high plummeted when Dev continued, saying that Jean had also been interrogating several women I'd slept with to find out if I was a fanner. I believe these days the term is *pillow queen,* and I can only imagine she made that assumption because I still proudly stood out as femme. I told Dev to assure Jean that I was not, nor ever had been a fanner, and that she'd never get a chance to find out for herself.

All sorts of adventures happened out at the bars. Affairs, police raids (thankfully, I was never present for one), even death—one night a woman stole her lover's car and ran off with the bartender. They sped down the street, only to crash a block away, and both were killed instantly. It was all anyone talked about for weeks.

The scene was evolving. I could sense it. Societal disgust was still the rule, but I felt that gays, at least in New York City, didn't seem to be hiding as much as they had when I'd first arrived. I began to see pockets of activism reported in the papers, small groups of protesters organizing over incidents like the draft records of homosexuals being made public, and picketing outside a prominent psychiatrist's lecture on homosexuality as a mental illness. There were glimpses of visibility, except when it came to me.

I divided my time between two worlds. My social life couldn't have been more different from my work at IBM, where my career was rapidly advancing in the programming standards department. I was often assigned special projects to investigate technical programs like character codes and printer graphics. I'd identify bugs in the systems and implement the way to fix them throughout all departments. As a core member of the company's SHARE program, our purpose was to take all the new research and information being discovered in different internal branches and find ways to implement them into IBM's overall goal—to create large, fast computers that would benefit science, engineering, and education.

I could clearly see the future promise of technology and where the world was headed. I knew without a doubt that computers were going to be essential tools in our development as a society, and being in the middle of that tide swell was everything I could have hoped for in a career.

What I didn't see was a future for my personal life. I'd grown exhausted with my male colleagues always inquiring about whom I was dating, and I continued the tiresome heterosexual charade of accepting the occasional dinner out with their single male friends.

I lived in near-constant fear of being discovered. One Friday night out at a bar, I saw four men who worked on the same floor as I did at the Time-Life Building enter and take a table near the front. It seemed as though they were on a sightseeing trip, coming to look at the gays after a dinner and too many martinis.

I was there with Dev, and I shrank into the wall, positioning her in front of me so the men wouldn't see me. Since they were so close to the front door, I was trapped. They only stayed for one drink, but as I peeked to watch them gather their coats, I accidentally made eye contact with one. I turned away fast but still saw his surprised gape of recognition.

I considered calling out sick that Monday but decided to brave the office and relaxed when the man who'd seen me passed by in the hallway and barely acknowledged my presence. It was only then that I considered perhaps they hadn't been queer watching—maybe they belonged at the bar. But even if that were the case, he definitely didn't seem to want to share any details of his personal life.

This upset me, because I'd grown so close to my other coworkers. I often went to dinner with them and their wives, and when we'd travel together for business, we always had so much fun, visiting casinos and playing blackjack well into the night, as though we were on an actual vacation.

I turned thirty-five in 1964, and that was far too old for me to be a single unmarried woman. (It didn't help that my hair almost overnight had developed a premature silver streak, but I actually quite liked the look and didn't try to hide it.) Being single wasn't just a problem in my coworkers' eyes but the entire world's. Cele never failed to comment on my lack of a husband when we spoke on the phone or when I visited, but she never dragged the subject out and remained as loving and devoted to me as ever. She was extremely proud of my job, and I think by that point everyone in Philadelphia knew about my IBM career through her constant bragging.

Dolly was too busy with her own family to pry too deeply into my personal life. Her children were all growing up fast, and she was back in school, studying for a Ph.D. in French literature. Blackie was the same old Blackie, still doing odd jobs, with a different girl at his side every time I saw him. I knew how smart he was and tried to get him a job at IBM. They gave him an IQ test, and he scored off the charts (higher even than I had—I was well over 140; he was 172), but he wasn't interested in a desk job in New York.

He did ask about Abby every now and then when no one else was around, but I'd glare and refuse to answer him. I continued to catch up with her over dinner every few months but was still convinced they'd had an affair behind my back.

I distracted myself from loneliness with shopping. I made good money, enough to keep my closet full of clothes that still had price tags on them. I was finally given my own office at work, a moment I took great pride in, and the first item I bought for it was an enormous glass ashtray. Sunnie came by to see my new digs during a stop through New York—she'd gotten married and wanted to introduce me to her husband. She was very impressed with the office, and I was smitten with the red Ferragamo heels that she'd picked up in Italy on their honeymoon. After they left, I promptly went searching for a pair of my own.

The dissatisfaction with my personal life began to manifest at work. During my yearly employee evaluation, I received many glowing remarks about how I'd earned the respect of the entire SHARE team, but under the self-improvement goals section, I was advised to learn how to "curb my emotions."

I made a decision to take that advice one step further and suppress them entirely. My love life had flatlined. It was growing more and more painful to see Thea at parties. I ached for her not even from afar, but close enough that I could see and smell the sweat glistening on her skin when we danced. *Torture* is the only word to describe the end of each night when her lover would pull her away and usher her out the door.

The final straw came at a New Year's Day brunch Dev invited me to, held at the house of a friend of hers, when Thea arrived with her girlfriend. It was quite chilly, but for dessert, the hostess served us all ice cream that had been mixed with vodka. I was so nervous about Thea being seated in the same room that I'd barely eaten a thing during the meal, but I devoured all the ice cream, and the alcohol went right to my head. I found myself wandering over to the record player in the next room, where an old Dinah Shore song played softly. Her voice reminded me of my early years of college, of my time with Caroline, and I swayed slightly to the music, staring out the window at the skeletal bare trees that lined the street, wondering what had happened to her, if she was happy, if she was still with Michael. The needle on the record suddenly skipped. I turned around to see Thea switching out the vinyl.

"You don't like Dinah Shore?" I asked.

"I do," she answered. "But this is far more fun."

The Beatles filled the room with their cover of "Twist and Shout." She turned the volume up as other women came dancing in. Beatlemania wasn't my thing, but I didn't care—Thea had sought me out to dance, and I matched her move for move. Someone else took over the turntable and continued a string of similar up-tempo songs to keep everyone going, until the party finally began to break off. Before long, it was just Thea and me, still dancing.

Dev approached, wearing her coat and holding mine. "Time to go," she said, and I could hear the warning in her voice. Thea and I turned putting on our coats into part of our shimmy.

"One more song," Thea said. It wasn't a request, so her date and Dev stood by the door, frowning and watching us continue to go at it until our hostess walked in and turned off the player. The only sound left was the clinking of dishes being stacked as a housekeeper cleared the table in the next room.

At home alone that night, I tried to tell myself the day had been a victory. The attraction was clearly still there on Thea's part.

So why was I all by myself?

Over the next few weeks, I grew more and more depressed. Rather than let myself wallow in my feelings, I tried to view them as I would any sort of math or computing problem. I identified each area of concern:

I was alone.

I wanted someone to love.

I wanted someone to love me.

The person I wanted to love and to love me back was unavailable.

It was an indefinable and unanswerable equation. To compound all of that, the world I lived in didn't approve of my homosexuality, and that's putting it mildly. That past summer, the Civil Rights Act of 1964 had passed, which outlawed labor discrimination based on race, religion, color, national origin, or sex. There was nothing in there about sexual orientation, and while I didn't think IBM would necessarily fire me if I were ever outed, it was certainly within their legal right to do so. And even if they discovered the truth and kept me on, I didn't doubt for a moment that my being gay would halt my steady rise within the company.

There was only one logical conclusion. The answer to my problem was to not be gay.

Or at least to not *act* on being gay. I know I couldn't change that fundamental part of my being, but I'd suppressed it once before with Saul, and now that I was older, I felt I had more control over my impulses. I thought about how much easier my life would be if I had a husband. I'd be accepted at work and could continue my career track unburdened. Boosted, even, with a man by my side championing me the whole way. A combined income would ensure stability. I'd no longer waste time and emotions

EDITH SCHLAIN
6120 Christian Street
SHAW
Poetic "Edie" likes good music and Dr. Mahaney. In her spare time she does Trig problems and breaks hearts. She lives for the day when her poems are published.
ACTIVITIES: Senator; Victory Corps Chairman; 101 Aide; Library Aide; Patrol; Senior Assembly Committee.

Born June 20, 1929, Edith Billie Schlain was around six years old here, and already a musical buff with a proclivity for getting kicked out of movie theaters due to playing harmonica along with the songs.

A rare portrait of the whole family taken in Atlantic City sometime in the late 1940s. CLOCKWISE FROM LEFT: older brother Blackie (*Edmund*); older sister Dolly (*Delphina*); mother, Cele (*Celia*); father, Jack; and Edie.

When Edie (*second to right*) took up tennis during her freshman year of college, she met her first girlfriend, Renee Kaplan (*far left*).

Edie was an associate editor at *Rittenhouse Review*, her first college's newspaper, but swore she had nothing to do with this glowing write-up in their "Bouquets" column.

Edie didn't know it at the time, but her friend Marty Cohen was also gay, and would go on to become an essential part of her social life in New York City years after this picture was taken.

During Edie's summers off from school she lived with friends in Atlantic City, where she found work as a waitress.

Saul Wiener and Edith Schlain married on May 5, 1951. Both of them walked away with a new last name—Windsor—but only Edie kept it after they divorced.

Edie tended to pace when she was anxious, a quirk she inherited from her father, Jack.

Marty Cohen introduced Edie to her core friend group in New York during the 1950s, several white-collar gay men she called "my boys."

After graduating from NYU with a master's degree in mathematics, Edie quickly began moving her way up the ranks at IBM.

As a core member of IBM's SHARE team, Edie took information and research from the company's divisions and helped decide how it could all work together as a whole.

Edie is often cited as a female pioneer in tech, but she was always quick to add that IBM was great about hiring women before she arrived there. (One of their early campus recruiting brochures was titled "My Fair Ladies.")

Edie first met Thea in 1963 at Portofino, a downtown restaurant with a popular, but unofficial, lesbian night. It took two more years for them to finally get together in 1965, when this picture was taken.

Thea, posing on the Yamaha Twin Jet 100 that Edie bought her. Edie only drove it once and ended up careening into oncoming traffic.

After homophobes targeted Fowler Beach, a popular gay hangout in the Hamptons, locals mobilized to form the East End Gay Organization.

Edie once said, "Everyone thought I was good at sports, but I wasn't at all." Thea's love of shooting her in various poses like this one likely contributed to the rumors.

Thea loved softball, but golf was her true passion.

The couple toured Europe in 1969 as Thea's birthday gift to Edie. Unbeknownst to them, the Stonewall riots were in full force back home in New York.

Whenever Edie looked at this picture of their ample matching luggage, she'd just laugh and shake her head.

Edie lounging in a Venetian gondola.

Edie's family threw her mother, Cele, a big bash for her eightieth birthday in 1973. That's Edie's sister Dolly on the right.

The couple's wild patterns come courtesy of the mid-seventies. This picture was taken just before Thea began to stumble due to her developing Multiple Sclerosis.

This photograph from Edie and Thea's fifteenth anniversary is the same one Edie used as their wedding cake topper twenty-seven years later. Her green dress was a custom gift from her friend Stan Herman.

Edie and Thea's annual Memorial Day Backyard BBQ was (and remains) a can't-miss Hamptons event that evolved into a fundraiser for various LGBTQ charities. Here, they celebrate circa the early 2000s.

A prophetic Halloween in the early eighties. Edie recalled, "So many people thought the sign was real!"

By 2006, Thea was in home hospice care but continued to see her own patients until she passed away in 2009.

The couple never once let Thea's wheelchair get in the way of their favorite pastime—dancing.

After Thea's death triggered a massive inheritance tax that would not have applied to a married heterosexual couple, Edie and her lawyer, Roberta "Robbie" Kaplan, sued the United States and won, paving the way for marriage equality in all fifty states.

Edie greets friends, family, and press on the steps of the Supreme Court in March 2013, right after Robbie made her winning arguments.

Meeting First Lady Michelle Obama was a highlight of Edie's White House visit.

After her historic win, Edie was invited to the White House to celebrate with President Barack Obama. Obama was a big Edie fan, and the feeling was more than mutual.

Edie and Jim Obergefell, whose landmark 2015 Supreme Court case completed the work she started and made same-sex marriage legal in all fifty states.

Days after her Supreme Court win on June 26, 2013, Edie was Grand Marshall at the New York City Pride March.

Judith Kasen-Windsor and Edie began dating in 2015. "She was the love of my life," Judith says. Here, they pose on the red carpet for the premiere of Dustin Lance Black's *When We Rise*.

Judith's best friend Danielle Reda served as the witness at their 2016 city hall wedding.

Legendary anti-war activist and author David Mixner became close friends with Edie and Judith during the last several years of Edie's life.

Edie and Judith wave from the Heritage of Pride float at the New York Pride March in 2017. (Note Judith's "Edie Windsor taught me how to code" shirt, created by Lesbians Who Tech.)

Edie and her cousin Sunnie were only a year apart and grew up extremely close; it was a friendship that lasted throughout Edie's entire life.

"Sunnie's Week" was a long-running annual event for Edie's cousin and her family to vacation in Southampton with her.

Karen Sauvigné (*left*) met Edie and Thea in the mid-eighties and soon became an extremely close and trusted friend to both. Here she is with Edie and Wendy Stark, executive director of Callen-Lorde, in 2012.

Her sense of humor on full display, Edie took to the streets for the 2017 New York Dyke March.

Edie's long history with The Center dates back to 1983 when she wrote a check to help them buy their current headquarters.

Edie adored the Lesbian & Gay Big Apple Corps and helped keep them in new uniforms—as long as they maintained the unofficial nickname of "Edie's Band."

chasing after a woman who was not only taken but almost seemed to be flaunting that fact in my face with her abrupt exits after every encounter. I felt too old to continue prowling the bars, and I didn't see my lesbian life leading anywhere except to more grief. I convinced myself that if I were truly meant to be with a woman for the rest of my life, I would have already met her when I was much younger.

I'd sowed more than my share of wild oats, and maybe that part of my life should end. I decided that I could live without sex. But I could not live without love.

I came upon what I believed to be the perfect solution. I'd try to find a widower with children who needed a mother. I could funnel the love I had to give in my heart into the kids, and hopefully this nameless man would remain so heartbroken over the loss of his wife that he'd want to stay faithful to her even in death. We'd create a marriage of more than simple convenience; it would be one that could benefit an entire family.

In order for my fantasy scenario to realistically work, I'd have to completely tamp down my feelings for women so there'd be no urges to stray. I didn't think that one-on-one reparative therapy was the right way to go for me; I knew most of those doctors were quacks. But there had to be other people out there like me, ones who wanted to give up the sadness in their lives and try to live among normal society. Having friends by my side that were experiencing a similar struggle would make it easier; I'd have confidants who could relate, and we could help each other.

It didn't take me long to find a support group. It wasn't technically designed as a conversion organization, but was for people with a variety of sexual issues that got in the way of the lives they wanted to live. There were around ten of us in the beginning, and the majority were heterosexual philanderers and serial cheaters, but there were a few gay men attempting the same path to a straight lifestyle as I was.

We met on Monday evenings in the Park Avenue office of one Dr. Mullins. We'd sit in a circle, drinking coffee and smoking, each taking a turn talking about what we wanted to change about ourselves and offering advice to the others on how to achieve specific goals. Dr. Mullins rarely intervened and seemed content to let us work through our own issues together. He acted more as a moderator in case a conversation got heated.

That winter was the gloomiest of my life. I'd spent Thanksgiving and Christmas in Philadelphia with my family, envious of Dolly's large, happy family and Blackie's ability to freely date whomever he wanted, whenever he wanted, with no repercussions from the family or the world at large. My own life consisted of work and therapy. I began to ignore lesbian friends like Dev and Abby, and I avoided walking down any block where I knew I might be tempted to duck into a women's bar.

Instead, I spent more time with my coworkers, attending lots of dinners with men and their wives. I agreed to go on more blind dates, but none remotely resembled the scenario I'd set my sights on, and it was too awkward to ask friends to only set me up on dates with men who happened to be recently widowed.

In the beginning, all the therapy really did for me was provide a distraction. Listening to depressing stories of failed marriages and recurring cases of the clap were enough to make anyone uninterested in dating, regardless of sexuality. All the members took a vested interest in my situation, though. The few gay men all dropped out after the first several weeks, so I was the only homosexual left. In the remaining patients' minds, I was a much worse deviant than any of them. They felt morally superior about their infidelities and self-destructive behavior, because at least they weren't gay. They weren't mean or cruel about it, though. If anything, their concern for my future fed my need for acceptance. A few of us began to socialize together outside of group, meeting for even more coffee and cigarettes to continue our conversations about everything that was wrong with our lives.

As the dreary months rolled by, I became more and more defeated. Even the long-awaited arrival of spring couldn't lift my mood. Everyone at work talked about summer vacation plans, and I half-heartedly agreed to possibly tag along on a few couples' trips.

Then a call came from Dev. She knew about my therapy group and remained vehemently opposed to it. She'd tried several times to get me to stop attending, to no avail, but she finally dangled the right bait.

"Word around town is that Thea and Frederica are on the outs," she said. "And Thea will be spending Memorial Day weekend at their usual Hamptons rental alone. This could be your opportunity."

My heart skipped several beats. I looked out the open window of my apartment; the early-evening sky was still bright, and the noise on the street below seemed to grow louder, filling me with the same excitement that I'd felt when I first moved to the village. I felt giddy as the old me, the real me, began to rise back up to the surface.

"Well, we must go to the Hamptons, then," I said.

"I can't. I have family plans I'm committed to. Besides, it'll be close to impossible to find a place this close to the holiday."

"Then why on earth are you telling me?" I asked, exasperated, but still grateful for the news.

"Because I know you'll find a way to make it happen."

It was mid-May, which meant I had two weeks to figure out a plan. I began phoning friends and ex-lovers I hadn't spoken to in months but whom I knew would still take my call. None had a bed for me—they were either staying in already packed houses or headed to Provincetown or Fire Island.

In the course of my reaching out, I dug up a bit more information. Apparently, Thea and her friend Peggy planned to drive to the Hamptons late Friday night. Thea's summer rental was in East Hampton, but she was going to stop by a house in Southampton first on her way in, to drop Peggy off, because she was staying there with a different group of friends.

I had to be at that house when Thea arrived to drop Peggy off.

The ringleader of that particular clique was named Mary, and while I knew who she was in passing from bars and parties, I'm not sure we'd even said hello to each other twice. I learned that her rental had a spare bedroom, so I found her number, gathered all my courage, and cold-called her that night.

"I know this is presumptuous as hell," I said after some cautious chit-chat. "But I hear that you have an extra bed in your house for Memorial Day weekend, and I'd love to take it. I can bring a check, and of course, I'd share all expenses."

Whether she was simply a nice person willing to help out another lesbian or needed another pocketbook to help pick up the tab, she graciously agreed.

My next step was to quit the therapy group. I felt I owed it to them to tell them in person, since we'd shared so much with each other already. They didn't take the news well, which I'd expected. After several shocked protests from the circle, Dr. Mullins raised his hand to silence the room.

"Edie," he said. His voice oozed with concern, but the tone had the opposite effect of his intended one—I felt my anger flare. "This is a terrible idea," he continued. "And I think you know that."

"What I *know* is that I need to see this through to its conclusion," I said, looking around. "There's a pull between me and Thea that I have to explore. Even if it doesn't work out, I need to know that I tried when I had a chance. I know I'll regret it if I don't go."

"That pull you feel toward her, it's called the false breast," Dr. Mullins said. "You don't want that."

"The *what?*"

"The false breast. This woman, she represents your need for maternal affection."

I burst out laughing. Cele provided more than enough maternal affection. Always had and always would.

"I really don't think that's correct," I said.

The group made me promise to come back again the following Monday before Memorial Day. I agreed, but not for the reason they hoped. I wanted to say my final goodbyes in person, because I knew that even if my shot with Thea turned out to be nothing, I still wouldn't be returning to them. The mere potential of happiness was enough to jolt me out of my funk.

As my excitement grew over the next several days, I realized that I didn't owe them anything. I felt badly for many of the members—several really were in miserable shape—but I wasn't one of them. On Monday, I wrote them a note, begging off due to a terrible cold and apologizing that we all couldn't have been more help to each other. I arranged the delivery myself during lunch so my secretary wouldn't see it, and after work, I began the next step on my holiday preparation to-do list: swimsuit shopping.

That Friday, I left work early in an attempt to beat the traffic out of Manhattan, but so had the rest of New York City. During that slog of a drive, I had plenty of time to second-guess my impulsive actions. I had no idea if this woman truly liked me. What if it had all been in my head? What if I was about to make an utter fool out of myself? I was acting like a high school girl with a crush who'd decided to crash a party on the off chance that the object of her desire might take notice.

Each time I worked myself into a state of anxiety, I forced myself to remember the dance floors I'd shared with Thea. I hadn't imagined us staring directly into each other's eyes, or her snake-charmer ability to use her body to maneuver my own without ever touching it.

I finally arrived at the house around 7:00 p.m. The rental wasn't beachside, but it was close to the shore, and as I stepped out of the car and began unloading my luggage, I could feel the wind coming in off the ocean, cooling the evening.

Mary and the rest of her houseguests suddenly appeared en masse, filing out the front door, laughing. All the women looked vaguely familiar to me from the bars, and I felt a rush of relief that I hadn't slept with any of them.

"Edie! You're just in time!" Mary said. She greeted me with a hug. "I left a note for you in the kitchen; we're on our way to dinner, and we're going dancing at the Millstone Tavern after. Here, let me help you take your stuff inside. You must join us."

"Oh, no, I'm fine," I said. "I'm actually exhausted from the drive."

They badgered me a bit more, but I insisted, so Mary showed me inside to my tiny closet of a room before taking off. In the sudden silence, I nervously explored the rest of the house, too anxious to fix myself any-thing for supper. I checked the clocks every five minutes and kept a con-stant eye on the front windows for the sight of headlights turning into the driveway. The night felt interminably long, and when it reached midnight, I stretched out on my twin bed and fell asleep.

I awoke to the sound of everyone stumbling in from their evening out, and I ran downstairs, worried that I'd missed the drop-off, but when I casually asked Mary if Peggy had already arrived, she said she'd heard out at the bar that Thea ended up having to work late at her residency, and they wouldn't be arriving until the following day. I was disappointed, but also mildly relieved since I was still a bit woozy from my nap and knew I wouldn't be in top form. I said my good-nights and fell back into bed.

I woke early, and it was still chilly, so I dressed in a cream-colored cashmere sweater with a mock turtleneck and light gray flannel slacks I'd brought because they were extra tight in the ass and flatteringly tapered from the thigh down. I topped it all off with a strand of pearls.

Everyone else woke up not long after I did, hungover but still full of energy. They began to pack up a picnic lunch to spend the day at the beach.

"Come," Mary urged. "Join us!"

I declined the invitation, pretending to feel mildly ill but promising to join them later if I felt better. Thea had to see me as soon as she arrived, so she'd know I was in town.

As the morning turned to lunch hour and stretched on to midafter-noon, I began to grow tense, pacing from one end of the house to the other. My nerves about seeing Thea evolved into a more familiar feeling—I was starting to become annoyed as hell. The holiday weekend was closing in on the halfway mark. What if it was all a waste of time? To top it off, I hadn't even had a chance to work on my tan.

Around 2:00 p.m., I heard a car pull into the driveway, and I froze mid-stride. Doors slammed, and from my post in the living room, I watched Peggy burst into the kitchen and get straight to work making coffee.

Thea entered the house a moment later. She wore a tan linen shirt and white pants with a braided rope tied together as a belt—the picture of summer-casual lesbian chic. She leaned across the counter, facing Peggy, but didn't see me. I approached her quietly from behind, extended my hand, and almost touched her. I hovered, my fingers an inch from her back, daring myself to make contact, before I quickly pulled my arm back.

"Is your dance card full?" I finally asked.

She didn't turn around, but I could feel her smiling.

"Now it is."

Without looking at me, she walked toward a turntable sitting in a corner of the living room. I followed. She kneeled down to put on a record. I don't remember what, only that it rollicked. Maybe Martha and the Vandellas. As she started to stand back up, I stopped her. I turned her body and held her head, pulling it to my breasts, where she rested for a moment.

We rushed out of the house, leaving Peggy behind without saying a word. I caught a glimpse of her jaw dropping open slightly. Thea drove wildly with one hand on my thigh, and I felt like I couldn't breathe during the entire ride.

Maybe twenty minutes later, she turned onto a small, quiet side street. The road was unpaved, and there were no houses to be seen, until eventually a barn rolled into view. It had been converted into living quarters and painted white, though it was already flaking a bit at the corners. It wasn't anywhere near as large as the house we'd just been in, but it had a rustic charm and a mild sophistication to its shabbiness, as though it were intentional, because the energy spent there was meant to be devoted to enjoying life, instead of worrying about perfection. Thea opened the barn doors so that the living room and the yard became one, and she led me by the hand to a small bedroom built into the back of the structure.

We fumbled with our clothes, and once they were off, they stayed off for the rest of the day.

The phone rang periodically for long stretches, but Thea didn't get up to answer until the sky began to grow dark, and she left the bedroom to close the barn doors against mosquitos. It was Peggy on the other line; she and the rest of the girls wanted to know if we wanted to go dancing. Thea didn't have to ask me to know my answer.

———— ✺ ————

The story of Edie's "Is your dance card full?" pickup line is legend among those who knew Edie and Thea well, but the location of their long-awaited consummation is also legendary. Provincetown and Fire Island were the much more well-known East Coast destinations for gay vacationers, but since the 1950s, the Hamptons had also been building up a strong queer community, albeit a rather niche one.

Clothing designer Stan Herman initially met Edie through Abby in the 1950s, and though they were friendly, they lost touch when Edie went back to school at NYU, but reconnected and grew extremely close later in life. He describes the Hamptons of that period as much different from how it is now. "It was an arts center," he says. "A small one, but it attracted people like Philip Roth, John Ashbery, Pollock, Capote. I had a small place that I rented to de Kooning's mistress."

Almost any area known as a center of the arts will inevitably draw a queer crowd, but the difference with this place was money. Stan invokes a popular phrase about the wealthy end of Long Island but infuses it with double meaning: "The Hamptons were behind the hedges."

By the mid-'60s, the Hamptons had a thriving underground gay community. Lesbians and gay men rarely comingled except on the dance floor at the Millstone or at Fowler Beach, the unofficial gay spot for swimming and sunbathing, and even in those spaces, men and women tended to stick to their own gender. It was an affluent, privileged, upper-class crowd of not just artists but people who could afford to buy the art.

Money wasn't any sort of driving force in Edie's quest for love, but it's fair to say that security was; Cele had put that in her head from the very start. That Thea frequented a well-heeled vacation destination likely didn't go unnoted by her.

Edie's observation that gay visibility was increasing was spot-on. The Stonewall riots were only four years away. Inspired by the civil rights movement, activist groups like the Mattachine Society and Daughters of Bilitis were becoming more and more visible. (The former took its name from a masked group of performers and protesters in medieval France; Bilitis was an obscure fictional inhabitant of the Isle of Lesbos.) But at this point in her life, Edie was much more focused on personal growth than community. *Prior to her post-Stonewall activist awakening, she's often admitted that she had disapproved of people who flaunted their gayness. "I didn't see why I had to be associated with those queens," she said on more than one occasion, referring to Stonewall's patrons. "But then they turned a car over in the street in protest, and everything changed for me."*

No one can blame her for an initial internalized homophobia. It remains incredibly common, especially for people like her who've spent their lives successfully moving unnoticed in heterosexual society. It cannot be overstated that Edie didn't stand out as a lesbian. "She always had the most makeup on in any room," Stan recalls. "She may have been a Judy Garland fan, but there was a big part of her that was Ginger Rogers. The flossy hair, the frozen-in-time look . . . a showbiz glitter. No righteous lesbian would wear low-cut blouses like she did. And the more buttons she opened, the more desirable she became. She was famous for her breasts, and she threw them around."

He's teasing and describes her physical appearance lovingly (even pretending to juggle her breasts in the air like balls), but there's no question that Edie's natural femininity made her a nontarget, unlike "those queens." Queer people almost always craft early identities in a state of fear about being discovered, even if it's subconscious. Edie had the perfect disguise in both her physical appearance and taste in clothing. She did not want to be found out. She was a staunch supporter of the civil rights movement, but when it came to being gay, she felt safest with those most like herself: upwardly mobile white women. It was self-preservation and, at the time, the only way she could imagine leading a safe and happy life. The allure of the Hamptons' lesbian scene, with its promise of less glitter and more golf, was strong.

Eleven

There were signs from the very start that Thea was nowhere near ready to settle down with a new girlfriend. Take our first night out dancing at the Millstone Tavern. The area's only gay bar was a mysterious little place, located on the northern end of the island in Noyack, close to the Bridgehampton Race Circuit. If you went early enough, you could hear cars zooming and loud cheers in the distance, but late night was the time to arrive, and despite its desolate location, the hidden bar sometimes got so crowded that the doorman would turn people away. That never happened to us, though. The Millstone drew a primarily male audience, so it helped if there were some women on hand in case of a raid.

The Millstone was little more than a cement bunker with a concrete floor. A wooden bar ran along one side, and a jukebox on the opposite wall was filled with hits you couldn't escape that summer. The floor was packed with people doing line dances like the Hully Gully and the Madison.

I'd been there a few times before on previous brief weekend trips to the Hamptons, but arriving with my arm on Thea's was an entirely different experience. I felt like I truly belonged, especially when she introduced me to several handsome gay male friends whom I thought looked incredibly sophisticated, with nary a shirttail out of place or sweat stain to be found, despite the heat and bodies pressed together.

The admiration wasn't shared. They all seemed appalled by my presence, and it quickly became apparent that they'd brought along a woman of their own to introduce to Thea on her first weekend out as a free agent. She chose to stick with me, though, and we tore up the dance floor all night with Peggy and Mary and the other women from the rental house.

The rest of the weekend is a blur of sunbathing and wild sex. Thea had brought along a violin and climbed up to the barn's second floor loft to serenade me from above—she was working her way through Mozart's Concertos nos. 23–27. As I listened, I wished that Cele could hear her play. She'd always adored classical violin, and Thea was superb. She told me the story about how she'd been passed over as first violin at Sarah Lawrence and how she changed her major because of it.

I thought it a shame that she'd quit playing professionally, but more importantly, I took note of the story behind the story. She had an ego—a well-deserved one—but I sensed that if I wanted a future with her, I might need to tread carefully at first. She only wanted the best out of life, and I needed to show her that's exactly what I was.

At the end of the weekend, she drove me back to Mary's house so I could pick up my car. We embraced and exchanged numbers, and she promised to call me the next evening, which she did, and we made plans to meet for dinner later that week.

Thus began a pattern that would continue for the rest of the summer and well into fall—she canceled on me.

I didn't think anything of it at first. I was disappointed, but it wasn't the end of the world. She promised to call me back and reschedule, but then didn't. I was pissed and refused to call her to find out what had happened. When she finally reached out the following Tuesday, she invited me to the Hamptons for the weekend, so I accepted her apologies and the vague excuse she gave for her sudden disappearance.

The weekend was as glorious as our Memorial Day holiday had been, with a few small exceptions. The sex was just as fantastic, if not better, but each day that we were at the barn house, the phone would ring in the early morning and she'd slink into the bathroom with the receiver, tucking the cord under the door and shutting it behind her.

It's not as though we were officially dating, but I did find her behavior rude. It was clear to me that I wasn't the only woman she was sleeping with. Not only that, but there were apparently others waiting in line. At the Millstone, her male friends weren't any nicer to me than before, and in fact acted outright hostile. I overheard one of them say, "Just promise you'll meet her for a drink this week. She's perfect for you."

I confronted her about the man's request that night when we got home. Not aggressively, I just explained that I wanted to know the score between us. She was very frank.

"I'm not interested in being tied down," she said. "I've been with the same woman for a few years now, and it's time for me to play the field. If you can handle that, I think you're sexy as hell, and I hope you'll continue to see me."

"I'll do more than just see you," I told her.

I understood the logic, and the last thing I wanted was to be her rebound relationship. If she needed time, I'd give her that. I threw myself even more into work, but found that I needed a hobby to keep me distracted on the nights I stayed in alone, something to occupy my mind rather than imagine all the other women Thea might be out with. So when I saw an advertisement in the back of *The New Yorker* for a build-your-own harpsichord kit, I sent away for one.

Thea's violin playing had already reawakened my appreciation for classical music, and I signed up for piano classes to try to pick back up all the lessons I'd learned as a child while Blackie and Dolly were away at the army base. I convinced myself that by the time I finished building my new harpsichord, Thea would not only be done with her roving, perhaps we'd play music together.

She continued to ask me to join her at the barn on weekends, but sometimes I'd feel as though I'd suddenly been demoted to friend. She'd disappear for hours to play golf, which she was mad for, or tell me that

she needed to have a private dinner with an old acquaintance and leave me there alone, and then try to sneak back in around dawn with some story about how she'd been dragged out to the Millstone against her will.

I tried to invite her into my world, but she always had an excuse to say no. One weekend, Dolly threw a birthday party for one of my nephews, and I asked her if she'd like to go, but she declined. During the party, surrounded by children and family, I grew lonely, so I called her up at the barn just to hear her voice, even though I decided ahead of time I'd keep the conversation light and casual. She picked up on the fourth ring, sounding slightly out of breath.

"Hello, it's Edie," I said.

"Oh! Hello," she said, and I heard a familiar click in the background— the sound of the bathroom door closing behind her. This time, I was the woman on the other line.

"I didn't realize you were entertaining," I said icily.

"It's just a friend," she said. "You'd love her." The name she dropped was a woman mildly famous at the time for her repeated wins on a prime-time television quiz show. I knew that she was beautiful and hadn't realized she was a lesbian. I quickly made up a reason to hang up.

I began to lug whichever section of my gigantic harpsichord kit I happened to be working on to the Hamptons every time I received one of her invitations, so I'd have something to do in case she wandered off. She teased me mercilessly about it and even went so far as to "accidentally" spill water on some of it when I was sanding a piece of wood while sitting on the ground next to some plants, but I could tell she was impressed with my dedication.

In early August, I was due to fly to Seattle for an IBM conference mid-month, and since it ran Tuesday to Thursday, some coworkers and I decided to stay through the following weekend and rent a house near Olympic National Park. I wrote a check for my share, but when I mentioned the trip to Thea, she begged me to fly home on Friday instead and spend the weekend with her. I was surprised by her insistence and thought that maybe we were turning a corner, since I was already supposed to spend the upcoming weekend with her. So I canceled on my colleagues and changed my flight.

I picked her up that Friday night to drive us out to East Hampton, and I could tell by the look on her face that something was wrong.

"I'm so sorry, but I have to cancel next weekend."

"Oh no! Why?" I pretended to take the news in stride, but I was furious. I couldn't change my flight for a second time, and besides, another coworker had already taken my slot in the rental. I'd be stuck in the city during the hottest month of summer.

"I have to work," she said, handing me a letter. I scanned the neatly typed paragraphs on letterhead from a psychology institute I'd never heard of, informing her that she was required to take on additional shifts at her residency.

"Tell them you're unable to, that it's too short notice," I said, finally making my annoyance visible.

"I can't. It's a direct request from one of my former professors who advised on my dissertation. I'm so sorry. I promise I'll make up for the missed time this weekend."

She slid her hand up my thigh, and by the time we arrived at the barn, I'd all but forgotten the bad news.

The weekend was as dreamlike as ever. We'd have sex for hours and then head to Fowler Beach, where she'd socialize while I sunbathed, reading and smoking behind a pair of sunglasses. Thea loved to cook, and she boiled up lobster fresh from the sea. Best of all, there were no mysterious phone calls I had to pretend to ignore.

On Sunday, before heading back to the city, we decided to stop off to say goodbye to a few women we'd run into at the beach who were staying an extra day and throwing a barbecue that afternoon. The house was in the middle of nowhere, and as we turned onto a narrow road, I saw a large pack of motorcycles lining one side like a gleaming black fence.

"I'd love to own one of those," Thea said longingly, staring at the machines as I parked the car on the opposite side of the road, a bit farther up.

I didn't want my bumper getting scratched by someone suddenly zooming off.

"Then you should buy one," I said. I knew by that point that she could certainly afford it. "I think you'd look fantastic on a motorcycle."

She wrinkled her nose a bit. "A person must ride the *right* kind of motorcycle. One that looks good on her." She had a habit of jokingly referring to herself in the third person at times, particularly when discussing material goods or commenting on proper manners.

"We shouldn't stay too long, or traffic on the way home will be a disaster," I said as we walked to the back of the house, following the sound of music playing and loud laughter.

I don't think I'd ever seen so many butches in one place before in my life. It felt like a biker club full of women wearing leather vests despite the heat. I could feel eyes all over me, and what can I say, I loved the attention. Thea seemed to as well and took great pride in showing me off and introducing me around this new crowd. I finally spotted a familiar face, Mary, and went over to say hello.

"Memorial Day seems to have worked out well for you," she teased. "I'm happy I could be of service to help kick things off." I knew that rumors had been circulating among the Hamptons' lesbian crowd of my ploy to use her house to meet Thea, but I couldn't have cared less.

"You and me both, dear," I said.

"Just be careful with that one. I've heard things."

"We're doing quite fine, thank you." I didn't realize how cold the words sounded, and she looked taken back.

"I didn't mean anything by that," she said. "I just . . ."

"It's fine. I should get going. I'm sure I'll see you soon."

I walked away abruptly and went inside the house looking for Thea. I found her deep in conversation with a striking woman with short dark hair, wearing a plain white T-shirt and jeans. She had a bottle of beer in her hand, with her thumb hooked onto the belt loop so they tugged her pants down a bit, exposing a strip of milky-white skin below her waist. I could see why Thea was listening so intently to what she had to say.

"We need to get going," I interrupted.

Thea looked startled to see me for a moment, but recovered fast and kissed my cheek. "Yes, let's go. Oh, this is Aileen. Aileen, this is Edie."

We smiled tightly at each other, and I gave her a curt *hello* nod before spinning on my heel and marching out of the house. Thea followed right behind.

"Don't be jealous," she said. "We just met. It turns out she's the cousin of one of Peggy's oldest friends."

"I'm not jealous at all," I said, keeping my voice light. "I'm just worried about getting back too late."

Right when we got to my car, I heard a door slam behind us, and I looked up. Aileen was bent forward on the front porch, her hands leaning on the rail. She cocked her hip, accentuating the curve of her behind. "Hey, Thea!" she shouted. "I'll see you here next weekend! Can't wait!"

Thea pretended not to hear. We both got in the car, and neither of us said a word as I turned on the engine and tore off down the road. I took the next several turns wildly and careened on toward the highway.

I finally couldn't stand it anymore. "Perhaps I heard wrong, but did that woman say she'd see you 'here' next weekend?"

"Hmm? No, I told you, I have to work."

I glanced down at the seat and saw the letter Thea had shown me on Friday. I grabbed it and unfolded it with one hand, reading it over in between quick glances at the road.

"This is utter garbage!" I said. I couldn't believe I hadn't realized it before. The words read exactly like a fake doctor's note that a teenager might forge to get out of school. "My god, did you actually write this yourself?"

"Don't be absurd," she said, not very convincingly.

"Well, then, since you'll be *working,* I'm happy to take the barn off your hands next weekend, seeing as how I canceled my vacation plans for you and have nowhere else to go."

She opened her mouth to say something but saw the look on my face and thought better of it. "Sure," she said meekly. "It's yours."

We rode in painful silence the rest of the way home. When I dropped her off, she reached to take back the letter, but I snatched it first.

"I'll hold on to this. And I'll take the keys to the barn."

She looked miserable as she pulled them from her pocket and placed them on the seat next to me before exiting to remove her bags from the trunk. She left the passenger door open like usual so that she could climb back inside and kiss me once she'd unloaded her suitcases, but I reached across the seat and slammed it shut.

The whole car shook as she closed the trunk, and I saw from the rear-view mirror that she was coming up to my window to say something. I slammed my foot on the gas and left her standing in the road.

The following night, I finally took the phone off the hook to end the constant ringing. I refused to pick up. When I arrived at our hotel in Seattle on Tuesday, there was a wire waiting for me. *Please let me explain. Please call.* I crumpled it up and threw it in the trash before heading up to my room.

The conference was a nice distraction, but everyone could tell something was troubling me and tried to get me to open up. "Family problems," I said. "I'd rather not discuss it."

They urged me to stay with them at the end of the week, offered up the couch at the house rental, but I declined. I'd have felt like a burden out in the open, in the middle of a room, and I didn't want to spend the extra money to change my flight because of *her*.

I took the red-eye home Thursday night, and I could hear my phone ringing from the hallway before I even got my door keys out. It continued to ring all morning as I unpacked my work clothes and repacked weekend outfits. Once more, the only solution was to take the phone off the hook.

I had no idea what to do with all the anger I felt. I took a long walk around the neighborhood, chain-smoking the entire time, because I knew it was probably a bad idea for me to get behind the wheel of my car just yet. After I felt a little calmer, I returned to the apartment to collect my things and placed the phone back on its hook. It immediately began to ring. I picked it up and held the receiver to my ear, not saying a word.

"Oh, thank god," Thea said. "Please don't hang up. Just let me say something. I don't expect it to fix anything, but I need you to know why I did it."

I didn't say a word but made sure she could hear my loud, angry sigh.

"It was such a stupid thing for me to do. It's just that I didn't want to hurt you, and I thought that having you think I was working was a better option than you knowing I was with another woman. I wanted to spare your feelings, and I've always been clear with you that I'm not ready to settle down yet, but—"

"I know you're not interested in settling down," I snapped. "I know the situation we're in, and I accept that, and I'm the one who's being the adult about it. I can't for the life of me understand why you won't be a grown-up as well. My god, Thea. *A fake letter?* You must think I'm an absolute idiot. And I was an idiot—I fell for it! I should be thanking Aileen."

"I won't be seeing her ever again," Thea said. "If that helps."

"You can see whomever and do whatever you want."

"What I want is to spend the weekend with you. Please let me join you."

That was all I wanted too, but the days would be tainted. Her betrayal was too fresh, and I told her as much.

"I swear I will make it up to you," she said. "I need to see you. You're all I can think about."

"Only because now you know you can't have me."

"No, that isn't true. It's because you're sexy and brilliant, and I was a fool to ever think there's anyone out there more beautiful or as fascinating as you."

I could feel myself start to relent, and that only made me angrier. "I need to think about it."

"Peggy is giving me a ride out to the Hamptons. I'll stay with her. Just let me come to the barn to see you tonight. Please, Edie."

Hearing her say my name did the trick. She filled the word with so much genuine emotion, but I still wasn't ready to let her know that I could forgive her yet.

"Fine, you can stop by around 9:00 p.m., and we'll talk."

"Thank you, Edie," she said. "You don't know what that means to me."

I thought about our situation for the entire drive out, trying once more to take my emotions and put them into a form of logic. What she'd done was despicable, but if she'd truly done it to try to spare my feelings, then it meant she cared, that she had feelings for me beyond the fantastic sex. There wasn't really any other answer aside from that; she was open about not wanting to get serious, so there was no reason for her to not just tell me the truth——that she was going to be with someone else for the weekend.

But then I'd remember this all happened *after* she'd made plans with me, after I'd already changed my plane ticket. It was one thing to want to sleep around and plan accordingly, another thing entirely to be passed over after plans had been made. There's a staggering difference between accepting that you're one of many women but then discovering you're considered second best of the available options.

I still didn't know how I was going to handle the problem when I arrived at the barn. I moved through the house, turning on lights and unpacking my things; it felt disorienting to be there without Thea. Our place of joy took on the deadweight of silence. There was no reason for me to be there without her, and I felt my resolve to keep her visit to a casual one, a chance to assert my will and simply talk things out before sending her on her way, begin to slip.

My strength disappeared entirely when I heard the rumble of her car along the road. I watched her pull up, get out, and look at me warily as she approached the door where I stood. I wondered how it was possible that she'd become even more beautiful after a week of feeling nothing but fury for her. She folded her arms around me and kissed me, and we stumbled backward through the house toward the bedroom, tearing at our clothes.

The last few weeks of summer passed without incident. Whenever we were at the beach or the Millstone, Thea would stay focused solely on me, making me feel as though I were the only desirable woman in the world. While I suspected there still might be others on the side in the city, I didn't press the issue. I told myself that as long as she didn't lie to me, I could handle that knowledge for the time being.

But it begged the question—where were we headed? I certainly wasn't going to wait around for her forever, but I was deeply, madly in love. She was the most impressive woman I'd ever met. Driven in her career and never willing to rest on the knowledge she'd gained in school—she kept up with all the medical and psychiatric journals, studying advancements in her field and figuring out ways to work the ones she believed in into her own fledgling private practice.

Once fall came and we were back in the city full-time, she began to sleep over at my house a lot. I knew that she lived downtown somewhere with a male roommate named Robert, but she never invited me to her place, insisting that she didn't have much privacy there. That was something we definitely required, as our sex life somehow kept getting better and better.

I was curious about her male friend, though, and suggested many times that the three of us should get dinner, but she always pushed the idea aside. She in turn repeatedly asked to come see my office in the Time-Life Building, which I also refused to commit to. I was too nervous that someone might suspect we were sleeping together, since all our mutual friends commented constantly on the clear physical attraction between us, even when I wasn't aware either of us were doing anything.

"I've got it," she said one day. "We can kill two birds. I'll bring Robert to your office. You'll finally get to meet him, and it will deflect any suspicion because I can pretend he's my boyfriend. You can give us a little tour, and then we'll all get lunch."

I thought this was an excellent idea. Despite my nerves, I did want to show off my workplace; I was still supremely proud of my large office.

They arrived promptly at noon. Robert was tall and attractive, but rather aloof. I didn't get the impression at first that they were particularly close friends, although that was all about to change. I gave them the grand tour and made a few cursory introductions to coworkers who hadn't already ducked out for lunch. I saved my office for last. I ushered them in and sat behind my desk, gesturing to the two chairs in front of it for them to sit down.

"Very impressive," Thea said, and I beamed. "Much larger than I expected."

"I'm very important," I teased.

"I can tell," she said. Robert sat down in one of the chairs and gave me a mischievous smile. Thea shut the door behind her and joined him in the second chair. "You could get away with all sorts of things in here."

I laughed, a bit embarrassed about how flirty she was being with me in front of Robert. His smile suddenly started to look less mischievous and more lecherous.

"Where should we go for lunch?" I asked, lighting up a cigarette.

"Why leave at all?" she said.

"Because I'm hungry."

She reached across the desk and took my hand in hers. To my utter shock, she then reached out for Robert's hand as well. "I think the three of us could have much more fun in here."

I'd already guessed by that point that's where she might be headed but had been hoping I was wrong. I had no idea she'd ever even been with a man, and I wasn't about to ask her if she'd planned on this proposed three-way to be her first. I wrenched my hand away. "Get the hell out of my office," I said icily, repeatedly stabbing my cigarette out in the ashtray.

"Darling, don't be a prude," she said.

I was shocked that she seemed to have no idea just how far over the line she'd crossed.

"Get out," I said as loud as I dared. "*Now.*"

Robert shrugged as he stood and left the room without a word, but Thea lingered in the door. "I just thought it might be exciting." She started to say something else but decided against it after she saw the look in my eyes. I was so angry that I was shaking. "We'll talk later," she said and quickly left.

Don't count on it, I thought.

I really thought that was the end of us. I tried to concentrate on work for about another thirty minutes but gave up and went home, claiming I was sick.

How *dare* she! It was awful enough that she'd so thoroughly disrespected my office, the place at which I'd worked so hard to arrive, but she'd opened up an entirely new door of paranoia and fear. She and Robert were *lovers* and not just roommates? The whole thing had come so far out of left field, I felt like I'd been socked.

My phone began to ring right at 6:30 p.m., when she knew I'd normally be arriving home from work. I yanked the phone cord out of the wall and tried to fight back tears. I couldn't eat and spent the entire night in bed, smoking and staring at the ceiling, wondering how on earth I could have been stupid enough to fall in love with Thea Spyer. I felt like a goddamned fool.

The next day at work, every single person I interacted with asked me what was wrong. They could see the dismay and anger on my face, and I insisted that I was just still feeling under the weather. I stayed late at work every night, not wanting to go home, where I'd be alone with my dark thoughts.

After three days of not reaching me, Thea finally dared calling the office, even though I'd always told her to never call me there. I told my secretary to inform her I was unavailable.

After about a week, the phone calls stopped, and I knew we were over. I didn't have the heart to ask any of my friends if they'd heard anything about what she was up to, and like I always did when times were rough, I threw myself deeper into work. On weekends, I went to the movies by myself and cooked sad little dinners for one.

Sometime in mid-October, I awoke around 2:00 a.m. to the sound of my phone ringing. I reached over and picked it up, my first thought being that something terrible must have happened to one of my family members.

"Hello?"

I heard a muffled sigh, the sounds of cars honking, a small sniffle.

"What do you want, Thea?" I lay there in the darkness, listening to her breathe. I heard a clicking sound and realized she must have been calling from a pay phone. I heard a siren and then realized I could hear the same one from outside my window. She was close by.

"What do you want?" I repeated.

"You," she said. "I want you."

"You're not ready for me."

"I am, I swear it. Please let me see you."

This was abuse, pure and simple. I wanted her so badly it ached, I could already feel her legs wrapped around me in bed, and I knew I was a goner. "Go ahead, then," I said. "Come up."

The phone went dead, and less than a minute later, my buzzer began to ring.

I didn't ask her about Robert. She'd already apologized profusely for her proposal a number of times, but I didn't press for any details about him. I didn't want to know, didn't want anything to fracture the joy of having her back in my life. She said that she'd already moved out and into a new place, that after the day in my office, she knew she'd made a terrible mistake and wanted nothing to do with him since he'd become a constant reminder of why I was no longer in her life. She swore that she'd been trying to be kinky, that there was nothing else behind her insane suggestion. She had absolutely no desire to be with men. From her enthusiasm with me in bed, I believed her, but I felt the need to remind her often that I was not going to put up with any more of her shit.

"If you want this," I reinforced more than once, "then you've got to have it, period. No more others." She swore up and down that she was all in.

Looking back, I can't believe how much I put up with from her. She grew into such a glorious person, but she wasn't always that way. She was human, and I would never fault her for that. And in the end, all the waiting, all the mental torture, was worth it a million times over.

———◦◦———

There were a few more brief breakups and makeups aside from the Robert incident during that bumpy fall of 1965. Edie shared a letter that Thea wrote *after one of their many breakup sex sessions during this period that provides good insight to where Thea's head was during this time. Edie had fallen asleep when they'd finished and woke to find an empty bed and the following note:*

Edie,

Be proud of being yourself! I don't know how much happiness you'll get in return for it but it seems that your way should pay off.

There are few who can create, rather than settle for what happens (I'm not one of the creators yet) and from what I can see of your dealings with the world you'll carve out something good.

Although I behave absurdly, I have changed, or am changing from having known you, mainly in that I have tasted moments of nearly unmodified joy as never before . . . no, that's not true. It's because I have been given something which is marred somewhat by my not having really done likewise for you in a sustained way.

I have spent the last hour or so savoring some of the most glorious moments with you. I began with your body, your deep sensuality, and ended with your commitment to living which is really what you're about. Your putting an end to the affair was again commitment to defining, limiting, and hence really having what we had (reality and potential both). I am deeply grateful to you for having done that for both of us.

Yes—that's what I wanted to say. I wish I could really be something for you, something substantial, but I can't, not now, probably never.

You're a magnificent woman, fully deserving of a golden five iron.

Thea was clearly being affected by Edie's good influence. She wasn't ready to fully commit just yet, but Edie's way of looking at life had begun to change the way Thea saw her own. Each breakup brought Thea closer to realizing what she wanted, or as one of their friends put it, "Thea's heart finally started catching up to her intellect."

Twelve

I want to take you somewhere special for the holidays," Thea announced one evening in bed.

"That sounds lovely," I said, wrapping the blankets around me tightly. "Can we go somewhere warm?" The temperature had recently dipped into the midthirties, and even with Thea finally by my side—she was spending almost every night at my place while searching for a new apartment—I wasn't looking forward to another dreary winter.

"How does South America sound?"

"Just perfect! Brazil? I hear the beaches are gorgeous. Argentina?" I was already mentally sorting my bikinis.

"Suriname," she announced.

"Never heard of it."

"It's on the northern end of the continent. Coastal, but it stretches inland, so there are jungles to explore."

"But there are beaches?" I asked, trying to sound casual. I didn't want to come across as ungrateful.

"Yes, yes," she assured me.

I gave her a kiss. "I love that you've sought out someplace unique and off the tourist path."

I thought it was a symbol of her thirst for adventure but soon discovered her destination of choice was almost the opposite. It turns out that Suriname was colonized by the Dutch in the late seventeenth century, and it became a plantation state that was dependent on African slaves. At the time, in 1965, it had only been its own constituent country of the Netherlands for about a decade and wouldn't become independent for another ten years.

Thea's particular interest in it was that the population largely spoke Dutch, which would make the trip easier for us to navigate and, more importantly for her, provide a chance to impress me with her language skills outside of a standard European destination.

It meant so much to her, in fact, that I later discovered she'd been spending time at Suriname's consulate offices in New York, mapping out an adventure with the aid of a diplomat. She wanted to ensure we'd not only see the most beautiful parts of the country but also have the most authentic, non-tourist experience.

My excitement grew as our departure date approached, but so did my nerves. In the early stages of any relationship, there's that one big trip that becomes a symbolic make-or-break moment. The couple sees each other outside of the immediate comfort zone they've built for themselves. Mettle is tested, true colors are revealed, and the journey either becomes part of a couple's origin story to be told at cocktail parties or the sad punch line of a breakup discussed over brunch with friends or in a therapist's office.

Luckily, ours was to be the former, and I never had another experience like it.

We caught a flight to Caracas, and from there, we transferred to a tiny plane that brought us into Suriname's small capital city of Paramaribo. We were met by a guide at the airport who took us to a semi-Americanized hotel for the first night, to prepare us for our journey deep into the jungle, where we'd be staying as the guests of various families on our trek into the heart of the country.

Thea had been right—her ability to communicate impressed the hell out of me. And I was so grateful for it, because I knew that she was able to adequately express our thanks and gratitude to all the lovely and warm people we met as we journeyed deeper and deeper into the rainforest. I was a bit concerned at first that our hosts might find it suspicious that two women were traveling together without men, especially since we stood out as decidedly masculine and feminine.

That's not to say that we didn't look fabulous. Thea wore tailored khakis with shirts full of sensible pockets and topped it all off with a domed pith helmet.

I, however, had brought my standard vacation clothes. A couple of light shift dresses in pink and navy blue, white shorts with airy pink blouses, and many bathing suits. These weren't ideal clothes for rural villages and jungle adventures, but I borrowed a pair of proper walking shoes from Thea whenever we knew we'd be hiking any sort of long distance. She was dashing, and I was the damsel, but no one raised so much as an eyebrow. Out of respect for our hosts, we didn't dare have sex in any of the small thatched-roof huts that we slept in over the course of our stay.

The temperature was brutally tropical, but I quickly became an expert at applying my makeup flawlessly in the ninety-eight-degree jungle humidity. I just had to do it more often, but I became so good at it that it never hindered any of our day trips. "I'll catch up," I'd call, pausing along a trail to trace on my pink Helena Rubinstein lipstick. Thea would wait for me anyway, exasperated but quick to steal a kiss when no one was looking.

Midway through our trip, our guide arranged for us to travel down a portion of the Tapanahony River. Thea, our guide, and I sat in one narrow little boat, with some local friends of the guide's in another. We spent the morning drifting lazily downstream to where a truck was waiting to drive us back to the village where we'd stay the night.

The journey downstream was tranquil, and I stared at the shoreline, lulled into a near trance as the trees slid by. I was watching for birds and wildlife, so I barely registered the first few gentle rocks of our boat. After a particularly hard jolt that thwacked my hand against the side, I looked ahead and realized with sudden unease that we were entering into some fairly heavy rapids. Our guide paddled on with a grim look on his face, following in the path of the villagers' boat as they navigated their way through angry white crests. I was just about to good-naturedly remark to Thea that our adventure seemed to be picking up, when the boat hit a rock and capsized, hurling the three of us into the river.

The water surrounding the lower halves of my legs was colder than the layer closer to the surface. My feet scrambled to find the bottom, but I couldn't touch it—we were too deep. I flailed my arms upward to reach the surface and gasped as my face hit the air. For all the time I'd spent at the beach in my life, I'd never become a particularly good swimmer, preferring instead to splash around in the shallow waves. I began to panic as I felt my body clumsily try to stay afloat as the rapids forced my entire body forward, and a sudden dip caused me to go completely underwater again, but only for a split second. I felt a sturdy arm circle my waist and yank me up so my head was above water.

It was Thea, in the water as well but holding on to the side of the boat with her other arm. It was right side up again, and as I blinked runny mascara from my eyes, I saw our guide had gained his footing on the other side of our long wooden boat, where the water was shallower. He dragged us toward shore. My feet touched the rocky bottom, and before I knew it, I was standing, stumbling alongside the vessel with Thea's arms still around me.

When we got to firm ground, I collapsed onto the bottom of the boat into about an inch of water. I was too shocked to say anything, so I concentrated on my breathing and tried to get my heart—which felt as though it might explode at any moment—to slow its beat to a steady pace. Thea and our guide appeared above me, concerned, and I gasped out that I was fine and only needed a moment. The guide disappeared from view, but Thea stayed by my side, kneeling outside the boat beside me and holding on to my hand.

I stared up at her worried face as my heart steadied, and I struggled to sit up. I saw the villagers who'd accompanied us on the other side of the river and gave them a feeble wave.

"You saved my life," I said, turning back to Thea. "You know what that means, don't you?"

"Tell me."

"You're responsible for me until I die now. That's what you get when you save a life. The burden of forever having to protect that person."

"That's no burden," she said and shifted her body so our guide wouldn't see as she caressed my cheek.

Several days later, we were back in Paramaribo. We'd wisely decided to end our trip with two days of rest in a hotel. I was grateful for hot running water, freshly laundered sheets, and most of all, the privacy to let loose a week of pent-up sexual tension. I paddled around the edge of the overly chlorinated pool, clinging to the edge with one hand but determined to learn how to properly swim once we returned home. Thea stretched elegantly in a poolside lounge chair, one knee up, wearing a black bikini and sipping a bright green cocktail made from Pisang Ambon, a Dutch banana-flavored liqueur rumored to be based on an old Indonesian recipe—just one of many little signs of the Netherlands' continued influence in the small country.

I caught her eye, and she raised her glass to me. I lifted an imaginary one back. I thought back to my misery a year prior, the lonely existence I'd led. It was beyond me how I ever could have imagined that I was willing to give up on finding this, these waves of love for another human rolling through me. We hadn't said the three magic words yet, but I knew she felt the same, and it was only a matter of time. She'd saved my life, after all. After the fear subsided that day, I'd realized that her rescue was one of the most romantic moments to ever happen to me, and I ached to tell the story to my family and coworkers, but I knew it wasn't possible. Even if I lied and retold the story, casting her as just a close friend, I knew that my voice would reveal my true feelings.

Hell, I couldn't even keep my feelings off my face. As soon as I returned to work, everyone began asking me who the lucky guy was that I'd spent my vacation with. I was blissfully happy and unable to hide it, which presented a problem. I couldn't play coy forever. I discussed the conundrum with Thea one night in bed. She'd finally moved into a place of her own close to me so it would be easy for either of us to swing by right after work, but she'd yet to unpack, and her bedroom was lined with bags and boxes.

"Just invent someone," she said. "That's what everyone else does."

"It would need to be someone connected to you, though," I said. "You're the only one I mention."

"Say it's my brother," she suggested and swung her legs out of bed, crossing the room naked and rummaging through an old box. She pulled a large doll out, one that had seen better days. He had a rather dour expression on his face, perhaps due to his unkempt onesie, chipped-paint hair, and bits of what looked like straw or horsehair poking out of a small tear where his ceramic head met his cloth body. "Meet Willy!" she said. "He was the only toy I had time to grab when we fled Amsterdam." She held him at arm's length and gazed fondly at the ragged thing. "He wasn't even my favorite doll, really. Just the closest within reach."

She turned and tossed him to me, and I held him gingerly.

"Give him a kiss," she teased. "He's your man, after all."

I left the doll propped up on her dresser when I left the next morning, but I carried his name on my lips to work, where I finally revealed to my coworkers that I'd been dating my close friend Thea's wonderful older brother, Willy. I even told the story of Thea's river rescue, but placed him in the starring role. In an effort to discourage any offers of double dates, I elaborated that he traveled a lot for work, so we preferred to spend time alone together as often as possible. Regardless, everyone was happy for me, and I was forced into making several dinner plans that I absolutely intended to cancel.

Another set of canceled plans involved our summer. Thea learned that the barn wasn't available to rent, and even though it was firmly established that we were together by then, I was still overjoyed when she asked me to rent a place exclusively with her.

"Just the two of us," she said. "I don't want to share it with anyone else."

"It's a deal," I said, kissing her. "Except for Willy. He can come, too."

———◦◦———

In 1966, that same year Willy became Edie's imaginary boyfriend, Time magazine— located in the building where Edie worked, and a publication that would one day go on to name her as a runner-up to Person of the Year, second only to the pope—published an unsigned essay called "The Homosexual in America." It stated:

> [Homosexuality] is a pathetic little second-rate substitute for reality, a pitiable flight from life...it deserves no encouragement, no glamorization, no rationalization, no fake status as minority martyrdom...and above all, no pretense that it is anything but a pernicious sickness.

The New York branch of the Mattachine Society was busy fighting this kind of blatant discrimination when activist Dick Leitsch and two other members staged a "sip-in" at the still-standing Julius' a few months after this article was published. The trio traveled to several bars across the city in an attempt to be served alcohol after stating that they were gay—a form of protest modeled after the lunch counter sit-ins at diners that segregated their black customers. Any establishment was allowed to refuse service to gays because they were considered disorderly.

The protesters brought several reporters along with them, and the ensuing press coverage helped get the Commission on Human Rights on board, whose chairman told The New York Times, "We have jurisdiction over discrimination based on sex. Denial of bar service to a homosexual solely for that reason would come within those bounds." And when Mattachine sued bars in New Jersey the following year for refusing to cater to gays, the state's Supreme Court ruled that "well-behaved apparent homosexuals" deserved to be served.

Being extremely well read, Edie was no doubt following all of this with keen interest. But she was still deeply in the closet and nowhere near ready to add her voice to any kind of movement for visibility and rights. She was happy and in love, and for the time being, that was enough.

Thirteen

A summer rental in Southampton is a terrible amount of money for a working person. It's much, much worse today but was still the case in 1966. Even though I was doing quite well for myself at IBM, the cost of every place we looked at was exorbitant, and since we'd already ruled out the idea of a share, our choices were extremely limited. We'd been spoiled by the luxury of the barn from the summer before—not its physical state but the privacy.

Thea finally offered to pay for an entire house so we wouldn't be as hindered by cost in our search, and I gratefully accepted. Once that decision was made, we ended up choosing the first property we looked at. For all of her wealth and privilege, Thea was never interested in any of the excess that comes with the Hamptons; we'd seen a listing in a Long Island newspaper and both fallen in love with the place at first sight—a charming little one-story cottage, with painted white clapboards and an elevated, screened-in porch that looked out over a bay. The reedy shoreline meant the water was no good for swimming, but we'd be able to push the canoe that came with the house through the marshy grass. The owner, who showed us around, was a kindly old lady, and after we wrote her a check on the spot and drove off, we immediately began referring to our new temporary home by her name: Mrs. Fordham's.

I felt like I needed to contribute something of significant monetary value to our summer experience, though, and despite my lingering anger about the party we'd stopped at the summer before that had been populated by all the dykes on bikes, I wanted to buy Thea a motorcycle. She had continued throughout the year to mention every now and then how much she'd love to own one, but there weren't any she felt she'd look good on or feel right riding. After some nudging about what exactly the problem was, I learned that she felt they were too bulky and that she didn't like the standard color of black most came in—they were too much like the ones every other lesbian had. She wanted something that would stand out and represent the individuality of her taste, something more streamlined and elegant.

Elegant wasn't a word I ever would have associated with motorcycles at the time, but I finally found one that I thought might work at a dealership on Fifty-ninth Street, on the West Side just off Tenth Avenue—a Yamaha Twin Jet 100. It was a sporty little two-seater, small enough to scoot around the city, but strong enough to handle the long ride out to Long Island. And best of all, the in-house garage could do a custom white paint job on the exterior.

After I caught Thea earmarking motorcycle advertisements in a sporting magazine, I told her what I'd done so she wouldn't pull the trigger and buy one herself. She was delighted, but I was pretty sure I detected a glimmer of worry in her eye, that the one I'd chosen might not be up to snuff, but when I showed her a photo and told her to picture it in white, she threw her arms around me.

On the day we picked the bike up, we both gasped when the mechanic rolled it out. It gleamed like a pearl, with round mirrors that arched up and outward from each handlebar like antennae. I could see my reflection in the surface of the chrome fuel tank. Thea and I both agreed it was awfully sexy.

I'd met her at the garage after work, having come straight from the office, so I was still dressed in my work clothes. I wore a tight navy dress that landed just below the knee, with a pair of leather sandals. Not exactly the most appropriate outfit for riding a motorcycle, but I didn't let that deter me as I hopped on and kicked down on the lever the way I'd seen it done in movies about rebellious teens. The engine revved to life, and without warning, I shot across the sidewalk and careened into the road. I screamed as I angled my body and the front wheel to the left so I wouldn't run headfirst into the brick building across the street, and I realized that I had no idea where the brakes were located. I felt one of my flats slip off my foot and caught a glimpse in one of the mirrors of it bouncing away into the gutter.

The corner of Tenth Avenue approached fast, and with it, waves of oncoming cars. I turned the front wheel again to enter into the flow of traffic—it was either that or run smack into the side of a moving target. Over the roar of the engine, I heard myself screaming, *"Please, somebody stop me!"*

Thea chased after the runaway bike, and as I made the turn, the machine slowed slightly. She shot diagonally across the corner, leaped into the street, and with lightning speed wrenched the steering column and squeezed a lever on the right handle. The bike and I both jerked to a stop.

So that's where the brake is, I thought, from a place in the back of my mind still capable of rational observation.

Thea caught the full weight of both the bike and me, bracing her body to keep us upright so we wouldn't topple to the ground. My one bare foot scraped against the sharp pavement, but I laughed through the fear and the stinging pain as I clung to her shoulders as shrill horns sounded around us. It occurred to me that it was the second time in less than six months that she'd saved my life.

We returned to the garage, both of us full of adrenaline and me filled with more than a little embarrassment as one of the mechanics handed me my missing sandal, trying not to laugh after he realized I was uninjured.

"I'm buying us helmets," I announced.

Thea grumbled at how huge and bulky they were and selected a half helmet for herself that perched on the top of her head, one that would allow her hair to blow in the wind.

"You're the one here with the most knowledge about how the brain works," I said. "Tell me exactly what is and isn't protected by that wimpy thing if you get in an accident." She reluctantly picked out a safer but much less fashionable option.

Thea rode the motorcycle alongside my packed-to-the gills car on our first day out to Mrs. Fordham's. She'd left us the keys under the mat, and as we brought in all of our suitcases and boxes of various kitchen needs, I noticed that we weren't quite as isolated as I'd remembered—I could spot a few neighboring houses through the trees from the windows, which I'd also failed to notice lacked any curtains.

"You get set up; I need to run in to town for a few more supplies," I said and left before Thea could question me. I returned an hour later with arm-loads of shades and spring-loaded curtain rods and promptly got to work setting them up while Thea teased me about what a prude I was being.

"We don't know if they're a bunch of Peeping Toms," I countered. I knew she'd end up giving me guff about my paranoia, but I couldn't help it. I'd spent my entire life hiding my sexuality, and it wasn't a habit I seemed to be anywhere near growing out of.

Rather than continue her verbal teasing, she gave me a playful smack on the ass and then proceeded to make me forget all about potential voyeurs. If there were any, they got a damn good show, and after our romp, as I stretched out nude on my back on the bare floorboards, I realized she'd given me a very literal lesson in exposure therapy.

Thea dressed and got to work setting up the kitchen, which I'd known better than to touch. The room was strictly her territory and was anchored by a hulking antique stove with six top burners and two oven compartments. The walls were dotted with copper pots and several different-sized cast-iron pans, each sticky with years of seasoning.

Our first night there was chilly, so we camped in front of the stone-framed fireplace in the living room. I watched over the top of my book as she got to work making a fire, methodical in her placement of newspaper twisted into crumpled ropes and architectural framework of evenly spaced kindling. The level of care was her standard tendency in any project, but I suspected a bit more precision was being taken into account in an effort to wow me, since she knew I was spying.

Now that we were back in the Hamptons, where I'd experienced so much heartache the previous summer, the very smell of the salt air was enough to bring back feelings of unease that Thea might still have someone else on the side. We'd come so far in the past year, but a small part of me dreaded the thought of catching her behind a closed door, the phone cradled against her shoulder, a woman on the other line. The area was packed full of her ex-lovers. I tried to brush away fears and let my defenses down, but memories of the disdain she'd held for monogamy kept me slightly on guard in a way that surprised me. I'd thought we were past all that.

I'm in love with her, and we're going to live together for the summer, but then I'll have to go home alone, a nagging little voice inside my head whispered.

She soon made it clear I had nothing to worry about.

We established a routine. She woke with the birds and would hand-grind the coffee beans and have a pot of french press coffee waiting for me by the time I finally shuffled out of the bedroom to join her on the porch, cigarettes in hand and stacks of red-and-white boxes of Regents in ready supply.

Midmorning, we'd pack up wicker baskets with bread, cheese, and fruit and head to the gay section of Fowler Beach. We'd read and visit with friends, and I splashed in the ocean, attempting to get better at swimming but never venturing far enough out that I couldn't touch the bottom. I smoked cigarette after cigarette as my skin sizzled into a bronze-gold hue. (Years later, Thea looked back at photographs from this time and grumbled that I was trying to get two kinds of cancer at once.) Sometimes she'd leave me alone there for several hours while she went off and golfed.

Her male buddies had given up trying to separate us. We were a couple, and everyone knew it. Every now and then, we'd run into one of Thea's ex-lovers, and Thea always made sure to let the other woman, as well as anyone else in the vicinity, know that I was her girl. She was proprietary in that way I'd hated on my first trip to a women's bar long ago in Atlantic City, but in our case, now that I was on the receiving end, I didn't mind at all. No one could even take a photograph of me except for her. I basked in the devotion and returned it every chance I got.

Our friends spanned different cliques, from wealthy executives to starving artists, and we began to serve as a bridge between groups. It's not as though there were rivalries, but like any small community, the Hamptons gay scene had its social divides and boundaries. We crossed them all, and for the most part, we genuinely liked everyone. With one exception—Thea didn't take well to old friends of mine we'd run into, women I knew from my early days in New York. Her jealousy was severe, and because of that, she didn't leave a favorable impression on everyone we met. I accepted the occasional socially awkward moments as a small price to pay for what I got in return from her—a very public display of fidelity, which did much to alleviate any lingering fears about her being unfaithful. She did like Dev, at least. She knew she was funny and smart; she'd been the one who'd introduced us, after all.

The summer sped by in a blur. Returning to the city on Sundays was torture, and I used up all my remaining vacation days for the year so we'd have occasional full weeks together. One Friday afternoon, I was so anxious to get out to the island that I left my Chevy Corvair convertible running outside my apartment while I ran upstairs to grab something I'd forgotten, and when I came back down, it had been stolen! (It appeared in upstate New York a few weeks later, none the worse for wear.) And on a Sunday afternoon not much later, when I had to leave early to catch a flight for a work conference, Thea kept me so distracted in bed that I lost all track of time, and I knew I'd never catch my plane.

"Don't worry," she said, bundling me into the car. "We'll get you to the airport in time."

I braced myself for a terrifying, pedal-to-the-metal race across Long Island, but instead of getting on the road toward the city, she headed farther inland until we reached a small airfield, full of tiny private planes that belonged to the fabulously wealthy.

"Stay here," she instructed and then ran off, returning not ten minutes later and opening the door for me. "I found someone you can catch a ride with," she said. "He's flying to JFK now. You'll make your flight with time to spare."

No romantic gesture was too large or too small for her. From saving my hide by hitching me a ride on a private plane, to small poems she'd leave tucked inside whatever book I happened to be reading, she made me feel loved. I wish I could recall the first time that summer we each said that we loved one another, but at the same time, it seems unnecessary to mark that occasion. We slid into that phase of our lives so gracefully and naturally that it doesn't need a marker, a before-and-after moment when the words were finally spoken as if nothing that came before really counted. Her actions, the ones that proved she loved me, were what mattered most, not the words.

Dinner parties or backyard barbecues would give way to late-night dancing at the Millstone, and it was a banner year for music that kept us out on the floor. New releases, destined to become classics, played on repeat. We adored the lascivious wink of "Hanky Panky" by Tommy James and the Shondells and the sweaty joy that came with working our bodies to "Summer in the City" by the Lovin' Spoonful. Mambos were our favorites, but I wanted lyrics to sing along to, so Thea made ones up on the spot about her love for me.

Donovan's groovy "Sunshine Superman" played on the radio a lot too and hinted at the Summer of Love headed our way in three short years. A younger lesbian couple we'd grown close with, Anna and Corinne, were doing their best to prepare for it by smoking copious amounts of marijuana.

Thea and I weren't big partyers aside from the socializing aspects, but she did smoke pot with her friends from time to time back then, and I was curious to try it. Anna had been spending the summer making her way through Julia Child's *Mastering the Art of French Cooking,* so when Corinne invited us to a dinner party built around her latest successes, and then added (once Anna was out of earshot) that the food was much more palatable after a few joints, we gladly accepted.

We arrived at their rental on the designated night to find they had dimmed the dining room lights by covering the lampshades with fringed red scarves, which I suppose was meant to provide a French bordello vibe. We took our seats and introduced ourselves to those we didn't know and greeted the ones we did. Corinne lit up the first joint as soon as Anna bustled in with a starter course of stuffed tomatoes—a simple enough dish. I'd certainly eaten my share. I inhaled and exhaled my first puff of the joint after Thea passed it to me, holding the smoke in my lungs like she instructed. I briefly thought of Blackie, telling me nearly the same thing when he taught me to smoke cigarettes, but this stuff was much harsher. I disliked the sharp sting and coughed it out—it was nothing like the smooth pull I got from my beloved Regents.

I took a bite of the small bread crumb–topped appetizer on my plate to rid my tongue of the skunky film left behind. The flavors began to bounce like tiny Ping-Pong balls through my mouth, and I'd eaten three tomatoes by the time the joint made its way back around to me. I took a perfunctory hit and blew it out fast before it could hurt my lungs too badly and passed it on, eager for the next course that was being set before me—a large bowl of bouillabaisse, full of fish, clams, and mussels pulled fresh from the ocean, probably early that afternoon. As I rolled the broth across my tongue, I heard someone on the other side of the table say, "Oooh, can you taste the orange peel?" I found that suddenly I could.

The light grew hazier as several more dishes were brought to the table. Crisp little cheese tartlets, a salad of buttery greens lightly coated with a barely there vinaigrette that didn't distract from the freshness of the leaves. Each new taste held countless wonders from a country I was suddenly determined to visit. *How have I lived this long without ever seeing Paris?* I wondered.

I continue to take tiny tokes each time a new joint was rolled, but I could no longer follow any of the conversations. I clutched Thea's hand under the table from time to time with sheer delight over the miniature explosions inside my mouth. She squeezed it back and smiled at me each time, and I wondered if my eyes were as glassy and red as hers.

Every now and then, a roar of laughter erupted around the table, and I'd look up sheepishly, wiping away a stray bit of food from my face with my napkin. I'd try to make sense of what was so funny before quickly giving up and returning my focus to whatever new experience had landed on my plate.

I could hardly move from my chair by the time the night ended, after a chocolate mousse that I insisted Thea must re-create for us. I felt a wobbly smile plastered on my face as we tumbled out into the street, grateful that Anna and Corinne's house was within an easy walking distance from ours, just a twenty-minute stroll that took us along the outskirts of East Hampton.

Thea ran ahead along the road, pausing to serenade me beneath every lamppost, as if each beacon was her own private spotlight. "*Oh, Edie, come on and dance with me,*" she sang to the tune of "Sweet Pea" by Tommy Roe, another unavoidable song of the summer. "*Oh, Edie, come on and be my girl. Come on, come on, come on and be my girl?*"

"Always."

I grabbed her hands, and we spun in circles as Thea continued her re-write of the song. "*We took a little walk, I held her close to me. And underneath the stars, I said to Edie——*"

"I'm hungry," I interrupted, and she stopped.

"How on earth is that possible?"

I shrugged and pointed over her shoulder. She followed my gaze to a bright sign I could just make out in the distance at the edge of the village: an orange triangle, with the magical word *Pizza* spelled out in neon inside of it.

"You're joking."

I shook my head and headed toward the light. I felt like a moth, determined but unable to fly straight toward my shiny goal.

A few moments later, we were back on the street, stuffing ourselves with slices doused in oregano and black pepper.

"How did we get into this crazy eating thing?" I wondered aloud through a mouthful.

"Edie Windsor, you are stoned," Thea teased.

"What are you?"

"In love."

Summer rolled on. Some weekends, we'd take the motorcycle to and from the city, my arms wrapped tightly around Thea's waist, squeezing the breath out of her. I was determined to learn to drive the damn thing myself, but the closest I ever got was Thea nabbing a few stylish shots of me posing on it in a bikini. I much preferred taking the convertible, putting the top down and my sunglasses on, a white kerchief holding my hair back and a lipstick-stained cigarette dangling from my mouth.

She liked to ask about my marriage to Saul. She'd tease me and say things like "What on earth were you thinking?" but I never indulged those barbs, gentle as they were. Saul still held a special place in my heart, and I wouldn't let her sully that affection by making light of what I'd gone through with him. But it turned out that I misunderstood her intent. She was genuinely interested in the institution itself and what it meant for a relationship. *Married* was a word we used for gay couples we knew who'd been together for ages, who were true life partners. It summed up their situation, but in the emotional sense only. *Marriage* was the only term we knew that defined what our future could be like, even if it had to be lived mostly in secret and not legally recognized. We told ourselves that it didn't matter if there was no word to cement our reality. *We* were the ones that made it real.

And yet, the sense of otherness loomed.

One night, we were stretched out, head to feet on the sofa on the screened-in porch, when she said, "If you ever got married again, to a woman this time around . . ."

I poked her cheek with my big toe, and she swatted my ankle.

"Would you wear a ring?" she continued.

"God, no," I told her. "Think of the stories I'd have to make up. Or I'd have to hire someone to play the role of Willy."

I took a deep drag of my cigarette and thought of Cele and the power she placed behind the idea of marriage. We hadn't discussed it in years, but I felt sure she no longer believed it was the only way for a woman to be financially secure. Marriage, for her, had been introduced as an anchor—a clearly defined status that both established and guaranteed her place in America. It had meant that she finally belonged. But since my father died, her business sense had only grown shrewder, and no one ever expressed concern about her living independently now. She'd have laughed in their faces if they had.

"I suppose I'd want to wear something," I decided. "A pin, maybe. The physical symbol of attachment would feel good when I'm alone. What about you? Would you wear anything?"

"I'm still too angry that you've absolutely destroyed my plan of playing the field for the foreseeable future to think of how to answer that," she said. "I had it all figured out, then you had to come along and ruin everything."

The last weekend of the summer came far too quickly. On the drive out that last Friday afternoon, I made list after list of everything that needed to be done while Thea drove, wondering how on earth we were going to get it all done in time. At one point, she asked me again about the idea of a pin as an engagement ring. She spoke of styles and gems and size and cleverly manipulated me into conjuring up an image of a circle lined with diamonds. I wondered why she was fixating on it, but not deeply enough to suspect anything. When we pulled into the driveway, I leaped out of the car and started to head straight for the house.

"Edie, wait," I heard from behind me.

I turned, and she had one knee on the ground, a small box held in the palm of her outstretched hand. I felt a rush of adrenaline and gasped. Everything was silent for a moment, just a tiny hair of a second.

"Edie Windsor, will you marry me?" she asked, but didn't get a chance to finish her proposal because I had already begun shouting, "Yes! Yes! Yes!"

I understood her earlier conversational maneuvers when she held out a circular pin, lined with twenty-two diamonds that appeared to move on their own as they caught the day's last tiny flashes of sunlight. I'd never seen anything so exquisite, a piece of jewelry that appeared delicate at first but radiated strength the longer you stared at it.

All my plans for packing up the house disappeared as she pinned it to my shirt. We stood in the driveway, embracing in silence, before I grabbed her hand and rushed inside so I could admire the diamonds in a mirror. I watched in the reflection as she wrapped her arms around my waist.

"We'll need to find an apartment," she said. "I've already started looking."

"You were that confident I'd say yes?"

"Of course," she teased.

Thea's desire to signify their engagement with something physical mirrors a long history of coded symbols gays used to either secretly declare their love or even just subtly identify themselves to others—like Victorian men wearing a dyed-green carnation on their lapels. At the time, neither Edie nor Thea seriously considered that they would ever be able to get married. "It was a statement of what was happening between us," was how Edie described it. "It was the only way we knew how to describe the intent behind what we felt for each other." Theirs was a commitment that would go on to change American history, but at the time, engaged and marriage were borrowed language, the only words that carried the weight of their emotions and legitimate only in their hearts.

Fourteen

Our search for a home to share began in earnest as soon as we returned to the city, and we found one fairly quickly, thanks to a friend of Thea's from her graduate program. This woman's husband was a lawyer, and he had a client who was stuck with a lease he needed to unload for some reason or another. Whatever his situation, his loss was our gain, and we moved into a grand ten-room apartment with arched windows on Fifth Avenue and Twelfth Street, at a monthly rent of $600. It was an absurdly low cost; even calculating for modern-day inflation, it was only a fraction of what rent on a similar place would have been.

I spent the following months decorating it with furnishings and textiles that epitomized the height of late-'60s chic. Thea had several pieces of antique furniture in storage, as well as some Dutch artwork, including a five-foot-long waterscape filled with merchant ships bobbing in the North Sea Canal. Just across from it sat my harpsichord, finally completed after two years and a source of great pride for me. I left much of the parquet floors bare to show off the wood designs but carpeted the hallway that led to our bedroom in a jolly bright red. I wallpapered our closet with a Liberty of London–esque floral print and hung a rack specially designed to hold the collection of wigs I'd bought to wear when I felt like changing things up for a night on the town. They were beginning to go out of fashion by the late '60s as hippie culture influenced softer, more natural hairstyles, but I loved my classic coifs and that I could effortlessly alter my look without spending an hour or two in the salon.

I decorated our bedroom entirely in pink. Maybe *decorated* is too gentle a word—I doused the whole damn room with it. Pink walls, pink curtains, pink linens, a pink bedspread, and even a pink half canopy that hung above our white filigree headboard. Thea shook her head every time she entered but indulged my love of the color. I think she secretly liked it.

Cohabitation was nothing new for us by that point, so there were no major red flags when it came to adapting to each other's idiosyncrasies on a 24-7 cycle. That's not to say there weren't occasional surprise flare-ups beyond household basics like the proper way to fold a fitted sheet. One day, I arrived home to find a small stack of Rorschach blots on a side table. Thea's back was to me, but when she turned around and saw me scrutinizing one, she shrieked.

"Stop!"

"Why on earth not? It's just a little butterfl—"

"No!" she interrupted, placing her hands over her ears. "I do not want to know what any of those cards look like to you." She marched across the room and snatched them from my hands, disappeared into her office, and came out a moment later.

"What the hell was that about?" I asked.

"I don't ever want to know anything about you that you don't already know yourself. Or to realize something that you do know, but you don't *want* me to know."

This always stuck with me. It wasn't a question of simply wanting to separate her work from her personal life. She respected my privacy, even if I wasn't aware I was revealing something.

Thea truly loved her work, even when acquaintances would come up to her and ask for psychological advice when she was out and about. Her lot in life was no different from that of a general practitioner at a cocktail party in terms of people seeking free counsel, but she was always gracious about it. Her office was nearby, on Tenth Street, and while she couldn't tell me a thing about her patients, what I did know is that she cared for them.

Obviously, I didn't tell anyone at IBM that I was engaged; they would have demanded that I bring Willy in to meet everyone immediately or, worse, try to throw some sort of party. I did brag that the impressive diamond pin I now wore daily was a gift from him.

We spent the holidays separately that year, her with her family and me with mine, though by then, she had already met everyone during a brief visit to Philadelphia. At the time, I told Cele that she was my new roommate and ignored the knowing glance between Blackie and Dolly. When I finally got them alone together later that evening, I elaborated and said that we'd moved in together as a serious and committed couple. I didn't use the word *engaged*.

Dolly didn't have much to say about it. She seemed unsure how to respond except for a flustered "Well, I'm happy that you're happy."

Blackie took a deep drag on his cigarette and drawled, "I'm happy to hear you found yourself another dark-haired Jew," alluding to Saul. I swatted him, but could tell he was genuinely happy for me.

For the rest of the visit, I watched enviously the ease at which Dolly and Rick maneuvered through their life, with their love in plain view and three healthy, handsome boys to show off to the world.

A benefit to not having children meant more disposable income, and as spring approached, Thea and I began discussing where we should rent in the Hamptons the following summer. Mrs. Fordham had decided to stay for the season that year, and I stumbled across a listing for the sale of a small house in Southampton that seemed far below market rate.

I rang up the real estate agent so that we could book a viewing. She warned me that offers were already coming in, but I didn't let that deter me. We drove out the following weekend, and it was love at first sight. The small peaked-roof cottage had a cast-iron woodstove smack in the center of the living room, with a metal chimney that rose straight up and out the roof. There was just one bedroom that sat off the kitchen, which was really only a wall along part of the living room with a stove and a refrigerator. A small sleeping loft was wedged up against the vaulted ceiling. Below that was the home's one tiny bathroom. I nudged Thea when we saw the size of it.

"If we can survive with just that little thing between the two of us, then we've got it made," I whispered.

The owner was home (much to the distress of the agent), and it turned out that he'd had a long career as a famous hairdresser, but he'd been letting back taxes pile up. He needed a fast money infusion to get out of hot water but was sad to give up his little vacation spot that he'd spent so many years putting together.

"It comes with everything," he said. "Dishes, sheets, towels, furniture . . . I've got no other space for it all. You'd think that would be an incentive, but every offer that's come in so far keeps trying to knock the price down by saying they don't need any of this."

It was immediately clear that this was my chance. He was house-proud, which I could certainly relate to after all the work that had just gone into our own apartment. It was insulting to him that anyone wouldn't want his things. And there really were some marvelous pieces, including a grand hutch full of cheery red-and-blue hand-painted dishes. I made sure to effusively compliment his taste before we left.

As soon as we arrived home, I called in my offer: $35,000 cash, and I wanted everything. It was still a bit below the asking price, but I felt confident that he'd accept, and he did.

Thea wanted to pay for it, but I refused. "Let this be my gift to you," I said. "I can afford it." I knew that she was charmed by the place as much as I was, and it made me love her more. She certainly could have afforded something much bigger and nicer, but she didn't need that sort of excess. Like me, she considered the little house's rudimentary outdoor shower an ultimate luxury.

We threw a party for all our friends on Memorial Day as a housewarming (an event that would go on to become an annual tradition), and while we were preparing for it, I proudly showed Thea the little sign I'd painted that read, "Edie and Thea's."

"I'll mount it out by the road so people will know they're in the right place."

"You absolutely will *not*."

"What do you mean?"

"I have clients that live out here and who know that I spend time here too! I can't have them drive by and see that I'm living with another woman!"

"That's absurd. You're not the only Thea in the world, and the only people driving by are going to be people who already know us."

"You don't know that! No sign. Absolutely not. I cannot believe you almost hung that without conferring with me. My god, what is a person to think."

She stormed inside the house, leaving me crushed. She'd spent the previous weekend (and a small fortune) planting bright tulips all along the border of our driveway, as well as a flower bed around a big tree in the center of our backyard in circles of varying colors. I'd been so excited to show them off, to show *us* off. Even here, in what was supposed to be our safe place, we continued to have to hide from the world.

I sat in the sun for a bit, thinking, and then picked up a new piece of pasteboard and began to draw. I entered the house quietly and saw her standing on the other side of the living room, staring out the door into our backyard.

"I know it isn't fair," she said without turning around. "But I can't risk it."

"Is this all right, then?" I asked, feeling rather timid. I held up the new sign, on which I'd painted "Edie & T's," and anxiously awaited her response.

She read it over her shoulder and gave me a sad smile, then turned and strode across the room, wrapping her arms around me. I let the sign fall to the floor. "It's lovely," she said. "Of course you can hang it. And I'm so sorry it's not my full name. You know I love you and how proud I am to be with you."

I did know. And at the time, it was enough.

——◇◇——

Edie did quite well for herself at IBM, but that she just happened to have $35,000 in cash sitting around (adjusting for inflation, that's roughly

$250,000 today) didn't go unnoticed among her friends and family. Edie often spoke of her love of playing cards during our interviews, but what she didn't mention was that she knew how to count them, a skill corroborated by many firsthand witnesses.

"It seemed so out of character," says Debbie, the wife of her cousin Sunnie's son, Lewis. "She liked to play blackjack, and she told us a story about how one time she was in a casino when she realized that the dealer was onto her and she was about to get in trouble, so she quickly left. I was shocked!"

Lewis and Debbie's daughter, Maya, even remembers Edie trying to teach her and her twin brother, Ben, how to count cards. "When she explained it, I remember being dumbfounded about the amount of skill you had to have."

"She could do it with four decks!" Lewis marveled. "You had to remember so many things."

"Obviously, none of us learned how," Maya added dryly.

Others told of trips to casinos. The stories go that Edie would fly out somewhere for a weekend and gamble until she'd made enough to cover the cost of her flight, meals, and hotel. Anything beyond that was presumably a bonus, and her card skills might explain why Edie was able to afford the house on her own, out of pocket. Indeed, more than one person said exactly that to me. As a woman in a casino in the '60s not wearing a showgirl headdress, she was likely very unassuming—wide-eyed and sweet, no doubt delighted by her sudden good fortune with the cards, charming everyone at her blackjack table until things got hot and she'd have to scoot. One friend recalled Edie telling a story about being escorted out of a Las Vegas casino. "The way she described it, they didn't make a big fuss. A couple of tall, well-dressed men approached her, offered her some sort of perk, like a free dinner at a restaurant, and then walked her out. She was just winning too much."

Edie's years' worth of calendars contain many days marked off for visits to casinos throughout the world. "My guess is she taught herself how to count cards," says Sunnie. "She was brilliant!"

Someone else recalled Edie proudly admitting that she'd been contacted by one of the world's most notorious card counters to join his now-legendary crew, but she declined. No loss there—she had more important things to do in life that would bring her fame.

Fifteen

L et's tour Italy in June."
        I'm not sure I'd ever heard sweeter words. It was 1969, and the
trip was Thea's gift for my fortieth birthday. "First class, all the way," she
announced. "The only rule is that each of our hotel rooms must have a
water view, no matter where we are."

Who was I to argue?

It felt impossible that I'd been alive so long. I certainly didn't feel my
age—no one does once that particular milestone arrives—but I understood the weight of that marker. It had taken me time, much longer than
most, but I was confident that I was finally where I was supposed to be.
I had the career I wanted, friends I adored, a fabulous apartment in New
York City, a vacation home, and I was in a committed relationship with a
woman I was madly in love with. My life was seemingly perfect, but the
need to hide my relationship began to grate on me more and more. For
the first time, not being able to show affection anywhere except among
our friends really started to bother me. I'd been willing to be discreet for
so long because there was simply no other choice.

There was one bonus to the need for discretion—just like in Suriname,
it meant that once Thea and I were behind closed doors, all the built-up

tension from forcing ourselves to keep our hands to ourselves exploded in the bedroom. And the living room, kitchen, bathroom . . . wherever.

One of the most exciting aspects about our upcoming vacation was the idea that we might not need to be quite so hidden. Europe felt much more open and carefree, the idea of two women together was no big deal.

We left in mid-June with an absurd amount of enormous matching luggage, and looking at photographs now, I have no idea how we managed with all those bags. We flew first to Amsterdam, Thea figuring that she should visit family members since we were going to be in Europe anyway. Our first night there, we dined at an oyster bar, and I spent the next three days horrifically ill with food poisoning in our hotel while Thea made her social calls. (The picturesque canal views from our room were utterly lost on me.) Not the most illustrious start, but I was back on my feet by the time we arrived in Venice.

Our suite at the Regina overlooked the wide Grand Canal with sleek black gondolas bobbing everywhere, guided by handsome young men in striped shirts. We immediately hailed one that glided silently through the quieter back channels, past abandoned palazzos that seemed ready to crumble into the water. I doubt our guide was shocked when Thea placed her hand over mine from time to time or when I nuzzled her shoulder. If he was, he didn't show it.

We went to bed early that first night, because Thea was determined to get a photograph of the normally mobbed Piazza San Marco without the crowds. "The only way it can happen is if we get up before dawn and arrive just as the sun is rising," she told me. At daybreak, we ran through the narrow streets until the basilica rose before us. We were indeed alone, except for an elderly man who seemed to be nodding off against a wall, but the square was teeming with pigeons. At the sound of our footsteps, the man shot to attention. He seemed to know exactly why we were there.

"I will get rid of them for you!" he shouted in his thick Italian accent and suddenly tore across the square, waving his arms wildly and making whooping sounds, scattering the birds away from us. He followed us over toward the basilica and repeated his crazy dance so I could get a picture of Thea standing in front of it looking calm and serene, while the reality was anything but with this elderly man jumping all over the place just off frame, shouting, "If you love her, kiss her!" We tipped him well for his efforts, and after wandering narrow alleys for the rest of the day, we parked ourselves at a casino for the rest of the evening.

We arrived in Florence and checked into our room at the Excelsior, with a view of the glistening Arno that flows between the two halves of the city. We strolled through the Uffizi Gallery, gazing at Botticelli's *The Birth of Venus,* but after a few days, we had to leave the city when the sheer volume of Renaissance art threatened to blend into one giant collage of the Virgin Mary in my mind.

Next up was Rome, for the majestic Pantheon and a public prayer service with the pope at the Vatican, because, well, when in Rome, as they say. We shopped at Pucci for wildly patterned scarves, toured the Forum, then flew to Tangier for a quick shopping trip in the city's maze of souks, packed with brilliantly colored treasures. I picked up more scarves, as well as slippers in shades of fiery red and deep blues that matched not just the stunning ocean views from our hotel, but our plates back in Southampton.

As we sipped champagne on our hotel terrace, we had no idea that back home our neighborhood had erupted in the roiling turmoil of the Stonewall riots. We were clueless that not far from our apartment, a car was overturned and protestors were flooding the streets. When we landed in New York, we still knew nothing of what had been happening. We were quiet on our cab ride back from JFK, exhausted but content. As I reflected on how supremely fortunate I was, I remember noticing what seemed to be a larger presence of openly gay men and women roaming about the Village with determined looks on their faces.

After we arrived at the apartment, I went out to the store to pick up milk and coffee, and that's when I learned about the raid on the Stonewall Inn, a place I was familiar with, as it was well known as one of the main gay bars in our area, but it wasn't a place that I frequented. Its patrons were mostly made up of drag queens and homeless gay kids, worlds I knew nothing about. Thanks to the efforts of the Mattachine Society, gay patrons could now be served at bars, but homosexual *behavior* in public was still illegal, so the Mafia continued their hold on gay bars, and on the books, Stonewall ostensibly operated as a bring-your-own-bottle private club.

But I'd settled down by then—the majority of my gay social life involved intimate dinner parties, backyard barbecues, and dancing in the Hamptons. And when I had been frequenting the New York bars, I'd gravitated to the ones that felt safest, even though I knew none really were. I didn't like the rowdier ones simply because they drew more attention, opening themselves up to the possibility of a raid.

This most recent one at Stonewall had turned into a standoff against the police, with the queens I'd so actively avoided my entire life fighting back against arrest and a crowd gathering to cheer them on. A fire had broken out, there were injuries, and then the protests had continued for six consecutive nights.

I ran home to grab Thea, and we walked together to stare at the now-closed building from across the street. We felt the electricity in the air, still crackling despite the protests having wound down a few days earlier.

I took a long walk alone through the neighborhood later that day. My body tingled, and I felt both exhausted and wired, but not just because of the jet lag. The 1960s were almost over and I felt a sense of being hurtled forward through time at a pace that was both frightening and exhilarating. When I'd first moved to New York, the idea there would be this sort of visibility—that the Village would be plastered with signs about gay rights instead of people furtively ducking behind closed doors—was an impossibility. A wish, certainly, but not anything I dreamed I'd see in my lifetime. Yet here were the very people I'd actively avoided my entire adult life, the queens who flaunted their gayness through loud dress and affectations, already proud long before the word was adopted as a way to celebrate our community, doing the fearless work that set in motion a swell that would go on to carry me into a future unfathomable to me at that moment.

I was in awe of these early soldiers, and I knew that I had to join them.

E die always readily admitted how different her life was compared to other
LGBTQ+ people. It's an important detail to remember because it not only
speaks to the strength of her heart that she made such an about-face later in life to
devote her time and resources to helping those in need but also to remember how
divided gay communities were at the time. She and Thea could afford the reclusive
safety of the Hamptons, but most of the Stonewall patrons had nowhere else to go
for the deeply necessary bonds of socialization that people who live most of their
lives in secret both crave and need to survive. Stonewall was the first step at not just
demanding equal rights but also the beginning of bringing different gay communities together.

Edie's close friend Barbara Rosen, whom she wouldn't meet for another thirty-
three years despite the fact that they both worked at IBM and frequented the same
women's bars, was there for the riots. "There were signs posted all throughout the
Village the next day after the first uprising, calling people to come back to Stonewall," she remembers. "My girlfriend and I stood on a corner and watched police beat
on the guys, the transvestites, anyone who was there. It was violent, and it was scary.
We watched as much as we could before we got frightened and left."

Perhaps because Barbara was in the thick of it, rather than stumbling on the
aftermath like Edie, she wasn't convinced at the time that anything was going to be
different following Stonewall. "I didn't feel like things were going to change. It felt
reactionary," she explains. "I remember sometime after Stonewall another bar was
raided and a guy jumped out the second story, and he was impaled on a fence below."

She's referring to an Argentinian immigrant named Diego Viñales who, eight
months after Stonewall, leaped from the second story of the jail he was brought to on
Charles Street after being arrested during a raid on the Snake Pit, a bar located in
a basement on the corner of West Tenth Street and Bleecker. After rumors spread that
Diego had died (he in fact survived, after five spikes were removed from his thigh
and pelvis), the incident sparked a demonstration of almost two hundred gays and
lesbians in Sheridan Square, an event credited with inciting even more homosexuals
to get involved with the growing movement.

It's possible, but doubtful, that Edie was there. Sheridan Square is just a few *blocks from the apartment she shared with Thea, and while Stonewall lit a spark in her, she was still very much afraid of word getting back to IBM that she was a lesbian. After all the newspaper attention that Stonewall had gotten, she likely would have known that press would be present at the Sheridan Square protest as well.*

Barbara had only come out herself a few months prior to Stonewall. "I'm not sure how, but I was aware of Daughters of Bilitis," she says. "It wasn't exactly an ac-tivist group; it was more a way for gay women to get together and socialize without having to go to bars. One day, I saw in The Village Voice *that they were having a meeting someplace in the West Thirties or Forties. I was living in New Jersey with my parents, so I borrowed their car, drove into the city, and sat in the driver's seat for a while outside the building where it was taking place. It was this dumpy area, full of factories, all run-down."*

Too nervous to leave the car, she watched for a while to see if anyone else was headed inside. "All of a sudden, this motorcycle comes roaring down the street, and this really dykey woman gets off and goes in. I thought, Well, I guess this is the world I have to join. *She steeled herself and went inside, where she met a woman named Grace, the girlfriend by her side at Stonewall. They were together for five and a half years.*

Trying to hide her relationship with Grace from her coworkers at IBM mirrored Edie's problems trying to keep Thea a secret, but fortunately, also like Edie, Barbara got along well with her coworkers. She worked first in programming and then as a systems analyst and says that the people were very nice. "I was always happy with my colleagues and managers," she says, even if she did have to wear pantyhose and skirts. "It was hard to not tell people there anything about my life. I shared an office with a guy who asked me out a couple of times, and I always said no. It got uncomfortable sometimes."

Grace used to come and meet her for lunch, but she'd have to wait for Barbara several blocks away from the offices lest they be seen together on the regular and raise suspicions.

In the early 1970s, Edie began to carefully open up to a few close work friends about Thea, including her female boss, Pat. The two got along well and occasionally got together outside of the office. One night, they went to the theater after work. Pat's husband came to pick her up after, while Thea came to collect Edie. Introductions were made all around, and they went their separate ways.

The next morning, Pat approached her and said in a low voice, "Lee told me to tell you that you two are a gorgeous couple."

Edie turned away, pretending that she hadn't heard, but Pat touched her arm. "Edie," she pleaded, "there's no way that we can be true friends if you don't at least acknowledge what I'm saying."

So Edie did, and one can only imagine the relief she must have felt to finally have someone in her office know the truth about Willy and what her pin truly symbolized. The four began to double-date soon afterward, and the couple often drove out to the Hamptons to stay with Edie and Thea for the weekend. Edie paid it forward when she hired a new secretary, a young man who wasn't quite as adept at hiding his homosexuality as Edie and who immediately became a target of barely disguised ridicule from many of the male employees in the office. With no HR department that would dare get involved, Edie protected him as best she could. When she discovered that one coworker in particular was bragging to the rest of the staff that he could get the "little fairy" to do all kinds of errands and work for him because he believed the kid had a crush on him, Edie took the young man aside and told him, "The next time that bastard tells you to fetch him coffee, you say no, and then you come to me. You work for me, not those assholes, and I think you could go far here." And he did. She rallied for his promotion, and after a while, he became in charge of a department of his own. Edie was proud of this story and always added, "One of my talents is finding talent."

Sixteen

In the wake of Stonewall, I watched the growing gay rights movement with increasing fascination. Neither Thea nor I were ready to fully come out of the closet, but things were certainly becoming easier. Aside from work, our life was full of other lesbians. Although I suppose I can only speak for myself—due to client-patient confidentiality, I have no idea if Thea was treating lesbians at her practice; it's entirely possible her work was full of them. All of this to say, we weren't active participants in the movement yet. Our method of helping gay people at the time was financial, and for the most part on a personal level, when our friends found themselves in need. They were our chosen family, long before that phrase became popular.

Navigating our birth families became tricky business. Thea still had a contentious relationship with her stepmother, Jetty, but out of respect for her father, who'd passed away a few years earlier, she kept in touch with her. Jetty would drive out to Southampton every now and then, and while the visits tended to be strained, we all tolerated each other's company, even when she'd do gauche things like show off the large diamond engagement ring Thea's father had given her and then announce, "You'll never get it when I die." When she'd leave on Sunday afternoon, Thea's relief was obvious.

We made sure never to act physically affectionate with each other around Jetty, but she at least knew the score. That's not to say she approved, but she accepted it in her own limited way. Cele, on the other hand, remained oblivious. In her mind, Thea and I were roommates and close friends. To be fair, I never sat her down and came out of the closet, but since she no longer pressured me about my romantic life, I didn't feel the need.

Blackie and Thea got along famously, but that's no surprise since he charmed everyone he met. His mix of brilliance and utter disinterest in a normal career path fascinated her. Dolly and Rick never talked about the fact that we were a couple, and I took that she let my nephews stay with us every so often to mean that they were fine with us. We liked to celebrate holidays together as a family and usually gathered at Dolly and Rick's for Thanksgiving. One year, Blackie arrived looking rather lean, and when Thea asked if he'd lost weight, he shrugged and said, "Only about thirty-five pounds."

Thea looked unhinged at the news, so he quickly added, "That's not a lot of weight. Two tons is a lot of weight."

From that day forward, anytime a person commented on any amount of excess, whether it was a financial cost or an extra-large serving of mashed potatoes, Thea would turn to me and muse, "Yes, but would *Blackie* think it's a lot?"

We spent many evenings with my friend Dev, who often lamented her own lack of a love life, so Thea and I decided to try to set her up with someone. We heard about a party being thrown for a newly single lesbian from the West Coast who was visiting a friend in the Village. She was determined to sleep with someone as a rebound fling, so the house rule was that anyone who came to the party already coupled up must also bring someone unattached to guarantee a roomful of eligible women. We brought Dev—not to set her up with the California girl but to hopefully find someone local.

The house was crowded by the time we arrived, but Dev wasted no time, nudging me with her elbow and nodding across the room. "That one," she said. "She's beautiful."

"Where?" Thea asked, and after Dev nodded at the girl she'd become instantly smitten with, Thea wasted no time in facilitating an introduction. Her name was Shelly, and Thea suggested the four of us leave and have supper at a quiet little place on MacDougal Street. They hit it off immediately, and we welcomed Shelly into our lives as she and Dev fell deeply in love.

We met another new friend, Teddy, at a fancy party thrown by one of the Hamptons' biggest real estate brokers. She worked in finance and possessed a razor-sharp wit and a frank, no-bullshit attitude. We learned that she lived only a block away from us in the city, and she too became a staple in our social circle.

Life was more than just good; we were having the best time ever. If we weren't vacationing, every weekend was spent in the Hamptons. Thea had mastered the squat woodstove that sat in the middle of our living room and kept the house toasty in the winters. The Millstone was long gone by then, and the new gay hot spot was called the Attic. The line dances we'd loved in the '60s were now a novelty act (albeit one Thea still taught all our friends at classes she held), and a new sound was emerging as soul songs from Curtis Mayfield and the Jackson 5 gave way to the rise of disco, which Thea and I went absolutely mad for. All those goofy, joyful tracks that came dance ready with their own custom moves were right up our alley. The sound was silly and cartoonish and colorful and kept us on the dance floor for hours, well, in between the many smoke breaks I needed. It's bad form to wave your arms around with a lit cigarette in hand, in case you singe someone's hair.

Aside from sex, dancing was about all the exercise I got, but Thea loved sports, particularly softball and golf, both of which were plentiful in the Hamptons' lesbian scene. For some reason, many people had the mistaken idea that I was a good athlete when I was younger. I think it's because I liked to pose in my bikini with Thea's well-worn softball glove, but my only interest in sports consisted of a standing yearly bet with Blackie on the Army versus Navy game, and I always put my money on Navy simply because I thought their uniforms were sharper.

As the gay rights and sexual liberation movements grew in the early '70s, so did second-wave feminism. As much as I was in line with the values it fought for—equal pay for equal work, abortion rights, raising awareness about domestic abuse and the like—I felt deeply burned by Betty Friedan, founder of the National Organization for Women. She outright rejected lesbians because she was afraid we were a stain on the reputation of feminism, that we distracted from the movement's goals. In 1970, she even coined the phrase *Lavender Menace,* a worse phrase to me than *Lavender Scare,* the words that had stoked my fears when investigated by the FBI for my UNIVAC security clearance.

Many lesbians adopted her phrase to create their own protest group. In 1971, NOW finally included lesbian rights as part of their agenda, but for me, the damage had been done. I was so deeply hurt by that initial rejection that I never quite got over my grudge against the word *feminist,* even after Betty Friedan publicly apologized for her prejudice in 1977.

In addition to Stonewall, I think that early snub from a community that was supposed to be fighting for me also helped fuel my alignment with the gay rights movement, and I finally fully stepped into the fray when one day during the summer of 1974, Thea and I arrived at Fowler Beach in Southampton to find that the parking area everyone used had been closed down. As we turned around in confusion to try to find a spot on the road where we could park, an acquaintance drove by and slowed to a stop, waving at us. She gave us the scoop: an extremely wealthy and extremely prejudiced local who lived nearby had convinced the town to shut down the lot to curb access to our community beach. Ostensibly, the closure was due to the amount of trash we were supposedly leaving behind, but it was obvious this was bigotry, plain and simple.

"We've got to do something about it," she said, and we agreed. I was furious. We kept the cleanest area of the entire damn oceanfront!

A few brave people, led in part by my old friend Stan Herman from my early New York days, banded together to form the East End Gay Organization, or EEGO. They lobbied town hall and managed to successfully block the rezoning of Fowler Beach's parking area, and EEGO quickly became something of a local social club, hosting fund-raisers for all sorts of causes, not just gay ones. Thea and I began to attend all their gatherings, which widened our social circle and got me deeper into activism. Thea felt the same way I did about all of it, but it's fair to say that at the time, I was a much more active participant, because I suddenly had a lot more free time on my hands.

When IBM decided to transfer my division out of the Time-Life Building to their upstate offices, I balked. Pat had moved on to another part of the company, and I'd been promoted from senior systems programmer to manager of programming standards, and also served as the corporate programming language strategist. I loved my career, but I did not relish the idea of a grueling daily rail commute outside of the city.

"You don't have to work, you know," Thea said one night over dinner, when she noticed I was picking at my food. "I've got more than enough to care for us." I heard the caution in her voice, and she was right to be wary.

"I love my job," I snapped. "You know how damn hard I worked for it."

"Of course I know that. I'm just saying that I want you to know it's an option. You could think of retiring early as a chance to go back to school. Think of all the time you'd have to read, to study anything you like."

"And be a housewife?" I shot back.

"You know that's not what I'm saying. Just think about it."

So I did, and the longer I mulled the idea, the more enticing it became. I appreciated Thea's gesture, though I suspected more than a small part of her relished the idea of being the sole breadwinner. She could be oddly traditional at times, despite how much she liked bragging about my career to our friends.

Not having to go to an office every day would be a luxury, another piled onto what I already had. I loved my work, but to have an open schedule to do whatever I liked . . . no one could ever accuse me of being a time waster, and I began to fantasize about all the different projects I could start—like setting up my own consulting firm and devoting more time to gay rights activism.

After weeks of hemming and hawing, I pulled the trigger and retired from IBM in 1975 with a generous package and a promise to consider returning someday. My coworkers threw a large party for me, complete with cake and champagne.

"At least now I won't have to bring an extra pack of cigarettes to work every day just in case you've decided to quit again," one joked.

He had a point. There was really only one thing that Thea and I constantly argued about, and that was my incessant smoking. By the time I retired, I was up to two or three packs a day and had been puffing away for thirty years. Thea had been an occasional social smoker when we initially dated but quickly grew to loathe cigarettes after we started living together. I smoked more than enough for the two of us, and all my efforts thus far to quit ended in total defeat after less than twenty-four hours.

Cele couldn't wrap her mind around my decision to retire early. "What are you thinking?" she asked on one of her occasional trips to visit us in New York. I usually went to her, but every now and then, she enjoyed expanding her shopping options and would come up for the day. "I've socked away more than enough," I told her. "I'll be fine, and I'm sure I'll go back to work soon. I just need a break." I still had no idea what she thought about our living arrangements. Thankfully, she adored Thea.

The good vibes weren't mirrored at Dolly and Rick's, though. Increasingly whenever we'd visit, I noticed a growing tension between Thea and Rick. I don't think it was anything homophobic; I think she just rubbed him the wrong way. They began to spar passive-aggressively about news and politics, and Thea's dismissiveness didn't go over well with him. Things grew especially tense after we spent weeks planning a big engagement party for one of their sons and they all arrived extremely late. I reamed every last one of them out because Thea had spent hours cooking, and while Thea graciously didn't comment on it in the moment, there was iciness to all subsequent visits that ramped up the already strained conversations.

Aside from that unpleasantness, our life together was grand. We had to leave our apartment when the owner decided to sell the building, but Thea purchased a three-bedroom apartment at 2 Fifth Avenue, just above Washington Square Park, and after twenty years of bouncing from place to place, I fast settled into the security of knowing that I wouldn't have to move again unless we wanted to. We were living a dream, full of affection and sex and travel and shopping and filling our minds with intellectual and artistic interests. Our future seemed to stretch forward with endless possibilities.

I was filled with so much joy, and we danced and danced and danced—so much so that during the summer of 1976, when Thea's right knee began to buckle every so often when we were out tearing it up at the Attic, we joked that I'd simply worn her down.

Watching Edie and Thea together was like watching a film," says their friend Teddy. "It was fascinating to witness them maneuver through that relationship, because they were each such a strong character, but they always left room for the other to shine. They were two of the smartest ladies I've ever come across in my life."

"They were the golden couple, really," says Shelly, who lost Dev to a stroke in 2016. "Both of them smart and beautiful. They had money, and they were sophisticated. They epitomized something special. People looked up and admired them."

One of their close friends, the playwright Nancy Dean, immortalized their presence in the 1970s Hamptons crowd in a novel she wrote under the pseudonym Elizabeth Lang called Anna's Country, about a woman who falls in love with her female neighbor. The story is set in upstate New York but inspired by Nancy's experiences in the Hamptons, and during the title character's affair, she gets a crash course in the local lesbian scene. Nancy disguised Edie's and Thea's names but swapped in their real ones while reading from the book years later at Thea's memorial service.

"Wait until Anna sees Thea and Edie," one of the old guards said.

"They'll be an education for Anna. They go anywhere. They go to

golf clubs, health spas, Grossinger's casinos, anywhere." Thea, rav-
ishing in a tuxedo, and Edie, devastating in silver lamé. They sweep
down spiral staircases and stun the astonished locals. Thea is a medical person, a tiny beautiful woman. Her lover for nigh on fifteen
years is Edie, a dainty woman who is a computer whiz, when she
isn't playing Scarlett to Thea's Rhett Butler."

The book goes on to describe an evening inspired by visits to Pat Chez, a real
lesbian bar that Edie and Thea frequented in the Hamptons:

A white-haired woman in a black caftan turned slowly in the center
of the dancers. Two glamorous women in long gowns modeled
from Rita Hayworth's best days danced slowly by, clinging together, their eyes closed. A woman in a white suit and vest walked
from table to table, stopping for a moment to speak briefly to each
couple. The whole world seemed to be there. Anna didn't know
if she would have the courage to ask Hope to go out on that dance
floor with her.

She watched a striking couple, a small dark-haired woman in
black slacks and a red silk shirt dancing with a lovely woman in
silver lamé. Their dancing was perfect. Red blouse was leading, as
they swung about the floors slipping between other dancers, sepa-
rating, coming together again with practiced timing and suddenly
they stood before them. Thea and Edie had become real, and Anna
loved their ease. This was their world and they possessed it.

The people in Edie and Thea's circle saw them as a divine model couple, partly
because of the glamour and their devotion to butch/femme dynamics but also be-
cause they balanced each other out despite how different they were. "When you
have two people who are each so strongly particular like Edie and Thea were, it can
sometimes be very difficult," Teddy says. "In many relationships, straight and gay alike,
there's often someone stronger, but there was never a shadow of one over the other."
In order to maintain parity, Teddy remembers that when undertaking big projects

like renovations or redecorating, they'd take turns being, as she calls it, "the foreman and the peon."

"They'd decide ahead of time and adhere to the role throughout the entire project. And the roles would switch depending on the project. It was a way to get through things together without going mad, because with those two, it was like having Einstein and Hawking in a relationship."

Speaking of Stephen Hawking, Edie was fascinated by the man. Teddy recalls a Saturday evening in 1974, just after the publication of his seminal article in Nature called "Black Hole Explosions?" Prior to his research, black holes were considered to be static, but he posited that they emit radiation, and he was right.

Edie and Thea were discussing his research, and Teddy confessed to them that she didn't understand what they were talking about at all. Edie grew extremely excited and ran into another room and came back carrying a large easel with a giant sketch pad and a black marker. "Let me show you," she said and proceeded to teach an impromptu twenty-minute seminar on quantum mechanics.

"It was the best explanation of black holes I ever got," Teddy says, but Edie and Thea's whip-smart exchange of ideas could get a bit intense. "You had to be fully aware to follow them," Teddy says, presumably meaning nights when Edie didn't have an easel on hand to help people. "An evening with them was filled with intelligent statements and ideas. Most people would get to what seemed like the logical end point of a conversation, but they'd keep it going back and forth and back and forth. Eventually over the years, I got better at keeping up."

They were both extremely logic-driven, Edie more so since she tackled any task with a mathematician's precision. Thea's work as a therapist allowed more room for emotions to come into play, but she too maintained a specific rationality to them, tracing angry outbursts to their root, whereas Edie was much more prone to letting her temper roar. To help them navigate their fights, they employed a number system to gauge heightened anger and try to keep things in check.

"If a discussion got too heated between them, one of them would invariably say, 'This is a five,' or 'This is an eight,'" Teddy says. "If the number got too high, they knew to stop. It was like an escalation warning to a big red button that would blow everything up. If they had deeply profound disagreements, as I assume everyone does, they kept those in their own space."

They also designated specific numbers as signals to use in public situations to communicate a thought without anyone else knowing. For example, if Edie began discussing Thea's stepmother to someone at a party, and Thea didn't think it appropriate, she'd murmur something like, "Thirty-eighty" under her breath as a warning to zip it.

It's a relief to hear they fought like any other couple. (Well, maybe not like everybody—the number systems are a smart tip more people should probably use, and they often recommended it to their close friends.) Edie and Thea's relationship is easily romanticized; it's important to remember that even after their rocky start, they were humans like everybody else, with their share of bad days and partner pet peeves.

There was jealousy as well, but for the most part on Thea's end and allocated to Edie's past romances. From many accounts, once they were together, an occasional crush outside of the relationship was fair game. This was the height of the sexual revolution, and they had a robust sex life that at different points included multiple partners. "They were very, very sexual," Teddy says, and they were also quite open about their amorous adventures. "They'd say, 'Don't call us on Tuesday between four and six. We have a sex date.'"

Equally decadent were the gifts Thea showered on Edie. "Minks and diamonds," Teddy says. "Here were two beautiful, educated women, both so gorgeous and intelligent that when they entered a room, everything stopped. There weren't, and still aren't, many of those." She sighs, but then adds, "Although, I go to the Center sometimes for coffee, and when I see some of the younger people today, I think, Well, maybe there's hope.*"*

Seventeen

When Thea was a teenager, she fell during a softball game and hurt her right knee. The pain was strong enough to send her to the hospital, but she was told the injury was nothing more than some torn cartilage and that it would heal on its own. It did, although she tended to slightly favor her other leg from then on. During the summer of 1976, she blamed her occasional dance floor stumbles and issues with her golf swing on that long-ago incident.

Her odd teetering turned to occasional falls during the winter and early spring of 1977. At first, we chalked it up to slushy, slippery streets and sidewalks, and she was mortified each time it happened. A public tumble is always a little embarrassing no matter how strong your character. With the increasing frequency, though, Thea quickly began to notice a similar pattern. Each incident started with her right foot. If her toe caught the ground, her right ankle would bend to the right, and once the fall began, she had no ability to recover from it.

She continued to blame her teenage injury, but other mysterious physical issues began to plague her as well. A general stiffness in both legs, difficulty raising them when she tried to put on slacks while seated on the bed. She'd shuffle around the house in slippers whenever she was home, a frustrated look on her face. She began to complain of mysterious sensations, like two of her toes being stuck together when she wore shoes. Her feet were always freezing, and sometimes the front of her legs would grow numb, as did a vertical band between her breasts and waist. And I wasn't aware of this at the time, but her need to urinate became increasingly frequent, and she even experienced an isolated incident of incontinence.

I pushed her to see a doctor, but she kept brushing it off, insisting that it was just her body growing older, that she was experiencing the same general indignities and annoyances that everyone must face sooner or later.

She'd recently begun performing with a few other musicians in a small string ensemble at the Ninety-second Street Y. She still had her original violin from college, already a family heirloom to begin with, but by that point an extremely valuable antique and in perfect working condition.

One day, on the way to rehearsal, she felt the familiar buckle in her ankle. Her only thought in the second it took for her to crumple to the sidewalk was that she had to protect the violin, so she clutched it with both arms up in the air and let her body take the full brunt of gravity and concrete.

She arrived home covered in scrapes and bruises, but her violin intact, and I demanded she check herself into the hospital for neurological testing, but still she refused. It was getting to be a growing point of contention between us, her insisting everything was fine, me demanding she get checked out, and we were in the middle of arguing about it one day in April when the phone rang.

It was Blackie. "Can I call you back?" I snapped. "I'm dealing with an extremely stubborn woman at the moment."

"Edie, I need you to sit down," he said softly.

I must have looked terrified, because Thea was by my side in an instant.

"Cele had a heart attack. She hasn't woken up, and they're not sure how much longer she's going to hold on."

I think I cried out. I remember hot tears that came fast, and I was distantly aware that I could tell Blackie was trying to keep back his own. Thea gently took the phone from me and began speaking to him quietly. I grabbed the phone back.

"When did it happen?" I asked.

"This morning."

"Does Dolly know?"

"Yes, she's on her way over to the house now, and Rick has offered to come get you and bring you down."

"Just let me know when he'll be here. I'll start packing. I love you, Blackie."

"Love you too, kid," he said and hung up.

Thea held me as I wept. After a few minutes, she brushed the hair out of my face with her fingertips and pulled a tissue from her pocket to blot my face clean of smeared makeup.

"I'll come with you," she said.

"*No!*" I said, and I pushed her away. "You have to go to the hospital. You have to get this checked out. There is no other option. I will not lose you. Come down and join me if Cele doesn't pull through, but find out what is happening to your body."

I saw her start to protest. I knew that she wanted the chance to say goodbye to Cele if this was indeed the end. I felt terrible denying her the opportunity, but the thought of losing her as well was too much.

She saw the unyielding look on my face and nodded. She held me again and swore to me that she wasn't going anywhere.

Cele didn't last much longer after I arrived. I was able to see her one last time, in the hospital. She was unconscious as I sat beside her and moved the chair closer to her bedside. She looked much older, her hair thin and skin pale, but even hovering close to death, she still seemed like the same pillar of strength she'd been my entire life.

As I stared down at her, I wondered if she'd realized on some subconscious level that her wish for me had come true; if she knew that I'd found the kind of lifelong partnership that she'd always hoped I would. She must have. It was so strange to feel as close to someone as I did to her but not be able to talk about my relationship. And I hadn't, to protect her from what? Having to disown me? Being disappointed? Feeling shame? I realized with a start that none of these were things she ever would have felt about me.

As she'd always told me, I could do no wrong in her eyes, so why had I felt the need to hide anything?

Even if she'd been shocked to learn I was gay, she would have come around fast. Hell, she might have even gone out and marched in one of the pride parades that were now happening in cities all over the country once a year in June to commemorate Stonewall, before I'd even felt brave enough to march in one myself. I desperately wanted her to wake up one last time, to let her know that she'd never have to worry about me, that I'd found love. I wanted to thank her for everything, for every ounce of self-confidence she'd ever given me. I pleaded silently for her eyes to open, but she remained still and calm. I leaned over and held her cheeks in my hands, in the same way she'd held my face so many times and I'd seen her hold so many others. The gesture felt natural, and I could tell why she'd liked it—I felt my love for her flow through my arms, out my hands, and into her. If she couldn't hear me tell her that I loved her, I made sure she could feel it.

She died peacefully in her sleep later that night.

We scheduled the funeral for a week later to give relatives from out of town time to arrive. This also gave Thea plenty of time to check herself into Columbia Presbyterian to be examined, and I made arrangements for Dev to drive Thea down to Philadelphia upon her release.

Cele had already explained her will to Dolly and me several years earlier. She wanted to leave the house to Blackie. She explained her reasons why but hadn't needed to—he was still nowhere near as settled as the two of us. Or anywhere near settled, period. He still lived alone on the third floor, surrounded by towers of books. He'd taken to buying entire libraries from estate sales whenever he had extra money to spend.

Over the next several days, as we welcomed and embraced family members I hadn't seen in years, I grew impressed with how grown-up he was acting—playing the host, serving food, and offering guests drinks and tissues.

I checked in with Thea several times a day throughout the week so she could keep me updated on all the various poking and prodding by doctors, but nothing turned up any obvious answers, and of course none of her symptoms happened to manifest while under their care. She endured a spinal tap, and a few initial terrifying theories like spinal cord tumors were eliminated by various other tests.

By the time she was discharged, the working diagnosis was that she was experiencing a loss of nerve tissue and that her treatment was to include physical therapy and follow-up appointments. Doctors floated the idea of multiple sclerosis (MS) but said it was far too early to tell. I planned to begin extensive research as soon as I arrived back home about all the reasons why nerve tissue might deteriorate.

I missed Thea desperately and couldn't wait to see her. I'd been sharing so many stories about Cele with different family members, and the exchanges did wonders for helping me with the first steps of healing from her loss. But watching all the married couples around me lean on each other for support made my heart ache. I wanted to hold on to my own love for comfort, but even when Thea arrived, we had to keep our emotions in check, our displays of affection at a minimum. Her discharge process from the hospital in New York took forever, so she and Dev were late getting into town. They were so late, in fact, that they arrived a quarter of the way into the memorial service.

I'd saved seats for them next to me near the front, and they waited until there was a lull between speakers before rushing up the aisle to squeeze in next to me. As they sat down, a man behind me, a distant uncle I didn't know very well, tapped me on the shoulder.

"Who're they?" he snarled. "The front rows are for family. I've never seen them before in my life."

I turned and glowered. "That one," I whispered loudly, pointing to Dev, "is my dear friend. This one sitting next to me is the woman I live with, and the woman I expect to live the rest of my life with." I gave him the evil eye, almost hoping he'd say something nasty so I could explode and release the frustration and grief I'd been holding on to all week.

"Oh," he said, leaning back. He didn't seem the least bit surprised by my impromptu coming out. "Well, they're late."

Afterward, the house was mobbed with well-wishers, and I lost Thea and Dev while fielding waves of condolences from long-lost cousins and their families. One woman, a second cousin whom I knew Cele had grown especially close to in her late years, cornered me. "I'm so happy to see that Thea could make it," she said. "You know, my daughter is gay."

"How did you know I was?" I asked, wondering if news of my little fit at the funeral parlor was spreading.

"Your mother told me."

She registered the look of shock on my face and quickly added, "Well, she didn't know she was telling me. But she used to talk about the two of you constantly. Whenever she'd come back from a visit to New York, she'd be on cloud nine and say, 'Oh, the love between those two girls . . . the sense you get inside their house is just wonderful.' The way she bragged about how close you two were, well, pretty much everyone in Philadelphia got it. Except your mother, that is."

Thea and Dev and I laughed about the story the entire drive back to New York.

———— ◆◆ ————

Edie always insisted that her mother had no idea she was in a relationship with Thea, but many family members believe Cele knew and simply chose not to discuss it. Perhaps it was enough for her to know that Edie was loved, and she felt it wasn't worth wading into the finer points of what that meant about her daughter. Edie even said that when her mother called to explain why she was leaving the house to Blackie, she'd told Cele it was fine because Thea would make sure she was taken care of. Yet Edie still didn't seem to think that Cele understood what that truly meant. Cele was a gregarious woman with a thirst for knowledge, and it seems unlikely that she wouldn't have known. She knew her daughter was happy, and had she lived to see further social progress with the gay rights movement, she probably would have openly embraced Edie's life. She was already so proud of everything her youngest daughter had accomplished, and it's easy to imagine her standing alongside Edie on the steps of the Supreme Court, beaming with pride and holding Edie's cheeks in her hands.

Eighteen

O ver the next two years, Thea continued to visit specialists for a multi-
tude of strange ailments: blood blisters on her left hand, periodic in-
ability to bring her fingers together, electrical sensations running through
her arms, problems focusing her eyes, increased incontinence, and feeling
as though a belt were being squeezed around her rib cage. One evening,
she fell in the middle of the living room in Southampton and narrowly
missed splitting her head open on the corner of the cast-iron woodstove.
We immediately had the stove removed.

In the midst of all her illnesses, I began having periodic chest pains, and
Thea began to complain more and more about my smoking. I'd continued
to try to quit every now and then, but no attempt ever lasted more than a
day. I simply could not handle the nicotine cravings, and my temper would
flare out of control to the point that it was always best for both of us if I
just lit up again.

With Thea's mystery illness worsening, she finally put her foot down.
"Both of us can't be sick. I can't stand watching you kill yourself, and I
can't stand the smell. You need to choose. It's me or cigarettes."

I told the truth—I honestly didn't think I could do it and that her ultimatum meant that we might even be facing the end of our relationship, but my love for her prevailed. Quitting smoking was the hardest thing I ever accomplished, much harder even than gathering the courage to sue the United States, but the idea of losing her to my habit was so terrifying that I searched for outside help. My own willpower simply wasn't enough. I discovered a program called Smokenders that addressed the full range of psychological crutches that came with smoking, and looking at my addiction through that lens, as opposed to cigarettes simply being a physical need, appealed to the way my brain processed information.

It didn't happen overnight, but after the third time I completed the program, my cigarette sobriety stuck.

When we finally got the official diagnosis in 1979 that Thea had MS, it was almost something of a relief to finally have an answer about what was wrong. I thought that we were on the same page about what it meant for our relationship—absolutely nothing. This was a body issue that would have no impact on her mind, and to me, that meant we simply needed to buckle up for a ride we hadn't expected to go on together. But I wasn't the one with the disease, and I feel foolish now for being naïve enough to think it wouldn't initially affect how she thought of us. Being told that your body was going to progressively fail you would change one's outlook on pretty much everything.

Over the course of three short months, she went from needing one cane to walk to two canes. That autumn, her right leg was fitted for a spiral brace, and before I knew it, she required elbow extension crutches to walk at all.

One day, late into a quiet drive out to Southampton, she said, "You can leave, you know. I'd understand. In fact, I think you probably should."

"What on earth are you talking about?"

"This is only going to get worse. I'll be in a wheelchair soon. I'll no longer have any ability to use the bathroom by myself. I'll need to sleep with a catheter."

"They'll find a cure," I said firmly, and I believed it.

"Edie, no, they won't. Not in our lifetime. I'm willing to try experimental medications, I want to keep my practice going, but the one thing I won't abide is you looking at me with pity."

"Thea, don't be ridiculous. That would never happen."

We'd pulled off the main road by then, and I rolled into our driveway and shut off the engine. "Besides," I continued. "We're engaged."

"That doesn't even mean a thing," she snapped, but apologized when she saw the hurt look on my face. "I didn't mean that," she said, leaning over and holding me. "I'm just so goddamn angry. I don't want to pull you down with me."

"I never want to hear you say anything like that again. I'm yours, and I'm in this. And we will get through it together."

Thea decided that she wanted to go to Europe as soon as possible. "I have to make sure I see Amsterdam one last time," she told me. "Who knows how much longer I have before I'm wheelchair bound?"

Her cousin Dick, the artist she'd befriended in the West Village after getting kicked out of Sarah Lawrence, had left America and was living there with his family. Their house was our first stop when we arrived. Dick and Thea immediately disappeared up the stairs and began shouting over some sort of misunderstanding regarding her father's will.

I don't recall what their specific argument was, but Thea had plenty to yell about when it came to that particular document. The money she should have received upon Willem's death had been split into half cash, with the other half being placed in a trust that was controlled by two men in her family and a male lawyer, all because Thea's father hadn't wanted to indulge her lesbian life (i.e., spend it all on me). Despite the fact that she had a Ph.D. and her own private practice, she was deemed irresponsible simply because she was gay, and that rightly infuriated her.

I stayed in the kitchen and got to know Patsy and Ginny, Thea's teenage second cousins. Ginny had made a large plate of profiteroles in honor of

our arrival, and we sat around the table and nibbled on them as I asked
about their school. By the time Thea and Dick worked things out and
came downstairs to join us, I'd grown completely enchanted by both girls
and insisted that they must come stay with us in New York often.

After our visit to Amsterdam, we traveled to Israel to meet with a doctor who we'd heard was working on an experimental treatment for MS,
but nothing came of the visit. Thea was too far along, and besides, he told
us, we already lived in the country with the most cutting-edge science in
that particular field of medicine.

Rather than feeling tired once we returned home, Thea seemed rein-
vigorated. She began taking lessons at Jo Jo's Dance Factory, where she
learned how to drop her crutches and move to Donna Summer while
standing in one place, by leaning all of her weight onto her stronger leg.
The ability didn't last long, but while it did, it was glorious to see her
standing on the dance floor of the Attic or Pat Chez, her hips swaying and
arms waving freely. She soon moved to her first wheelchair, though, and
made the best of the situation by purchasing a sporty pair of leather gloves
to prevent her hands from getting dirty while operating it. She accepted
the transition with both grace and her characteristic no-bullshit attitude
when it came to requiring any sort of assistance. She wouldn't accept pity
from anyone, and if a friend didn't listen to exactly what she required
when it came to needing help, they were never asked to lend a hand again.

We renovated both the apartment and the Southampton house to better
accommodate her wheelchair. I donated bulky furniture that took up precious rolling space. She was still mobile in the upper half of her body and
continued to love to cook, so we had all the counters and shelves in the
kitchens lowered to make chopping and mixing easier for her. We installed
a ceiling lift to help get her in and out of bed. She'd moved her private
practice to our home and kept her office in the living room. Whenever a
patient came by for a session, she'd shut the pocket doors that tucked into
our walls for privacy, and I'd either leave the apartment or stay hidden
away in my own little back office.

. . .

One Friday evening in the early summer of 1981, we were in Southampton preparing dinner when something on the news caught our attention.

"The CDC reports that between October 1980 and May of 1981, five young men, all active homosexuals, were treated for pneumonia at three different hospitals in Los Angeles. Two have died."

I remember thinking it was odd, but not giving it too much thought. The report was on everyone's minds over the next few weeks; it kept getting brought up at various parties and dinners as a curiosity, but that's about it. A month later, though, when The New York Times published their now-infamous article RARE CANCER SEEN IN 41 HOMOSEXUALS, alarms began to go off everywhere.

We spent the next day taking turns on the phone, calling around to friends in the medical field. Thea confessed that one of her patients, a gay male, had been sick and canceled his last several appointments, but she clammed up after that, not wanting to break confidentiality. I learned that one of my male friends from the 1950s whom I'd mostly lost track of was also sick. Within the next two years, he and one of the other men in that group would be dead.

The speed with which AIDS took hold is terrifying to recall, and the memories of that period are horrid. By the end of 1981, there were 234 confirmed deaths in the United States, and in January 1982, our downstairs neighbor Larry Kramer held the very first meeting of what would become the Gay Men's Health Crisis.

Word got out to more people that Thea was a gay psychotherapist, and her client base increased. She would never tell me anything specific, but it was clear she was suddenly treating an alarming number of men suddenly facing their mortality, and I could sense the sadness weighing on her, compounded by her own body's deterioration.

Funeral invitations began to pour in, and by the mid-'80s, many of the gay men we knew were dead, including several of Thea's colleagues. Up until that point, gay men and women still rarely mixed. There had even been a bit of a social skirmish in the Hamptons in the '70s when, for a time, the Attic stopped letting women in to dance.

The door-enforced ban didn't last long. Many of our friends were furious and complained that most of the male patrons didn't even go there to dance but to have sex in the bathrooms and hidden areas. My stance had always been that if having a back room for the men to get their rocks off was the only requirement for me to have a dance floor, then by all means, let them have one.

Once gay men started becoming sick, though, the wall between them and gay women collapsed. Lesbians stepped up to become caretakers when entire families turned against their sick male family members. My friend Rose Walton hosted the first AIDS fund-raiser out in the Hamptons in conjunction with the East End Gay Organization, and I began to get more and more involved with the group, as did many other lesbians in the community.

It drove me insane every time I read an obituary that referred to a dead man's lover as his "longtime companion." What a bullshit formality that was, as if the survivor were nothing more than a butler with benefits. There was no emotion in that phrase, nothing that translated the same grief one would inherently understand when reading about a person who'd lost a spouse at a hideously young age to a horrible, mysterious plague that ate away at the body. To say nothing of the fact that we were hearing multiple stories about these longtime companions being refused entry to their partners' hospital rooms to say goodbye, because their love held no legal rights.

Thea and I both knew that wallowing in feelings of helplessness wasn't going to get us anywhere, so we began to attend demonstrations and small fund-raisers, donating money to different advocacy groups. Since we moved in fairly affluent circles, we had friends who knew to hit us up for money, and we gave. It was the least we could do.

We'd always missed the Pride March in June because it happened on the weekend, and we spent those in Southampton. Our regular departure time on Sunday nights was 11:00 p.m., and we'd arrive back home around 12:30 or 1:00 in the morning. One night, at some point in the early '80s, I suggested we take a quick drive around the Village before getting to the apartment to see what was left of the parade. Christopher Street was empty, but debris from the marchers and parties was scattered everywhere. I felt hollow and said, "Honey, let's not miss it anymore."

From then on, we didn't. I wasn't quite ready to join the march myself, but we'd watch from the sideline and cheer everyone on.

An organization we supported that had risen out of the Stonewall riots, called the Lesbian and Gay Community Services Center, was growing fast as need for their help increased, and we were friendly with the group's vice president, David Rothenberg. In 1983, a former school on West Thirteenth Street was put up for sale by the city, and after some initial resistance, Mayor Ed Koch agreed to sell it to the Center for $1.5 million, with a down payment of $150,000 due by the end of the year.

David immediately began a campaign, hitting up as many wealthy homosexuals as he could find for no-interest loans of $500 or $1,000 each. We, of course, donated the larger amount, along with almost two hundred others, and the Center met its goal. When they tried to pay me back, I tore up the check.

I wish I could say my reason was purely altruistic, but the check they wrote had *The Lesbian and Gay Community Services Center* right there in big words on it. I was fine being out in the community, but I wasn't about to let my bank know that I was gay. Homosexuals in New York City had no legal rights in terms of being discriminated against in housing, employment, and public accommodations and still wouldn't until 1986.

I had something else to offer gay rights organizations besides money, though—my tech expertise. Early AIDS and gay rights organizations were very bare-bones, made up largely of volunteers who used whatever kinds of office materials they could get their hands on. Even though I'd left IBM, I still kept up on everything they were working on. Earlier, in 1981, my former manager let me know ahead of time that their first PCs were about to be made available on the retail market, and I made sure that I was the

first person in all of New York City to receive one. (I also promptly identified several bugs and called up my former department to inform them
of the issues.)

I soon discovered user groups and found entire communities of people
whose minds worked like mine and saw all the same potential I did for
personal computing. Not just to make lives easier but to use programing
language as a cognitive discipline. Learning code wasn't just about computers; it was a way to teach people how to use operational logic as a
means of planning and the execution of just about anything.

I began to help both the Center and EEGO set up their early computer
systems. For EEGO, I debugged their address databases for fund-raising
mailers and newsletters, and at the Center, I wrote a program revision
to their central database that allowed it to create gender designations so
that mailings about events and services geared specifically toward women
could be easily sorted.

I became involved with the Center's social calendar, volunteering to
help with dances and events. Thea wasn't able to join me for the setups,
which involved a lot of physical activity like climbing ladders to tape
paper flowers to the walls for decorations, but she came to each event
with me.

In 1985, the same year that I founded my own consulting company
called PC Classics, the Center asked me to help overhaul their entire
database, which I quickly discovered had devolved into an absolute disaster. I spent hundreds of hours learning the language of the system they'd
purchased, repairing bugs in their mail list code, adding new information fields, establishing a backup system, and in general just stabilizing the
whole damn mess.

Since I was getting older, the organization SAGE (Services & Advocacy
for GLBT Elders) greatly appealed to me. Though they were a separate
organization from the Center, they operated out of the same building at
the time. I began volunteering for them and raised enough money that I
was asked to serve on an advisory and planning committee for their TLC

(Tender Living Care) Project and Center, which was conceived as a re-source center for lesbians living with life-threatening illnesses.

For one particular fund-raiser, I pitched the idea of throwing a 1950s-inspired prom. I'd been reminiscing more and more about the early flir-tations Thea and I conducted to the sounds of 45 RPM records and all the goofy line dances we used to do. She didn't once let the wheelchair keep her from heading out to the dance floor to spin around and lead me whenever we attended an event. Plus, we still made sure to go dancing in the Hamptons every chance we could. I never would have let her see it, because I was so proud of the way she was handling this next phase of her life, but it did pierce my heart to know that I'd never see her perform any of our old favorite dances like the Lindy and the Jitterbug from more than the waist up. I felt selfish for even thinking such thoughts.

On the night of the '50s prom, Thea only needed my help getting into her dark pants and shoes before she put on a white formal jacket she'd had custom made for the occasion. I dressed in a gown I'd purchased for some fancy event thirty years earlier and paired it with newer silver-sequined heels to match the pearly silver nail polish I'd recently started wearing constantly after Thea said she loved the color on me.

Once we were both dressed, I pinned a maroon carnation onto her la-pel, then bent down slightly and held out my arm so she could slide a white gardenia corsage on. As soon as it was in place, I crossed my wrists while admiring it and realized I was basically in second position of the Hand Jive, so I stood up fast and knocked my fists together twice. Thea's eyes lit up, and she did the same. We launched into the rest of the movements in perfect tandem three times before I collapsed onto her lap, laughing.

I nuzzled her neck, memories of preparing for countless nights out all swirling into one massive swell of anticipation for the evening ahead, proud as ever to arrive somewhere on her arm. We began to slowly sway in each other's arms as she hummed a song I quickly recognized as "Some-where" from *West Side Story*. We both began to sing softly.

"There's a time for us, someday a time for us, time together with time to spare."

Thea began to spin the chair in a gentle circle. "See?" she said. "Who needs legs to slow dance?"

My dress caught in the spokes, and the chair jerked to a stop. So I changed into tapered silk pants, and as soon as we arrived at the Center, we were the first couple out on the floor.

We never acknowledged it, but we had an unspoken rule that neither was ever allowed to see the other cry over what was happening to her body. We counted ourselves lucky that her disease wouldn't affect her mind, that she'd always be present, but that didn't mean we weren't each mourning in our own way. She'd tell friends that the only thing she was truly sad about was not being able to press her whole body against mine while we slow danced. Of course, that wasn't all of it, but she kept those other thoughts to herself. There were many times when I had to leave the apartment, overwhelmed with emotion and calling out that I was just running downstairs for some made-up pantry need. I had a Ray Charles song stuck in my head for months, and I'd find myself wandering through the West Village whisper-singing it under my breath. The tune was meant to be silly and tongue-in-cheek, but the lyrics had taken on all new meaning for me: "*Look what they've done to my song.*"

I was singing for Thea, but also our entire community. The freedom of the '70s felt like ages ago. Now there was always another struggle, be it political, with our government refusing to do anything about AIDS, or bureaucratic, with arguments within the gay organizations who, at the end of the day, were all trying to do the same thing: create change and acceptance of us. My new awareness of all the battles that needed to be fought always managed to snap me out of my sadness. I'd return to the apartment, energized and ready once more to mobilize and fight for our rights or make love with my beautiful Thea.

More often than not, both would happen in the same afternoon.

———◆———

E die's sudden burst of activism starting in the 1980s is dizzying, it's almost as if she were making up for lost time. Her work with EEGO, SAGE, and the Center are but a small portion of what she was up to. There was the phone tree hub she assisted with out of her home for GLAAD, to organize protests against negative depictions of homosexuals in film and television. She was one of the founding members of MATRIX, a nonprofit organization that attempted to create a retirement center for lesbians. While it ultimately didn't succeed, it paved the way for the idea of future LGBTQ retirement centers. She joined OLOC, Old Lesbians Organizing for Change, and arrived at their first West Coast conference wearing a button that identified her as "57 and ¾," since membership was restricted to those sixty and older. (She didn't want to be dishonest.)

Along with other representatives from SAGE, she organized workshops on coming out and awareness about ageism. She joined the New York Personal Computer Club, a monthly social gathering of several hundred tech lovers who shared their knowledge and skills with each other. She and Thea donated their convertible for the grand marshal to ride in during the New York Pride March. She ran nine-week Smokenders seminars for other lesbians who needed help quitting their habits (as well as to help keep herself honest).

It's no surprise that during this time, Edie and Thea began to get noticed more and more by a much wider circle of New York's gay community. Their visibility and philanthropy turned them into local celebrities of a kind. As their close friend Karen Sauvigné, who met them in the mid-'80s after first spotting them at the Attic, puts it, "They caught your attention because they danced great and one of them was in a wheelchair. Which is unusual among dancers. Never mind good dancers."

Karen developed a nodding acquaintance with the pair, but they didn't grow close until 1986, when she and Edie were both on the crew of a musical revue benefit in the city for the Lesbian Herstory Archives, the Astrea Lesbian Foundation for Justice, and the National Gay Task Force. The show was called Taking Liberties: A Lesbian Celebration of the Statue of Liberty's Centennial Birthday. (Karen notes that the numbers were only very loosely based on that fact.)

The wrap party was held in a cast member's apartment, located in a fifth-floor walk-up. Karen, a self-described gym rat at the time, answered a call for several strong women to arrive early and help carry Thea up the stairs. "She was strong-willed and willing to be bossy," Karen says. "She instructed us to cross our wrists and clasp each other's hands to create a human chair that would lift her, and she kept her arm around my shoulder the whole way up. She was worried for her safety, but she was worried for everyone else's safety as well. She had me in an eye lock, and by the time we got to the top of the stairs, I was in love. I got to know them because Thea needed to know who she could trust for these sorts of things, and I became a trusted person."

Since Karen also spent her summers out in the Hamptons, she began biking by their house on the way to the beach and stopping off for brief visits, during which she'd help with little things like getting Thea into the pool. The three of them soon became extremely tight friends, and from Karen's recollections, it didn't seem as though being in a wheelchair had much of an effect on Thea's personality. "She was very sure of herself, and she loved argumentation," Karen says. "She was so smart and could always out-reason you, and had the backup to do so. She'd say, 'It couldn't have been like that because . . .' or, 'But don't you remember when we read in the paper that it actually happened like this?' She never made a correction into any-thing personal, though; it was her way of having intellectual fun."

The trio began an every-other-Tuesday-night dinner tradition, with Karen bringing over takeout for an evening of long talks, and it was clear to her that Edie and Thea's relationship was strong as ever. "They were very loving to each other," she says. "I'd occasionally see them having little tiffs, but they were always short and not serious. They deeply understood that they loved each other and were deeply aware of each other's capacities and incapacities. They were honest and open and talked about when one angered the other so that they could process it. It was a relationship that I admired."

Not everyone felt the same. The tension between Thea and Dolly's husband, Rick, worsened with each family visit, until eventually, at some point in the mid- to late '80s, there was an irreparable falling-out. Accounts of what exactly happened vary, but after a dinner at Dolly's house one night, as Edie and Thea were packing up to go home, Rick pointed at Thea and shouted, "I never want to see that woman again!" And he didn't. Edie felt that Dolly and two of her nephews had sided completely with Rick, and she and her sister rarely spoke after that. This rift, combined with *her activism work and tending to Thea's increasing needs, also led to an unintended distance between her and Blackie, which affected her profoundly.*

"I felt suddenly shy around him," was how she explained it, and he may have been feeling the same—or simply protecting her—because he never told her that his own health had begun to decline.

Nineteen

The stock market crash of 1987 took a devastating toll on our financial security, so much so that I decided to return to work at IBM out of fear of Thea's rising medical costs. The company had always said they'd rehire me anytime I wanted, so I took them up on the offer, despite the grueling commute to their upstate offices and a salary that was significantly lower than what I'd made before. Still, the opportunity was worth it. Since I'd kept up on computer technology throughout my retirement, I had much to offer the company. I became a senior applications programmer and worked with supermarkets to enhance and grow their computer systems for scanning and tracking inventory and sales.

The excitement of working again—many of my former colleagues were still with the company—was marred by a sudden onslaught of mysterious physical ailments. I began to have trouble breathing that was initially chalked up to adult-onset asthma caused by my former smoking addiction, but additional issues like rashes and a persistent upset stomach came up. I spent a full year being examined by a variety of specialists who couldn't figure out what the problem was, and I finally got so fed up that I checked myself into the Mayo Clinic, and I told myself that I would not leave until they figured out what was wrong with me. The wait was a short one.

On my first day, I had a splitting headache and asked a nurse for some aspirin. Thirty minutes later, my entire body was covered in a horrible itchy rash. "Hell of a way to make a diagnosis," my new doctor told me and explained that I was allergic to salicylate, an organic acid found in everything from fruits and vegetables to medications to certain cosmetics. The relief at finally understanding what was happening to my body almost made up for the annoyance of having to reconfigure my entire diet, and alcohol became limited to vodka. Luckily, it didn't take long to find a brand of salicylate-free lipstick that precisely matched my preferred shade of pink.

Rick passed away in 1989, and I hoped that maybe the strain between Dolly and I would lift. I knew that she was just as much to blame for our falling-out by siding with him when he announced he never wanted to see Thea again, but I hoped that maybe without his dislike standing in the way, we'd grow close again. Sadly, that didn't happen, and my condolences were acknowledged by Dolly but at a great emotional remove. For a time, she worked at NYU's Center for French Language and Cultures, which is located literally across the street from my building—my living room looks directly down on it—and I'd often sit by the window hoping to catch a glimpse of her or that my doorman would ring up, announcing that she'd stopped by for a visit. Neither occurrence ever happened. I missed my big sister, my former mother figure when Cele had been busy working to support us, and I was convinced that time would eventually heal the crack in our relationship.

Thea's progressive paralysis began to reach her arms, and in 1990 I retired for the second time to spend more time with her. Luckily, the stock market had stabilized, and I felt more secure about our ability to handle her increasing medical needs. We hired a home health care aid named Barbara to help her with things like showering and using the bathroom throughout the day. We remained active as ever, though, and even won the grand prize at a SAGE dance marathon, both for our stamina and for raising the most money.

Our moves on the dance floor weren't the only ones we kept up. Maintaining a hot sex life had always been important to us as a crucial aspect of keeping our love alive. Just because it required a little more preparation than it used to didn't make things any less erotic in our eyes. She was as beautiful as ever. We bought a giant roll of red tickets—the kind you purchase for rides at a county fair—and doled them out to each other for impromptu rides of a vastly more exhilarating nature. "There are times when I'm so inside the desire," Thea once told me, "that once we're finished, I'm surprised to find that I'm in a wheelchair." Due to my expertise, I even helped curate a SAGE panel on "Erotic Safer Sex for Lesbians With (and Without) Illnesses."

Thea continued her home psychotherapy practice but preferred to hide her wheelchair. Before appointments, she'd have the aid get her settled into a chair behind her desk. Whenever papers and books grew too cluttered on it, she'd blame the mess on her imaginary secretary, Carol.

"Carol's out sick this week," she'd say, gesturing at the piles. Or, "Carol's father passed away, so I'm on my own at the moment. Please forgive the mess." Most of our friends knew she was joking.

Unbeknownst to either of us, fate brought Thea a new client into our living room for a couple of sessions—a young woman named Roberta Kaplan, who'd just graduated from law school and was preparing to move to Boston. She'd recently come out of the closet and was devastated by her mother's negative reaction. She was convinced that finally acknowledging her truth meant that she was doomed to a life of loneliness.

Thea calmed her by telling the story of us, showing her that a healthy and loving relationship was entirely possible for her and that she'd just taken the first brave step in getting there. I would have been tickled to know that Thea was using us as an example in her therapy work, but I wouldn't learn about this visit for another eighteen years, when Roberta told me herself, just before agreeing to represent my case against the Defense of Marriage Act.

I don't remember who called me to tell me that Blackie died. I think it's likely that it was my cousin Sunnie, although it could have been Dolly's son Rem. The news shocked me to my core. My beloved Blackie, tormenter and hero, the eternal ne'er-do-well, but one who'd always done right by me, now suddenly erased from the planet. Rem once repeated a joke he'd heard Blackie make at a funeral: "Always a pallbearer, never a corpse." The news didn't feel real; Blackie was forever in my mind, and I was instantly filled with a painful younger sister longing for my childhood idol.

He'd spent the last few years of his life working at a casino in Atlantic City but made far more money gambling. I heard from one family member that he'd scored $18,000 in a single night and that he had the discipline to cut himself off the moment he lost anything over $1,000. The former didn't surprise me, but the latter did.

He died while waiting for a bus back to Philadelphia from Atlantic City, with $6,000 cash hidden away inside his shoe. I burst out laughing when I learned this and for a moment felt some solace. I knew he would have loved going out like that.

Now that Blackie was gone, I was sure that Dolly and I would join back together as sisters. A flood of memories about our childhoods together began to come back to me in the days leading up to his memorial service. I had a flash of us chasing him around our dining room table trying to kiss him as he reacted appropriately with horrified shouting.

Instead, his death drove us further apart. At the service, I asked Dolly and her two youngest sons for a key to Cele and Blackie's home so I could go to the house and take one last look around before they sold it. They refused, claiming a new will had been found that gave them complete control over the building. I don't know why they didn't want me to go inside but it broke my heart, and I retaliated the only way I knew how—the first thing I did after returning to Thea was write my two nephews out of my will. (Dolly's eldest, Rem, remained dear to me; he had no part in the events that transpired around the fallout after Blackie's death.)

I did gain other family members, though. I began to grow close with Sunnie's son Lewis, my second cousin. He'd moved to New Jersey, and we began to have regular meet-ups in the city. Thea found him utterly charming, so along with him and visits from Thea's second cousins Patsy and Ginny, we did feel as though we still had blood family in our lives in addition to those we'd found ourselves.

In early January of 1993, the mayor of New York City issued an executive order that allowed gay couples to register as domestic partners. I was over the moon—I'd been making plans with my friends from SAGE to attend the gay rights march in Washington, D.C., that was happening that April, and I was upset Thea wouldn't be able to join us, particularly since there were plans for a separate protest to be held the day before to demand marriage equality. (The main demonstration focused on broader ground, like a civil rights bill that protected against discrimination on a state and federal level, the decriminalization of sodomy laws, and more funding for AIDS research.)

The new year had just begun, but 1993 was already looking to be a big one for gay rights, and as soon as I learned the date that the domestic part-nerships would go into effect, I hopped up and down in my excitement. "Monday, March 1," I told Thea. "We're coming for you, city hall!"

Thea, sitting at her desk, flipped a few pages of her calendar and shook her head. "I have patients booked all that day. It will have to wait."

I stopped jumping as I felt my temper flare, and then stomped my foot on the floor hard enough to shake a lamp on a side table. "I have waited close to twenty-eight years for this day to come," I said, staring at her right in the eyes. "And it has been twenty-five years and five months since you proposed. I refuse to wait one single day longer than necessary. Clear your schedule."

I'd never made that sort of empirical demand on her, but we weren't getting any younger. She heard the iron in my voice and quickly agreed. Two months later, 109 couples registered as domestic partners at city hall, and we were number 80.

Exactly one year later, Thea left a note for me on my pillow that read, "Congratulations. You have successfully completed one year of domestic partnership." She meant it lovingly as a joke about how long we'd already been together, but I also read the mild sarcasm as well, and she was right. It wasn't enough.

———◊———

Edie talked at great length about the final rift between her and Dolly after Blackie's death, but if the story feels vague in its telling here, it's intentional. After speaking to family members and reviewing back-and-forth letters between lawyers, as well as reading the contested will, it's best to let that sad saga go. Still, the takeaway is an important lesson for anyone: get—and keep—your legal shit in order.

Edie and Thea were already well aware of this need after what they experienced with Thea's inheritance initially being so tightly controlled in a trust, due to her family's homophobia. Knowing that they had no legal protection financially in their relationship once Thea's full inheritance came through, Edie helped her manage the money through shrewd investments. Ever the math whiz, she taught herself a complicated theoretical pricing model for stock options mostly used by professional traders and investors. And all of it is documented. Going through Edie's extensive file cabinets, it's easy to poke gentle fun at her hoarding tendencies until you realize that for her, every piece of paper stood as a protection measure so that if any family member ever challenged either of their wills, there'd be a clear trail that showed where every cent had come from and to whom it belonged.

Edie weeded anyone who might do such a thing out of her life. More and more throughout the 1990s, Sunnie and her son Lewis provided the strong family bond Edie missed and craved. "She was always an integral part of the family, in the way that everybody talked about her," Lewis recalls of his childhood knowledge about Edie. "I don't remember anybody in the family saying they were gay or lesbians, but *they weren't just roommates. It was understood that they were a couple. But I never paused and thought,* Oh, wait, they're two women."

His sentiment echoes his mother's——Edie's homosexuality was an absolute nonissue on that side of the family, and Sunnie even instinctively grasped their butch/ femme dynamic early on, in her own way. "Shortly after she and Thea moved in together, Thea and I were talking and she said she wanted to explain what their relationship was," Sunnie says. "I said, 'You don't have to tell me, I know how it is. Edie pays the maid. It's always the woman who pays the maid!'"

Lewis's first encounter with Edie and Thea came in the '70s, when he was attending college in New York and got very sick. Sunnie insisted that he reach out to them for a good doctor referral, and they continued to have sporadic interactions over the years, but it wasn't until the 1990s when Lewis met his future wife, Debbie, that the two couples began to socialize more and more. After Debbie and Lewis got engaged, both Edie and Thea could tell during one of their visits that the stress of wedding planning was taking its toll on them.

"Go to our house in the Hamptons," Edie insisted, handing them the house keys. "You two need to get away from everything and spend some time alone, away from it all."

Their intuition and kindness with the younger couple continued after the birth of their twins, Maya and Ben. "They visited us in the hospital, and after I returned home, I was so stressed that they sent us a baby nurse to help out," Debbie says. "It was really lifesaving for me."

Edie adored their children, and they considered her and Thea an extra set of grandparents. Edie and Thea had talked on and off about the idea of adopting children, but it never seemed remotely feasible. There was simply too much going against them as a gay couple, and later, the care that Thea's MS required made it impossible to imagine also caring for kids. But very soon, an annual Hamptons tradition was born, in which all three generations of their family would go to Southampton to stay for a week in August. "Edie would go above and beyond to make sure we were comfortable," Lewis says. "She'd buy enough food to last a month and always got all new floats for the pool in case the kids had outgrown the ones from the previous summer."

As the years went by, Debbie watched as Edie and Thea's relationship continued to flourish. "It was just phenomenal," she says. "They communicated with their eyes, *this total nonverbal communication, but at the same time they were very direct. Thea would tell Edie, 'I need you to do this for me,' and there was nothing Edie would not do for her. Her life was built around that. But at the same time, there was this erotic side to them too, very sensual. Even when it got to the point that Thea could really only just move her hands, the electricity between them was palpable."*

Understandable, considering that more than thirty years into their relationship, Thea was still leaving Edie sexy little love poems throughout the house:

"Roses are red / Violets are blue / Bring on the toys / For me and for you!"

Twenty

I turned seventy in June of 1999. Ask any older person, and they'll probably tell you how I felt—that I looked different, but I still felt exactly the same inside as I did when I was in my twenties. It's not like there was a stranger staring out at me from the mirror, but despite sticking to a signature style pretty much my whole life, I still wasn't quite the same person I visualized when I closed my eyes. Giving up my silver hair and going blond helped restore a bit of youthfulness.

Not that I needed to impress anyone. Thea still looked at me the same way she had in the 1960s, and I felt the same with her. My body was aging and changing but I still had energy, and I remained angry as ever about the lack of movement on the gay rights front. The Defense of Marriage Act had been passed three years earlier, defining the word *spouse* as only pertaining to heterosexual couples. It was a despicable federal law, and I wouldn't be surprised if it was that, and not my years of smoking, that caused my first heart attack that same year.

I recovered fairly quickly, but it deeply frightened me, especially since my family has such a long history of heart issues. It was a stark reminder to me that life is short and time is precious. I strengthened my resolve to fight for our rights.

I founded an improv group called Old Queers Acting Up along with five friends, and we put on shows about ageism, homophobia, and the rage that we all felt about how gays were still treated as second-class citizens. Our battle call was "Out of the closet and onto the stage," and we performed at high schools, colleges, and community centers.

Thea and I were now both a couple of old queers, and we acted up in our own ways. We'd bicker over silly things like the television volume and then make up. She knew my quirks inside out, and I knew hers, like how she insisted on having her tea microwaved for exactly one minute and twenty-three seconds, and I knew to set out real silverware whenever we ordered takeout. ("What is a person to do with *this?*" she'd fumed early in our relationship after she tried to slice through a piece of chicken with a plastic knife that snapped in half.) I attended SAGE meetings; she tended to her patients. She continued to leave me love letters.

Returning home from an errand uptown one afternoon in 2001, I saw from two blocks away that an ambulance was parked in front of our building. I broke into a run, not so much because I was worried that it was Thea lying there on the gurney, I told myself, but just to make sure it wasn't. But it was.

Earlier that morning, Barbara discovered Thea had developed a rash in the night, two scabrous blistering belts, one under her left breast and the other on her back. I'd called the hospital and tried to get a nurse to come by to investigate but was told that her doctor would have to put in a special order for that to happen. We were friendly with one of our neighbors, a doctor who ran his practice out of the first floor of our building, so after Thea saw her patients that were scheduled for the day, Barbara wheeled her down.

"Shingles, unquestionably," he said after one quick glance. "Has Edie had chicken pox?"

"I don't believe so."

"This is incredibly dangerous for elderly people. If Edie doesn't have the antibody and catches it, it could kill her."

With that, Thea passed out.

Barbara began to stamp her feet and scream, "Don't you leave me yet, Thea!" The doctor couldn't find a pulse and began administering CPR, shouting for his nurse to call an ambulance.

Around 11:00 that evening, I found myself in a hospital isolation unit, wearing a cap, gown, and mask to protect Thea from airborne contagions. Each of the rooms on our particular floor had its own ventilation system, and I felt cramped, claustrophobic, even with the city view that stretched out before me. Thea's soft snoring, proof of her oxygen intake, was the most gratifying sound I'd ever heard.

She'd had a heart attack. We knew she had aortic stenosis but hadn't been too worried because we were told that it would take five to ten years to progress. That had been less than a year earlier.

Usually, whenever our friends asked how they could help us in any way, my bravado took over. "We're fine, managing just fine," I'd say. "I appreciate knowing you're there."

That time was different. I called five different friends and explained what had happened, mobilized who could call Thea's patients and who could bring food and fresh clothing. I asked for counsel on the decision we'd been presented with—open heart surgery. Thea and I needed to assess all the risks against the potential rewards. Her neurologist hadn't even weighed in yet, but the hospital was pushing for it to happen fast.

Surgery was taken off the table as an option the next day when Thea developed a sudden fever. I helped the nurses continually sponge her down with cold water and replaced the ice packs under her arms and in her groin. Her genitals were painfully swollen, and since she was on immune-suppressing drugs for the MS, the infectious disease guys were always hovering around, taking blood.

Once she stabilized, she suddenly began to lose more and more muscle function. At first, she could no longer raise her arms high enough to feed herself, then she couldn't reach the hospital room nightstand. By the fifth day, she could no longer turn the pages of a book.

That night, after the nurse came by to give her nighttime pills and change her catheter, I held on to her hand and could see the strain on her face as she tried to squeeze it.

"I'm here," I told her.

I waited until she was fast asleep and snoring gently again—still such a sweet sound—before heading home. As I walked through our neighborhood, I realized the streets were eerily quiet, but every now and then, I'd pass a couple holding hands and feel a pang in my heart. I wanted to run up to each one and tell them to revel in that exact moment, the simple act of strolling together, skin against skin, because it wouldn't last. Whenever I saw a solitary figure walking toward another, I'd hope that their eyes would meet, that one would wink at the other, and they'd sneak off into the shadows together for a fast fuck—an impromptu celebration, hell, just an *acknowledgment,* of the simple fact that they were alive and young.

We decided against the surgery. "If we can get a couple of years, let's live like hell and then both pack it in," I told Thea. She made me promise that she'd never have to go back into the hospital, so I arranged for hospice to be always on call. Her body deteriorated to the point where all the mobility that she had left below her neck was some limited use of her left hand, and it was enough for her to power the new electric wheelchair we'd luckily already recently ordered for her. I bought a giant van as well, with a ramp she could wheel up and down in. The passenger seat was removed so she could lock securely in place up front.

Our evening routine became much more complicated and involved. We upgraded the mechanics of the body-lifting equipment in both houses. I kicked Barbara out every night so that we could do the evening rituals alone—bathing, arranging the c-pap, and suctioning phlegm from her breathing passages before bed. Everything took longer now, but it didn't matter—that just meant I got more time to spend with her.

As Thea reinvented herself with each increasing disability, I found or invented assistive devices to match. I introduced her to computer software and a special keyboard that she could manage with the limited use of her

hand. I created disguised padding on her chair to protect her legs from injury if they kicked due to a spasm. She hated when her spasticity presented
in public, so I affixed Velcro to the bottom of her shoes and the footrest of
her wheelchair. It was very important to both of us to make sure no one
felt anxiety or fear about Thea's MS, particularly if someone we knew or
their family member had been recently diagnosed with it. She resumed her
private practice, and before long, we were back to a new kind of normal.

We returned home from Southampton one night to discover around a
dozen phone calls from Dolly on our answering machine. She was hysterical in all of them, babbling about how her boys had taken her car away to
get it fixed but then never brought it back. I called her immediately, and
she sounded surprised to hear from me. "I didn't call you," she said. She
sounded distant but polite, and even though we hadn't spoken in years and
I wanted nothing more than to catch up with her, I made up an excuse to
rush off the phone. I knew something was wrong and called Rem, who
told me that she'd been diagnosed with Alzheimer's and was being moved
to an assisted living facility in Yonkers.

I knew that if the disease had progressed enough that she could no
longer live alone, then there likely wasn't much chance for a true reconciliation, but I had to try.

After she'd been in the home for about a week, Dev drove me up to see
her. She offered to come inside with me, but I declined. This was something I needed to do alone.

A receptionist announced my visit and then told me her room number.
I took the elevator to her floor, found the door, and knocked. Nothing. I
knocked again, louder. Waited. A third time, even louder, and after almost
three or four minutes had passed and I was turning around to return to the
reception desk, the door opened.

She looked just like Cele in her later years, only more fashionable, with
a maroon print blouse and an above-the-knee skirt in a similar color but
subtly different pattern. She would have looked perfect were it not for

the sheer stockings that rose to just below the knees, leaving two knobby round lumps exposed. She smiled but didn't offer a hug. Instead, she ushered me inside, saying, "Come, come! Blackie has already been here and gone, but he'll be back soon. Won't it be neat? The three of us together again?"

The living room was large, with a few pieces of nice furniture, but it felt distinctly empty. There was no artwork on the wall, and the air held the slight musty smell of a hotel room that hadn't been inhabited for some time. A radio from somewhere played current pop music very quietly, interrupted every so often by short bursts of static.

Framed photographs waiting to be hung were scattered across most of the surfaces, and I spotted two pictures of young men in army uniforms on the radiator. One was of Rick, the other Blackie.

She sat down on the couch and gestured for me to join her. There were stacks of loose photos spread all over the coffee table. "Will you help me identify some of these people?" she asked. "I'm not sure who they are. I have lots more. You'll let me know if there are any you want?"

Most were pictures of her boys and grandchildren and their extended families. I picked up one of Rem to tell her his name, but she was already riffling through a stack of stapled papers. I caught the title page: "University of Pennsylvania, Graduate Department of Romance Languages, Doctoral Dissertations."

"I'm in here somewhere, but I can't find it," she said. I leaned over and saw that she was searching the graduate class list of 1966. I took it from her and flipped a few pages forward to 1967 and then ran my finger down the list until her name popped up. I showed her, and she seemed pleased.

A cell phone began ringing in the next room, and she shuffled off to answer it. Before I could even start to comprehend the emotional weight of seeing her again, as well as the fact that she seemed happy to see me, she returned to the living room, looking elated.

"That was Blackie!" she said, beaming, but then she hesitated slightly and looked confused. The moment passed quickly. "When I told him you were here, he said he'd be right over to see you."

"Come, sit next to me," I said, patting the sofa cushion. "Let's look at some more pictures."

We flipped through another stack, a large mix of people both familiar and unknown to me. Every now and then, she'd smile and identify a cousin or an aunt correctly, but for the most part, they were strangers to her.

Two of Dolly's sons soon arrived, accompanied by a couple of their kids. They were all off to lunch, but an invitation wasn't extended, and with the appearance of her grandchildren, Dolly forgot about me. I said my goodbyes, and she nodded vacantly. I fought back tears in the hallway and wanted to get out of the building fast, so I walked away from the elevator toward the stairwell but froze when I heard her door open and the family exit. I turned and watched as Dolly walked off in the opposite direction, holding the hand of a grandchild on each side of her, followed by her sons. Three generations of a family I no longer felt a part of.

It was the last time I saw her.

———◆◆———

*S*helly was with Dev and Edie when they drove to Yonkers that day to visit Dolly. Dev knew Edie was nervous about calling on her sister, so she pretended that she and Shelly had a lunch date and invited Edie along, casually suggesting that the restaurant happened to be near where Dolly was now living. "That was all phony, though," Edie said. "They just said that in case I ended up wanting someone to come inside with me."

It was difficult for Edie to talk about painful memories; she liked to brush past them. Her pattern was to tell the story and then sort of wave her hand in the air, as if trying to get smoke out of her face, and then move on to something much more fun. She wanted to dig deeper in terms of expressing how she felt for her book, but there often got to a point during an interview when she'd get a look in her eyes that pleaded, "Can we come back to this later?"

These moments occurred most frequently when discussing her family, particularly the falling-out with Dolly. Sibling bonds are so powerful—there's often no one else on earth that knows more about the origins of you, not even parents. Alzheimer's robbed Edie of a proper reconciliation, but she witnessed a look of excitement on Dolly's face at the prospect of the two of them being together again with Blackie. It may have signaled that her memory had gone, but it also showed that there were fond memories still left in there, and for Edie, that held comfort.

Twenty-one

With Thea's decision to never return to a hospital, and faced with an end possibly in sight, I asked her if there was anywhere she wanted to go, anyplace she wanted to see in the world one last time. She didn't hesitate with her answer. "Paris, in the springtime. I want to see the cherry blossoms blooming."

"Then we'll make that happen."

She was hesitant about making it a reality at first; a cross-Atlantic journey was nothing she could undertake lightly. It would involve so much planning and many moving parts, as well as someone strong enough to move Thea in and out of bed without the help of the lifts. This was also complicated by the fact that she now had osteoporosis; she had to move gently because she was at great risk for breaking bones.

At first, Thea was convinced we would require the help of a man—someone with enough upper-arm strength to lift her. She'd worked on and off over the years with an occupational therapist named Mary, whom we both loved—we'd first met her when Thea needed to be taught how to use a wheelchair. She always listened and paid close attention to Thea's every need, and they seemed to have a sort of intuitive physical shorthand—so we asked her for recommendations for some male aides. We trusted her judgment of character when it came to her field of work. She had several suggestions, all wonderful and experienced boys, but the more we talked to her about the trip, the more we realized that she might be the right one, so we asked if she would be willing to take on the complications and join us. We had her over to the house, and she completed a successful practice run of all the necessary moves. Thea knew that she could handle the job.

Another important reason for bringing Mary is that we couldn't bring the motorized wheelchair on such a long airplane trip; we'd have to use Thea's old manual model, and she was extremely nervous about the Parisian cobblestone streets and being knocked forward out of her chair. She knew that was an issue Mary would be extremely watchful over.

We enlisted two other friends to join us, one of whom had lived in Paris before and made an excellent guide, and we had a wonderful two-week vacation—we visited all the museums and spent hours just sitting and people watching at little tables outside of coffee shops. All the cherry trees were in full bloom, the entire city awash with pink.

We returned feeling rejuvenated. Thea continued to see clients, and our lives resumed their former pace. She still left me little notes and cards throughout the house, sometimes in her very shaky handwriting, sometimes transcribed, even if the message was kinky: "*Baby baby that's your name / Sometime's mine's the very same / It doesn't matter who's called what / As long as we can keep it hot.*"

We never let her worsened paralysis disrupt our sex life, and if you feel like you need more information about how that was possible, then you're probably doing things wrong to begin with.

I rejoined the board of SAGE and quickly became close with a woman named Barbara when I discovered that not only had she also worked at IBM—we had overlapped at the same office building for several years but had never met—but she was a psychologist like Thea. We were involved with hiring a new CEO, and the man we chose, Michael Adams, got straight to work cleaning up the organization, which, it turned out, was in dire financial trouble. So much so that soon after he arrived, he came to us and said we didn't even have enough money in the bank to pay the employees that month. "Well," I said, looking around the room at the other board members. "We'd better all pony up, then." Once Michael got our financial state back in order, Barbara and I became strong advocates for creating SAGE events and programs specifically for women, and we were eventually able to get a portion of the budget dedicated to just those.

Barbara played piano and belonged to a classical music group that had initially formed some forty years prior as a sort of social club for lesbians who weren't into the bar scene. I loved the idea and wanted to attend one, but my nights were dedicated to Thea, and I often had to leave our board meetings early to get back to her in time for our evening together. This was no sacrifice, though; there was no place I'd have rather been.

When I got the news in 2005 that Dolly had passed away, I felt sad, but knew that I'd already said my goodbyes to her long ago. Of my immediate family, I was the last one standing, and it began to weigh on me more and more that Thea wasn't legally recognized as my spouse.

The following year, we grew hopeful when we learned that a case for same-sex marriage was being argued in New York (by my future lawyer, Roberta Kaplan), but ultimately, the case was lost. I proposed the idea of getting married in Canada since same-sex couples could do it there without a residency requirement, but Thea wasn't particularly enthusiastic about the thought. The trip would have been far too exhausting for her.

We felt like time was running out, and when we attended a town hall meeting at the Center hosted by Marriage Equality NY (MENY) regarding various upcoming election issues, I was incensed when a representative from the Human Rights Campaign dismissed an audience member who asked about marriage equality, telling him (in a very rude tone), "Well, that's a couple of years down the pike."

We were sitting in the front row, and I shot my hand up. "I'm seventy-seven years old, and I can't wait that long!" I yelled into the microphone handed to me by marriage equality activist Cathy Marino-Thomas. "What do we have to do?" But all I really *could* do was keep going to MENY rallies and events.

That next spring, during a visit to one of Thea's doctors, we were delivered a devastating blow. "Thea, your heart has weakened to the point that you need open-heart surgery to replace a valve," she told us. "Without it, you won't live another year." Despite our stunned faces, she felt the need to add, "*Max.*"

"No more hospital stays," Thea said when we left, both of us still numb with shock. "You promised."

"Of course," I told her. As gut-wrenching as that was to hear from her, it was also somewhat of a relief—we both knew that a year was a lot longer than we would get if she chose to undergo such invasive surgery at her age and in her condition.

Our bedtime ritual that night was markedly darker and less joyful than usual. I tried to cheer us both up by singing to her, but it didn't do much good for either of us.

The next morning, before Barbara arrived to help get Thea out of bed, she asked me, "Do you still want to get married?"

"Yes," I said. "I do."

"Me too. Let's do it."

The preparations for our trip to Paris were nothing compared to the amount of logistics that went into this journey. We were introduced to an activist named Brendan Fay, who had founded an organization called the Civil Marriage Trail Project, which facilitated trips to Toronto so gay couples could wed.

Many of our friends wanted to help, but we knew that having too many people might end up hindering things, so we narrowed it down to six, including Mary and Brendan, who videotaped the whole thing for us. The entire time, we joked that most people do this when they're first starting out in life together, but we were doing it at the end. At least, out loud it was a joke. Inside, we both acutely felt the unfairness.

As the day grew nearer, I could tell something was agitating Thea. She kept brushing it off whenever I asked, but she finally admitted that she knew in her heart it was the last time she would ever be on an airplane.

"Maybe," I said. "But if it is, I can't think of a better way to cap that part of your life."

We wanted everything to be traditional. The vows, the rings, the cake, the whole bit. I told the baker to leave the top of our wedding cake bare because I'd bring my own piece for it. We arranged for our officiate (Canada's first openly gay judge, Justice Harvey Brownstone) to meet us in a reserved conference room on May 22, 2007, at the Sheraton Gateway, located in Terminal 3 of the Toronto's Pearson International Airport. We stocked the small conference room with champagne and decorated it with flowers, including rose petals scattered across tables, and I crowned the cake with the topper I'd made, a cutout photograph of Thea and me from our fifteenth-anniversary backyard party in Southampton. In it, I'm wearing my favorite green dress, made by my friend Stan Herman. Thea is at my side, holding on to her elbow crutches and radiant in an emerald-green shirt and white pants.

For the ceremony, Thea changed into a dark suit with a white turtleneck, and I wore a cream-colored suit with a long string of white pearls, like the ones I'd worn the day we first made love. Our friends sat in a semicircle, and Harvey sat in a chair as well so he wouldn't be towering over us since I was perched on the arm of Thea's chair. He smiled and spoke his prepared words:

We are gathered together today to witness a very happy and long-awaited event. Edie and Thea, you are here to obtain legal and societal recognition of your decision to accept each other totally and permanently.

Over the past forty-one years, you have been dancing. You have come to know and love each other, you have found joy and meaning together, and you have chosen to live your lives together. Now you seek to unite in marriage, and to this moment you have brought the fullness of your hearts, the dreams that bind you together, and that particular personality and spirit which is uniquely your own.

Thea required help from two of our friends to get my ring on my finger, and we rewrote the last little bit of the vows, so that we each said, "With this ring, I thee wed . . . from this moment forward, *as in days past.*"

I used a tissue to wipe tears from Thea's eyes once Harvey pronounced us "legally married spouses and partners for life."

People always ask me if things felt different, and they did, immediately. I know that being married didn't change everything we had been through, and it didn't change the love we felt for each other. But it gave us validation. Our love was given recognition on a global scale due to one small word. Despite all my self-confidence, there was still always a lingering feeling of otherness, a need to shy away from public displays of affection with Thea unless we were in a place that was safe for gays, like a bar or the Center or at a friend's house. Even with all my activism work, I was still partially conditioned to that 1950s mentality of the need to hide. At the time, I wasn't sure it was something I'd ever completely shake.

Even though we were in our late seventies and had nothing left to lose, placing our wedding announcement in *The New York Times* was still an act of courage for both us. And we were both stunned by the waves of emails, letters, and phone calls we began to receive from people out of our pasts to congratulate us. I heard from old IBM coworkers I hadn't spoken to in forever. They kept asking why I had lied to them and told me that they would have been fine with the fact that I was a lesbian, which was very sweet of them and also a very different thing to be able to say now that it was 2007 instead of 1967. I was grateful for everyone who reached out, though. Old friendships were rekindled, distant family members that I hadn't spoken to since Blackie's memorial sent congratulatory cards, and even a few of my long-lost lovers popped out of the woodwork, much to Thea's mild annoyance.

"Better tell them you're officially off the market now," she warned and then began repeating it as a joke anytime someone began acting overly nice to me. Her other favorite line came whenever someone asked her how married life was.

"Too soon to tell," she'd answer.

***

Brendan Fay, the man who helped Edie and Thea get married in Canada, knew the documentary filmmakers Susan Muska and Gréta Ólafsdottir, who'd gained attention in the late 1990s for their documentary The Brandon Teena Story, about the murder of a young transgender man in Nebraska. The film went on to inspire the Oscar-winning feature Boys Don't Cry.

Brendan asked the duo to interview Edie and Thea about their wedding, and they took that a step further by pitching the newlyweds an idea about making a documentary about their relationship, which resulted in the film Edie & Thea: A Very Long Engagement. In it, you can watch the moment that Edie and Thea got married and listen to the couple describe their relationship. If you're reading this and haven't already seen it, consider it essential viewing. Their love for each other is on full display, and Thea's elegant and clever little wisecracks throughout are a pure joy to hear.

It's also touching to see the duality of the way Thea viewed her situation. Like Edie, she tends to be relentlessly rational about almost everything, at one point saying, "The fact is, I do things because I'm able to under absolutely optimal circumstances. Number one, I have the love of my life . . . I'm able to afford a huge amount of assistance. I have no pain, and I have no cognitive deficits. Put that all together, and if you don't make a life with all those things going for you, I would say there's something really very wrong."

The area where she does admit to feeling badly, though, relates right back to Edie: "The big thing that I always have felt awful about, still do, we would be traveling, we would be doing stuff, and I've got you stuck. And I feel it very strongly, and I'm very often sad about it. So I see Edie struggle, and I get terribly what we call self-referential about it. It's my fault. Well, the fact of it is, it is my fault. I'm the one that got paralyzed, so it is my fault. That's extremely primitive, I understand, but it feels that way. And then it makes me sad and ultimately annoyed and angry."

Several people recounted the same story about a day not long after Thea was told she was terminal. They were in Southampton and she was upset, shouting that she didn't want to die and refusing to allow Edie in the bedroom, yelling at her to get out anytime Edie tried to open the door. So Edie took her giant construction paper pad and created a big sign that said "I love you." She took it outside the house to the bedroom window, where she held it up so Thea could see.

Mary Shea, the occupational therapist who traveled with them to Paris and Toronto, remembers a particularly extreme and moving story about their relationship. During their Paris trip, she was with them on the second floor of the Louvre, when the fire alarm went off and announcements began that everyone must evacuate immediately. Mary quickly realized that meant that the elevators would be shut off and they'd have to take the stairs. She started trying to mobilize Edie and Thea to get them out, figuring that she'd just have to find a way to carry Thea down the stairs, but they both told her to leave without them.

"You go; we're fine," Edie told her.

"What are you talking about? Come on!"

"No, honey, we're okay," Edie said. "You have to get out of here. We're fine. We've already talked about this kind of situation. You have to get out now!"

A security guard appeared and barked at them all to leave. "I told him, 'Not a chance!'" Mary remembers. "The guard was shocked that we weren't moving. I was shocked because I was realizing that Edie and Thea had already made a plan that they'd die together if there were ever an emergency situation that Thea wouldn't be able to escape from, and they were shocked that I wouldn't leave the two of them!"

Thankfully, the alarm was false. For Mary, it was yet another reminder of the deep, all-in love between Edie and Thea. "I asked Edie once how they'd managed to last so long," Mary says. "I asked, 'It must be compromise, right?' And Edie just laughed and said, 'No! Not at all. We've had this one set of decorative plates for thirty years, and the only reason they aren't up on the wall is because we still can't agree on where to put them.'"

So what was the secret? Both loved to repeat their favorite mantras of "Don't postpone joy" and "Keep it hot" to anyone and everyone, and the phrases are no doubt excellent pieces of advice. In the end, Edie summed up the true secret during an interview for Time, in which she said, "If you really care about the quality of somebody's life as much as you do your own, you have it made."

Twenty-two

February 5, 2009, was the coldest day that month in New York City. It was also the day that Thea died.

Her angina had been growing steadily worse over the summer in Southampton. The doctors had wanted her to come into the hospital, but she refused. She'd meant it when she said she would never go back, even as the pain got worse. It lessened to a degree when we returned home for the fall—the bouts of intense chest pain, a squeezing sensation that made her feel as though her heart were being crushed, only lasted for about ten minutes at a time, and watching her struggle pained my heart as well.

It happened in the morning. I heard her call to me from the next room that she was having trouble breathing, and I went straight for the phone to call hospice, but the card with the number on it wasn't in its usual spot. I shouted out to Thea that I couldn't find it as I frantically started looking under pieces of paper, and I heard her calmly recite the number to me by heart. I dialed and told them to come quickly, and when I ran into the bedroom, Thea was gone.

I stared down at her, and all I could think was, *She had patients booked today. I have to cancel them.* I calmly walked back to the living room and over to her desk, found her datebook. She had used initials instead of names to protect their privacy, but the numbers were listed beside them.

Next, I called Karen, as well as Dev and Shelly, Thea's dear friend Virginia, and a few other close confidants. They all rushed over and waited with me until the funeral home director came and took Thea away. More friends began to come by, and soon the apartment was full of people, all talking and reminiscing, but I wanted to be alone, so I kicked everyone out around dinnertime.

Everyone left except for Karen. "I brought my toothbrush," she said. "I'm staying on the couch. I'll keep out of your way. Don't feel like you need to take care of me, but I don't want you to be alone tonight. And I want to be able to make you coffee in the morning."

Thea used to do that for me, so I allowed it.

I spent a couple of hours reading some of my favorite poems with Karen, and that gave me some solace. It took me forever to fall asleep that night, but once I did, it was deep and dreamless, and I woke early to the smell of coffee brewing. There was no moment of confusion for me. I knew immediately why the house felt different, and I braced myself for the onslaught of grief, but I felt curiously light. I made my way out to the kitchen still in my pajamas, where Karen was waiting for me with a strong hug.

"How are you?" she asked.

"You know," I said, suddenly understanding how to answer, "this is the first time in years that I've woken up not worried about Thea. And to be honest, it's something of a relief."

I felt horrible saying it out loud, but it was true. Karen was quick to tell me that it was all right, though, and a perfectly normal response to the sudden death of a loved one who'd required long-term care.

That feeling didn't last, though. The apartment felt dreadfully empty after she left. I stared at my fingernails; painted with Essie's Pearly White, the silvery shade Thea loved on me, and resolved that I would wear the same color for the rest of my life.

I kept myself busy with my friends over the next few days, making preparations for the memorial service to be held at the auditorium of the Center. I wanted to do it in May, the anniversary month of our first weekend together, but I also wanted to get the logistics done early. Everyone pitched in to help with tasks like printing programs and blowing up photographs to display. Karen accompanied me to arrange for the cremation, and we didn't know that I'd be required to select an urn then and there. Almost all of the ones available were far too ornate, but we finally found a simple and elegant model.

Several nights after Thea died, I ordered in Chinese food, and when the delivery came, I suddenly found I had no idea what to do. Before Thea's paralysis, one of the longest-running gripes we had revolved around takeout. She could not stand having the cartons on the table while we ate, while the inefficiency of moving takeout food into bowls drove me nuts. It's a waste of energy and time.

But Thea had always insisted on dining at a properly laid table, and she always won that argument; so that night, I scooped my dinner into a bowl and sat down to eat.

I thought about how much Thea had loved to put together exhaustive French meals down to the letter out of Auguste Escoffier cookbooks. I was always of the mind-set that you can waste three-quarters of an evening preparing dinner and cleaning up after. I loved her food, but I'd always joked that I was happiest eating a sandwich standing up. Then we'd have a whole evening in which to *be*.

I looked around the apartment and thought about all the other little things in life that we'd landed on opposite sides of, like our collection of classical music records. She preferred Bach and Mozart. They're okay, but I love the romantics. She liked soloists; I like orchestras. She thrived on second movements in symphonies; I feel dragged down by them. "If I'm lucky, I'll fall asleep," I'd mutter to her whenever we attended a concert and one kicked in.

Everywhere I looked, I saw a reminder of these dichotomies. She'd mention that the telephone on her desk had stopped working, so I'd say,

"Let me look at it." She'd wave me off, telling me not to bother because it had worked fine that morning and probably would again later.

"Damn it, honey, it's not magic," I'd snap. "There are wires in there. Maybe something got pulled loose." What I meant was, *Let me look before we're engulfed in inertia.* I laughed out loud, remembering how she liked to call me a "wire butch" because I was so good at figuring out what cable went where on any kind of machine.

Watching TV wouldn't help me as a distraction. We always grumbled about it. She couldn't stand background noise, and I often needed it, even while I read. She'd mute the commercials while I worried that we wouldn't be keeping up with the product world. I liked knowing what was out there.

When our fights had gotten big, she always wanted to talk it out, but the more we'd talk it out, the bigger risk I ran of saying the wrong thing and making things worse. I preferred to walk away and let things calm down. I'm still convinced my way was better: One time, I walked out of the room mid-fight and she hurled a book after me, hard enough to leave a dent in the wall. I covered it up with a giant red construction paper heart, and by the next morning, we'd forgotten what had started it all in the first place. There were lots of little tiffs, and the significant stuff always got resolved.

I knew I had helped give her the best life she could have possibly had. But I missed her so goddamn much.

About a month later, I began having intense chest pain and trouble breathing. After checking into the hospital doctors confirmed I'd had a heart attack, and I was diagnosed with stress cardiomyopathy, otherwise known as broken heart syndrome. Karen stayed by my side constantly, and all I could think about was what Thea had gone through during her heart attack, how she had no desire to ever return to a hospital again. I felt exactly the same way.

"I don't care if you're sending me home to die," I told the cardiologist. "I've had a great life, but I can't imagine one now." I felt flat inside, as if nothing could bring me back.

The team in charge insisted on putting in a stent, though. I was absolutely against the idea, but after much persuasion on their part I finally agreed to the surgery. I made sure to rewrite my will and have it rushed up to the hospital to sign off on before I was put under.

Everything seemed to go fine, and after being kept awhile longer for observation, the doctors determined it was safe to send me home. When Karen and another friend came to pick me up, I was already putting on my street clothes, ready to get the hell out of there.

A bit later, right in the middle of the discharge process, the stent inside me collapsed and I went into full cardiac arrest. I learned later that for a time there was no connection between my atrium and ventricle. My heart had completely stopped, which had been both my fear and how I'd already felt inside before being admitted.

My hospital stay was extended, and on my last day, Susan, one of the filmmakers who'd spent so much time documenting Thea and me, told me that the movie had been accepted into San Francisco's Frameline Film Festival that June.

I needed to see what they'd made of our lives first, though, and after I returned home, I told them I wanted to see it ahead of time. They initially said no, that I'd have to see it at the premiere with everyone else. "I almost collapsed when I saw the video of our wedding," I told them. "You don't want me collapsing in front of an auditorium full of people." That did the trick, and I got a private screening.

I cried throughout the entire film. It was such a gift to see Thea again, to hear her tell all our old familiar stories, to watch her face on a giant screen talking about how much she loved me. It felt so healing to have this record of our life, to prove it had all happened. But it also brought on a whole new wave of grief and missing her with every ounce of my being.

I'd been consumed with what I would say at her memorial service; what could possibly clarify my thoughts through the past three months. To top it off, when the day finally came, I lost my voice, so speaking was difficult, but I soldiered on. Karen ran the show as a sort of emcee, and I listened as all our dearest friends and family members spoke about their memories of Thea. Then it was my turn.

"May is our anniversary month, forty-four years," I started. "On each anniversary, Thea would present me with a contract stating the number of days so far, and provide me with two choices: Quit while we're winning? Or go for another 365? I can't do justice describing the joy and the love in each of those 15,953 days that we spent together. If Thea were here, she'd ask me to please be more precise and address the 382,872 hours we spent together."

The joke got the laughs I'd hoped it would before I grew serious. Ever since Thea had died, I'd been reading so much poetry, returning to old favorites and discovering new writers. Certain fragments and lines had stuck in my head, and I quoted Edna St. Vincent Millay to describe my state during the first month without her.

> We were so wholly one I had not thought
> That we could die apart. I had not thought
> That I could move,—and you be so stiff and still!
> That I could speak,—and you perforce be dumb!

There were bits of Auden too, single lines I'd cherry-picked that had kept repeating in my mind: "Pack up the moon and dismantle the sun." And, "For nothing now can ever come to any good."

I next read the Millay poem that best summed up my second month without Thea:

> Oh, there will pass with your great passing
> Little of beauty not your own,
> Only the light from common water,
> Only the grace from simple stone!

I told the room that a single line represented the third month. Again from Millay and that I'd written it out and hung the words above my bedroom door:

"I had you and I have you now no more."

It sounds so sad on its own, but that's not how I interpreted the words. For me, they had become a constant reminder to be grateful. As I explained to everyone, and most importantly, out loud to Thea, "But I *had* you. I *had* you, my sparkling, beloved darling Thea. I had you."

———— ❧ ————

By the time of Thea's memorial service, Edie had already done her taxes for the year and knew how much she owed due to Thea's inheritance. The property value of their apartment had ballooned to well over a million dollars, and cash gifts Thea had made to Edie over the years were taxed as well, despite being under the limit that would have remained untaxed for a heterosexual couple. The final count: a federal estate tax bill of over $363,000 and a state estate tax bill of more than $275,000.

Karen remembers being with Edie the day she had to sell off so many stocks and bonds to find the money to pay it off and the anger Edie felt. "She was outraged," Karen says. "They were married, but it wasn't recognized. Edie was a striver for justice in every way, and it felt unjust to her. She'd started looking for lawyers immediately, starting with Lambda, but they turned her down, told her it just wasn't the right time for the movement."

Edie then found another lawyer but grew frustrated with the expensive hourly rate and requests that she start handing over all of her financial information on a monthly basis.

She found Roberta "Robbie" Kaplan through Brendan Fay, and as mentioned earlier, it turned out that Robbie had been in their apartment before as a patient of Thea's. She agreed to take on Edie's case on a pro bono basis and got to work, bringing on James Esseks from the ACLU and Donna Lieberman from the NYCLU as cocounsels.

Meanwhile, Edie and several friends flew to San Francisco for the premiere of Edie & Thea: A Very Long Engagement. (Filmmakers Susan and Gréta recall

Edie pinning a photo of Thea to the headrest of the seat in front of her and to
to the picture throughout the flight.) The film received a five-minute standing ov-
tion, and Edie was invited onstage to answer questions. "It was an incredible moment,
and Edie was overwhelmed with emotion," Gréta says.

As the film got accepted into more festivals, it began something of a healing tour
for Edie as she traveled to each one. "One of the things our audiences loved about
Edie is that they could feel she was so present and there just for them," says Susan.
"She was loving and encouraged everyone to live life to its fullest and to never give
up, and to remember that being older does not mean you cannot live life. She was a
force of nature." The U.S. government didn't recognize their relationship, but these
audiences did. The world that she and Thea had inhabited for so long was suddenly
being celebrated by thousands of people who witnessed all the happiness the couple
had shared. For Edie, this was the validation she needed to help bring her out of
grief, and if you watch videos of her Q&As during this period in chronological order,
you can see the transformation. At the early screenings, she's obviously overwhelmed
and grateful for the outpouring of love, but you can also tell that she's a bit shy. Her
ability to hear was worsening, so the filmmakers had to repeat audience questions,
but she began to bask in the attention. She particularly loved a moment when a
woman stood up and asked, "Who's your jeans sponsor?" (She wore them that well.)
Her public speaking skills grew stronger and more confident as the months went by, a
fortuitous crash course in media training for everything to come.

Twenty-three

A s I traveled all over the country to help support the film, Robbie worked hard on building our case. With members of her team, she compiled a beautiful brief outlining the history of my relationship with Thea, but she also explained that one of the main approaches she wanted to take was to focus on the financial aspect.

I was concerned about that at first and told her, "People are going to say, 'She's too rich. Who cares about that woman and her money?'"

But Robbie was smart about it. She knew that if there was anything conservatives cared about it, it was paying less tax. She wisely pointed out that's largely what the whole damn American Revolution was about in the first place.

Not that there is anything wrong with paying taxes—they provide much-needed resources for everything from infrastructure to public health. They're absolutely a necessary part of life in the United States. But if I have to give up more than half a million dollars just because I'm gay, then I should at least have a say where that money is going to be spent and be able to parcel it out as I see fit—like to gay organizations in need. Thea and I deserved to be treated as any other married couple, and I did not want the government to benefit financially from hateful discrimination.

We filed the lawsuit in 2010 at the U.S. District Court for the Southern District of New York for a tax refund since I'd been blocked by Section 3 of the Defense of Marriage Act, which denied gay and lesbian married couples from receiving any federal benefits or programs, even if their marriage was recognized by their own state.

Overall, DOMA itself was a hateful law signed by Bill Clinton in 1996 that stated for all federal purposes, marriage was defined as a union between man and a woman. (He publicly renounced his decision and expressed extreme regret in an op-ed for *The Washington Post* seventeen years later.) Our lawsuit focused on the fact that legally married same-sex couples received "differential treatment compared to other similarly situated couples without justification."

It felt surreal to see the full name of the suit: *Edith Schlain Windsor v. the United States of America.* How had I gone from a woman so deeply concerned about making sure my coworkers hadn't known I was gay to suing America because of it?

Thea. That's how. So it felt right that we held a press conference announcing our legal action at the Center, in the very auditorium where we'd held her memorial service.

It was my first time speaking publicly about the case, and Robbie had been preparing me the whole time leading up to it, enforcing the point that while technically the case itself should remain about money in order to win, we also needed to show that as the plaintiff, I'd been in a deeply loving relationship for more than forty years. Which led to Robbie's second rule: I wasn't allowed to discuss sex. At all. That was going to be hard for me, so I enforced a rule of my own: Thea was never to be referred to as my wife. She would have hated it. She had to be called my spouse.

In February 2011, we scored a major victory when we learned that President Obama, Attorney General Eric Holder, and Assistant Attorney General Tony West had all come to the decision that the Justice Department would no longer defend the constitutionality of DOMA. The official statement from Holder read: "After careful consideration, including a review of my recommendation, the President has concluded that given a

number of factors, including a documented history of discrimination, clas-
sifications based on sexual orientation should be subject to a more heightened standard of scrutiny. The President has also concluded that Section
3 of DOMA, as applied to legally married same-sex couples, fails to meet
that standard and is therefore unconstitutional. Given that conclusion, the
President has instructed the Department not to defend the statute in such
cases. I fully concur with the President's determination."

This was such a rare move—for the government to choose not to defend
its federal laws—and it sparked so much hope in all of us. But the House of
Representatives decided that someone needed to defend DOMA, so their
Bipartisan Legal Advisory Group (BLAG, and bipartisan in name only) voted
to do so. They selected a conservative attorney and member of the Supreme
Court bar named Paul Clement. The firm he worked for, which represented
many high-profile companies, was immediately targeted by gay organizations
for aligning themselves with such a homophobic lawsuit. There was so much
potentially damaging fallout that Clement actually resigned from the firm to
argue the case.

During this whole time, all my friends, including (well, especially) Robbie,
were very concerned about my health. I'd been diagnosed with coronary
disease and also had a rapid heartbeat. I'd had a pacemaker put in and
everyone I spent time with carried nitroglycerin tablets in case my heart
acted up. Just a few weeks after we filed, it did. I had a small heart attack
while out in the Hamptons. A second, much more serious one followed
in 2012.

My strength slowly returned, though, and three months later, Judge
Barbara S. Jones ruled that Section 3 of DOMA was unconstitutional and
ordered the federal government to give me a refund on my taxes. Plus
interest. Later that same year, the U.S. Second Circuit Court of Appeals
affirmed that decision, and arguments at the Supreme Court were scheduled for March 27, 2013. The name of my case officially became *United*

States v. Windsor, and seeing those words for the first time caused the only moment throughout the legal process that I ever felt a flash of true fear.

My health was up and down over those two years, but I always managed to bounce back up after the next wave of appearances and Q&As for the documentary. In addition to those, I began to get all sorts of awards from different organizations for my activism. It started with a Lifetime Achievement Award from SAGE in 2010, which meant the world to me since I'd been working with them for so long. I also received a Trailblazer in Law award from Marriage Equality NY and a Medal of Liberty from the ACLU for "extraordinary contributions to the Defense of Civil Liberties."

As lovely as the awards were, what was better was that as I began to become a public figure, I realized that by associating myself with fund-raising functions for any kind of gay rights organization—everything from AIDS research to teenage suicide hotlines—just the mere fact that my name got added to event materials helped draw in more people. I was more than happy to get onstage and say, "Thank you for coming. You want to help? Then open up your wallets. You do it with dollars, and every single one matters."

It was, of course, also exciting when people started recognizing me on the streets or in the subway. The idea that my relationship with Thea could provide comfort and reassurance to other queer people searching for love or looking for support about their own relationships—or hell, their very existence—all helped me heal even more. I was beginning an all-new love affair, this time with the gay community.

But every night, I still went home by myself. I'd get invited to all sorts of wonderful parties and spend the evening socializing and laughing, but in the apartment afterward, I felt so alone. I watched a lot of MSNBC to begin with, but I began keeping it on all the time just so there'd be voices in the apartment.

I accompanied Robbie to the Supreme Court to hear the arguments in March and was unbelievably honored to discover that people had driven from all over the country to support us. And to meet me! I basked in the attention, but the real hero was Robbie. Her arguments were flawless, and we all felt we were off to a good start when Justice Ruth Bader Ginsburg interrupted Paul Clement and described how his argument against us essentially made the claim that there were "two kinds of marriages: the full marriage, and then this sort of 'skim milk' marriage."

At the time, I was being shadowed by Ariel Levy, a writer for *The New Yorker*, who was working on a profile about me and my case. "I don't know what will happen," I told her. "But I think it's going to be good."

As you all know by now, it was. Even if we had lost the case, the moment we left the Supreme Court would still have remained one of the most joyous experiences of my life. The sun was blinding, and it took me a moment to realize just how large the crowd on the steps had grown, but I could hear the cheers. I threw my arms open and let all of that love wash over me and then sent it right back out. I hoped so deeply that I'd be able to return something more tangible through marriage equality if we won our case, but I told myself that even if we didn't, hopefully we'd at least advanced the argument for why it was so necessary.

The three-month wait was interminable, but on June 26, the Supreme Court agreed with the lower courts and ruled in a 5–4 decision that Section 3 of DOMA was unconstitutional. The government was ordered to pay back my estate tax.

I was at Robbie's house, with her wife, Rachel, and their young son, Jacob, whom I'd grown extremely close to throughout the whole ordeal. Everyone was screaming and crying, but all I wanted to do was get to Stonewall, back where it had all begun, and share the moment with as many other gay people as possible.

———— ✦ ————

In those first few moments after the ruling, President Barack Obama called Robbie from Air Force One to congratulate Edie. She thought she hung up on him, but the glitch was on their end.

It took some time for her to get to Stonewall that day. First, they had to go to the Center for a press conference, where Edie read the speech she'd hoped she could. (In *typical Edie preparedness fashion, there were two others ready to go—one if they'd lost, and one if she'd won the case but the ruling only applied to her.)*

"If I had to survive Thea," she told the room, "what a glorious way to do it." In summing up the overwhelming sense of injustice she'd felt that had brought her to this point, she said, "On a deeply personal level, I felt distressed and anguished that in the eyes of my government, the woman I had loved and cared for and shared my life with was not my legal spouse, but was considered to be a stranger with no relationship to me. On a practical level, due to DOMA, I was taxed $363,000 in federal estate tax that I would not have had to pay if I had been married to a man named Theo. Even if I had met Theo just immediately before, married him, and never even lived with him before he died, the tax would have been zero."

Glennda Testone, the Center's executive director, sums it up well: "Edie had a special way of taking seemingly complex issues and pulling them apart to get to the core of what was right and what was true."

Next they traveled to Robbie's law offices, then on to an interview with Diane Sawyer, and finally to Stonewall, where everyone in her group worried for her safety as she tried to touch hands with as many people as possible in the massive crowd that had gathered there. Once she got up on the podium, dressed in a black suit and a shimmery purple shirt, Thea's engagement pin firmly in place, she told the crowd, "Now's the part when I try not to cry."

The Pride March in Manhattan happened to fall that weekend, and Edie was the grand marshal. As honored as she felt, she later admitted that she preferred marching the whole way start to finish, alternating sides of the street hugging and high-fiving all the way. She spent the rest of the summer hopping from one party and parade to another, much to the worry of her friends, who were growing more and more concerned that she was overextending herself. During the case, Robbie Kaplan had often sent associates to escort Edie to events, much to Edie's frustration—she liked to give them the slip by pretending that she needed to go to the bathroom.

One friend of Edie's from the Hamptons, Rena Rosenfeld, recalls Edie even temporarily icing her out because of her worries over Edie's health. Around the time of the victory, Rena had become the Hamptons' ambassador for the USA Pickleball Association—a sport that's sort of a mash-up between tennis, badminton, and Ping-Pong that's played with paddles and a Wiffle Ball. Edie called her up and announced that she wanted to learn how to play. "She was an icon with a heart problem!" Rena says. "I told her she needed to get a note from her doctor authorizing her first, and she said, 'I am never talking to you again,' and hung up. I looked at the phone and said, 'Oh god, what have I done!'"

The silent treatment didn't last too long. Rena's spouse, Marilyn, was admitted to the hospital due to a heart problem, and one day, Rena walked into Marilyn's room to find Edie holding her hand. "Edie looked up and said, 'Do you have anything to say to me?'" Rena explained that she'd only been looking out for her, because what if something happened?

"I understand that you want to protect me," Edie replied. "Everyone wants to protect me. But understand this. I do what I want, anytime I want."

"Edie got her revenge on me later," Rena says. She'd harbored an innocent crush on Edie since the day she first met her decades earlier, but was in a happily committed relationship with Marilyn, whose heart condition worsened. Eventually, Marilyn needed to be moved to a hospital in New York. Edie invited Rena to stay at her place, and after spending the day getting Marilyn settled, Rena arrived at Edie's around 9:00 p.m. "I was so tired that I didn't even look at the room she put me in," she says. "I took half a Xanax, went to sleep, and woke at some point in the middle of the night to find Edie standing over the bed! I looked up at her and said, 'Edie, we can't! I'm a married woman! I can't do this. Go back to your room, and I'm going to turn over and go to sleep.'"

She did just that and woke the next morning to realize that she'd spurned a life-size cardboard cutout of Edie, made for an event, that was propped up beside the bed.

Rena was mortified, but not so off the mark in thinking that Edie might be on the prowl. (Just not for a married friend.) As she became more and more loved as a public figure and gay rights hero, Edie wanted to share her experiences with someone on an intimate level. There were a few attempts at dating, one with a closeted woman who wouldn't kiss Edie in public, but told her that it would be okay for them to stroll arm in arm because people would assume they were mother and daughter. Edie was infuriated and insulted, and the affair ended fast.

Edie's next relationship was with a woman described by many as being a bit starstruck by Edie but who wasn't particularly interested in having sex with her. As Edie told the New Yorker writer Ariel Levy, "She claims I demand sex. I told her, 'Honey, I'm not demanding, I'm begging!'"

Not only did she refuse to put out, she was irrationally jealous of Thea. Edie's apartment was naturally decked out with reminders and photos of her everywhere, and the new girlfriend insisted that Edie get rid of them all, as well as redo her entire kitchen because she liked to cook but hated the lowered counterspace that had been installed for Thea. When she finally presented Edie with an actual list of everything she wanted Edie to change for her while still continuing to withhold sex, the affair ended.

Karen remembers a night when she helped Edie build a Match.com profile and tried to convince her that she probably shouldn't use a real photo of herself until she vetted a few options. Ultimately, Edie grew frustrated with the whole thing, and her W-seeking-W ad never ran.

During this whole time, courts in different red states like Florida, Oklahoma, Texas, and Utah began allowing same-sex couples to marry, citing Edie's case. In March of 2015, a Peoples Brief signed by 207,551 people, including Edie, was submitted to the Supreme Court regarding Jim Obergefell, who had married his partner, John Arthur, in Maryland just before John succumbed to ALS. All Jim sought was that Ohio recognize him as John's spouse on the death certificate. The State had refused, but the Supreme Court ruled in his favor. Justice Anthony Kennedy explained why:

> No union is more profound than marriage, for it embodies the highest ideals of love, fidelity, devotion, sacrifice and family. In forming a marital union, two people become something greater than they once were. As some of the petitioners in these cases demonstrate, marriage embodies a love that may endure even past death. It would misunderstand these men and women to say they disrespect the idea of marriage. Their plea is that they do respect it, respect it so deeply that they seek to find its fulfillment for themselves. Their hope is not to be condemned to live in loneliness, excluded from one of civilization's oldest institutions. They ask for equal dignity in the eyes of the law. The Constitution grants them that right.

Edie and Jim met for the first time before the decision on his case came down. They were both at an ACLU event held at the nonprofit's Manhattan headquarters, and Donna Lieberman, one of the cocounsels on Edie's case, introduced them. "It was electrifying to see them together for the first time," she remembers.

"*We were in the midst of this large room, probably about one hundred people,*" *Jim adds. "Donna brought us together, and everyone was talking and eating and drinking, and I forgot everyone else existed. Edie had this way of making you feel like you were the only person in the world when she talked to you. We hugged each other and both started crying. Edie said, 'You know what? Let's see if we can find a room somewhere a little quieter so we can talk more.' So Donna found us a conference room, where we sat and talked about our spouses and the cases, just being in each other's company.*"

He remembers them acknowledging that they were the only two people in the world who truly understood what the other was experiencing. Jim had even proposed to John on the day that Edie's ruling had been announced back in 2013. "*If it weren't for Edie getting the federal government to acknowledge lawful same-sex marriage, I never would have been able to marry,*" he says. Or then go on to get same-sex marriage legalized in all fifty states.

—————— ❦ ——————

E die was an absolute pro by this point when it came to talking about the case and Thea, but there was another essential piece of her history that she desperately wanted to share, a core part of her identity: her love of technology and particularly being a woman during the early pioneer days of computing.

Leanne Pittsford, the founder and CEO of Lesbians Who Tech, was initially at a bit of a loss when she decided she wanted to start doing more live content for her organization. When she put out the question "Who would you want to hear speak?" to the initial one hundred or so members, there were very few thoughts. Aside from Megan Smith, the former VP of Google and Barack Obama's chief technology officer during his administration, there weren't many other choices. "People had zero ideas of queer women in tech," she says.

When Leanne learned that Edie Windsor used to work at IBM, she invited her and Robbie to be the closing keynote interview at their annual summit in 2015. "It was a packed house, there were no seats left, people were sitting in the aisles," Leanne remembers. "I think that energy and that love, she immediately connected to it, and she was so confident in her ability—she dropped all these terms, and it was very clear that she still had all the language about how you talk about technology."

For her part, Edie finally felt like she had found her true people. It was one thing to be loved by the gay community at large but another experience entirely to find herself in a room with thousands of other tech-minded queer women. "There are very few spaces that are all women, let alone technical lesbians," Leanne says. "She told me, 'This is nothing that I ever thought could really happen. It's like a dream.'"

Leanne loved seeing the audience reactions to Edie's stories about life at IBM. "I didn't expect her to connect with our community as much as she did. To see that type of leader at her age, being able to connect to all the generations, that's just next level, especially since women in tech have very few role models, let alone lesbians."

From that day on, Edie was committed to Lesbians Who Tech and went to every event they hosted that she could. "I was very respectful of her time," Leanne says. Knowing that Edie would always be a star attraction, she didn't want to overburden her, but that was no concern for Edie. "She wanted to come to everything. I remember she walked into one of our events, and I was like, 'Edie, you didn't tell me you were coming!' She had our shirt on. She was ready."

In 2016, Lesbians Who Tech set up a fund called the Edie Windsor Coding Scholarship for gender nonconforming and LGBTQ women to help launch their careers. At the announcement ceremony in San Francisco, Leanne told Edie, "Forever, lesbians who tech will know you, will know your story, will know what you've done, but also know that you were a techie, through and through."

Edie was then brought onstage, where she wiped away tears. As she absorbed the news and looked out at the crowd, she was momentarily speechless, something few people have ever witnessed. And on the other side of the country, Edie's new love watched it all happen via a live stream from her office, filled with pride and moved to tears as well.

Twenty-four

My schedule had grown relentlessly busy. I wanted to show up for every event I was invited to, to personally accept every award so generously given, but truthfully, I'd been also saying yes to it all to help distract from my loneliness, which had worsened every day. It got so bad that I'd even considered getting a roommate.

I knew my community loved me, and I felt that deeply. I cherished my close circle of confidants and trusted them with my life and knew that they all watched out for my well-being. My friend Carla Grande, who spent a year helping me build my website, even called me every night at 8:55 p.m. (just before Rachel Maddow came on) to remind me to take my medications. But my bed was empty. I'd been waking up in the middle of the night in a cold panic about what would happen if my heart gave out on me and no one was there to help. I'd turn on all the lights and pace throughout the apartment, unable to go back to sleep.

It was scary, but frankly, I was also sex starved.

When I finally did meet someone new and fall in love, it was once again Edna St. Vincent Millay who best described my feelings, this time about opening my heart back up after a love that had become so deeply mythologized:

Oh, savage Beauty, suffer me to pass,
that am a timid woman, on her way
From one house to another!

Twenty-five

Edie passed away on September 12, 2017. She'd been admitted to the hospital for a minor procedure, was recovering well, and looking forward to her upcoming discharge date. She'd already scheduled appointments with many people, myself included, for the following week. Her death was sudden and painless, nothing more than the result of a body ready to let go.

During our last interview before Edie went into the hospital, she made one thing very clear about her book: "I do not want it to just be about Thea," she said. "I want people to know about what happened after she died, how much Judith has given me, and how much I love her. Nothing that I do now would be possible without her."

Edie's spouse Judith Kasen-Windsor, whom she married in 2016, is younger than Edie. Their age difference initially raised some eyebrows, but what most people didn't know is that Judith is deeply respected as a financial advisor and had a thriving life and career well before she met Edie. She's also been a powerful LGBTQ advocate in her own right for more than twenty years.

When she began her profession in 1997, she was not just a woman fighting her way up the ladder in a decidedly male-dominated workforce;

she was an out lesbian who would only accept a new job with a company if it was willing to support LGBTQ causes. Raised in an affluent Jewish family that valued philanthropy, giving back came naturally to her, and she quickly became known on the gay donor circuit as one of only a handful of out-of-the-closet Wall Street executives at the time who could be counted on for help. As her best friend, Danielle Reda, says, "She and Edie were destined to meet."

Judith had heard of Edie before the Supreme Court case, since they moved in similar circles, but she first laid eyes on her at the SAGE event in 2010 when Edie took the podium to accept her Lifetime Achievement Award for activism. Like most people getting their first good look at Edie, Judith was instantly taken by her glamour and charm, but also remembers taking note of Edie's relative shyness at the time, compared to the public speaking pro she soon became.

Judith was sitting at a table with her close friend Melora Love, who'd been a SAGE board member for the past seven years. "Who is that?" Judith asked her, and Melora filled her in on all of Edie's charity work for SAGE and other LGBTQ causes over the years. Noting the interested look in Judith's eyes, she then added, "I think she's a little old for you," but agreed when Judith said that Edie was gorgeous and sexy as hell.

Judith then shushed everyone at the table so she could listen to every word of Edie's speech and left that night captivated and impressed.

The following month, she was getting ready for work one morning when she saw Edie on television, in a local news story about the press conference at the Center announcing her case against DOMA.

"I remember thinking, 'Oh, that's Edie!'" As Judith listened to the details, she realized that she had even briefly met Thea in 2008 at a fundraiser for Callen-Lorde, the LGBTQ health center. (Callen-Lorde would later go on to name a new building the Thea Spyer Center, with services dedicated to mental health care for LGBTQ New Yorkers, because Thea had been such a respected member in the field.)

"The news story sparked this memory," Judith says. "It was a very brief introduction, and I think it was only to Thea, but Edie must have been standing right beside her because she never left her side."

Since both Edie and Judith attended many of the same events, she began to say hello to Edie every time she ran into her, but as the Supreme Court case gained more attention, fans always surrounded Edie, and Judith felt that she never made any kind of impression. Those groups of fans turned into mobs after Edie won in 2013.

Over the next couple of years, Judith kept up her flirting every time she saw Edie but noticed more and more that she was usually only showing up for the cocktail hour of any given event and then leaving early. Judith continued her efforts and finally managed to engage in enough casual chitchat that it didn't feel inappropriate to ask her out to lunch, but Edie replied, "Oh, I hate going to lunch."

"I was like, 'Wow, that hurt,'" Judith remembers. "But I later found out that was a true excuse. She hated how lunch appointments disrupted her day."

Judith was rebuffed for a second time not long after, but not by Edie. At the Center's annual Women's Event in 2015, Judith managed to get in a quick hello at the start of the night, but per usual, Edie left early, surrounded by a mob of well-wishers. "I remember she was wearing a white silk suit, and I called out, 'Bye, Edie! It was great to see you!' She heard me, looked up, and waved. When we made eye contact, I said, 'One of these days, Edie Windsor, you're going to go out with me!'"

The woman escorting Edie out turned her head and snapped, "You're not her type."

"I wish I could remember who that was," Edie liked to say. "I'd kill her."

The third big attempt was a charm, but with a hitch: at Callen-Lorde's Annual Community Health Awards, Judith managed to give Edie her business card and repeat her wish that one day Edie would agree to let her take her out.

"Edie put her pearly white fingernail in my face and said, 'Stop teasing me!'" Judith says. "I told her I wasn't."

Edie recalled slipping Judith's card into her jacket pocket and playing it cool, but felt a rush of excitement she hadn't felt in ages. Unfortunately, she lost the card when she got home that night and couldn't remember Judith's name. Karen remembers Edie desperately searching her apartment all the next day, and Karen even called Donnie Roberts, the communications director at Callen-Lorde, to see if he knew who Judith was based on Edie's description. The card never turned up, but at least Judith had finally gotten Edie's attention.

The stars finally aligned at the Center's annual holiday event a few weeks later. Edie and Judith bumped into each other as the evening wound down, and Judith offered to walk her home. She took Edie's coat-check ticket to get her things for her, while Edie made her goodbye rounds. From experience watching her, Judith knew that might take up to an hour, so she waited outside in the hallway of the auditorium. Edie didn't realize where Judith had gone and proceeded to ask several people, "Where did she go? I finally found her, and now I've lost her!"

Both of their faces lit up when Edie finally exited and saw Judith standing there, waiting with Edie's coat as well as the walker she'd taken to using. Edie was mildly chagrined that the coat-check clerk had also handed that piece of equipment over and later told Judith that she'd planned to leave it at the Center and pick it up the next day. Instead, Edie carried it the whole way back to her apartment to prove her sprightliness and refused Judith's repeated requests to take it off her hands.

That night, they sat up and talked for hours. Around 1:00 in the morning, Judith said her goodbyes; it was late and she had to be up for work. Edie followed her to the door like she did with every guest, with one exception. Instead of her standard hands-on-the-cheeks kiss, she pushed Judith up against the wall and went in for the kill.

"She kissed me hard!" Judith says. "She was a fantastic kisser. I kissed her back, and it wasn't brief."

Watching the two of them tell this story, they both teased each other about what really happened: Edie insisted Judith kissed her first; Judith insisted it was Edie. After witnessing this debate several times, the safe bet is on Edie as the aggressor. She always got an overly innocent "Who, me?"

smile on her face whenever Judith defended herself. Particularly when Judith would add, "And Edie did more than just kiss me!"

Judith didn't stay over that night, but later that week, Edie invited her to a Hanukkah party at Robbie Kaplan's house, followed by a dinner with comedian Judy Gold and her partner, Elysa Halpern. Neither realized that Edie and Judith were on a date, and Judith herself had no clue that the date would escalate as fast as it did, but afterward, she walked Edie home and received an invitation to come up. "Edie was clearly on a mission," Judith says. "I knew I was not getting out of her apartment alive, so I decided, let's get this party started. I'm telling you, I did not feel like I was with an eighty-six-year-old woman. At all."

They began dating immediately after, but kept things low-key since the relationship was brand-new, each only telling one or two of their friends. In a random coincidence, Judith was invited to a Christmas Eve party in Edie's building. "I called her when I got there and asked what she was doing. She said she was binge-watching *The L Word* alone. I jokingly told her, 'Could you be more of a lesbian?' then snuck out of that party and went right down to her apartment."

After Judith had been missing for some time, she got a call from the host, demanding to know where she'd gone. "I think that's when people really began to realize what was going on," she says.

They both had standing plans for New Year's Eve that they couldn't get out of, but Judith assured Edie over the phone that she'd be at Edie's first thing New Year's Day. "I need you to make me a promise," she then added. "I don't want you kissing anyone else at midnight."

She remembers that Edie seemed shocked and was quiet for a moment before responding, "Well, same goes for you."

From that point on, Judith slept over nearly every night except every other Tuesday, since Karen and Edie had continued their weekly evening takeout dinner tradition long after Thea passed away. Judith's near-nightly presence calmed Edie's worry that she might need to get a roommate.

(Which is just as well, considering she was already a one-woman episode of *The Golden Girls:* the ultimate mix of Blanche's sex drive, Dorothy's pragmatism, Sofia's sharp tongue, and Rose's kind heart.) In the beginning, Edie still often woke in the middle of the night with panic attacks. Judith would wrap her arms around her, hold her, and make her feel safe. She'd ask Edie what she needed—an ambulance, water, or even just to sit in the living room for a bit and talk. Within weeks, Edie's night fears ceased.

A few months into their relationship, Judith was at work when she got a frightened phone call from Edie, who'd fallen after her walker had hit a sidewalk crack and tipped her over. "I dropped everything and ran to her," Judith says. It wasn't long after that when Edie first told Judith that she loved her.

"It was the morning; we'd both just woken up. We were lying in a way where we couldn't see each other's eyes, and she said, 'I don't know how to tell you this, but I love you.'"

Judith was too petrified to say anything. "I was dumbfounded, and thought, *No, it couldn't possibly be me.*" In fact, she was so freaked out that she pretended not to have heard, but as the day progressed, she couldn't bear to not acknowledge Edie's admission. "It really caught me off guard," she apologized to her. "I didn't know what to say." It took Judith a few more nights before she gathered up the courage to draw Edie into her arms and return the words.

"I love you," she told her. "Of course I love you. How could I not?"

Edie was feeling much stronger and decided after her tumble that the walker was more nuisance than help. The couple began going out more, but as often happens when a friend starts dating someone new, some of Edie's long-term confidants didn't approve of the match. Due to their age difference and Edie's celebrity status, Judith was an easy target. To protect Edie, Judith felt it necessary she take on the role of scapegoat anytime Edie turned her back on a friend who angered her, and there were some hurt feelings all around.

It was painful for Judith when she got snubbed at parties or events, but what Edie wanted and needed was most important to her, not what others thought. It hurt Edie deeply when her friends made their disapproval of Judith clear. Once when discussing the problem with her friend David Mixner, the legendary antiwar and gay rights activist, Edie told him, "Judith is the least judgmental person and the one who makes the least demands on me. I don't doubt for a second how much she loves me. I don't think people realize how intensely in love with her I am and that this is one of the most important relationships I've had, that came to me at just the perfect time. I need people to know that, because they tend to brush her aside."

His response: "Tell them that longevity is not necessarily an indicator of intensity."

What no one could deny was that Edie had come back to life. She exhibited a renewed vitality now that she'd found a partner who took care of her in every way, from small organizational tasks all the way to the bedroom, and everything in between—like how whenever Edie got out of the shower, Judith would be waiting to wrap her in a fluffy bathrobe she'd just warmed up in the dryer for a few minutes.

"Often when I did something nice for her, she'd look at me and say, 'Do you want to be with me?'" Judith says. "And I'd tell her, 'Anytime, anyplace, anywhere.'" She gave the same answer when Edie would teasingly ask if she wanted to marry her.

Ilene Borden, a close friend of Edie's who'd been a firsthand witness to all her previous dating disasters (but remains graciously tight-lipped about all of them) marveled at the transformative effect the new relationship had on Edie. "Judith improved the quality of Edie's life immeasurably and filled it with love," she says. "She took care of everything, always thinking first and foremost of what would make Edie happy and stress-free. There is no doubt in my mind that Judith gave Edie an extra two years of life. She wanted to have one last big love, but hadn't been counting on it."

Needless to say, she got it.

After Thea's MS diagnosis, Edie spent twenty years caring for her in every way, and now Judith was able to help make life better for Edie. "Edie didn't need care like a nurse; she was fiery and stubborn," Judith is quick to note. "I just did anything and everything I could to make her life easier."

Judith also never felt as though she were living in Thea's shadow, despite her continued constant presence in Edie's life due to how mythologized their relationship had become. "I can't compare myself to her; there's no way," she says. And Edie took care to make sure Judith never felt as though she was. Judith even arrived home from work one night to find that Edie had packed away some photos of Thea in the apartment. "I noticed something different right away and told her that she should put them all back. I told her, 'I love you, and I know that Thea is so much of who you are. You were together for forty-four years!' I happily helped her put all of them back in their places, and could tell she was happy too. I said, 'That's where they belong.'"

In the mornings, Judith would make Edie coffee, and then Edie would grow anxious to shoo Judith off to work so she could get going on her own day—writing speeches, answering emails, examining the stock market, absorbing everything on MSNBC, and conducting interviews.

"Then always around 2:00 or 3:00 p.m., I'd get a call from her and she'd ask, 'When are you coming home?' And then tell me something like she'd lost all of her glasses, hinting that she wanted me to come back as soon as possible," Judith recalls. "Over the phone, I'd guide her through the whole apartment until she could find at least one pair and then ask her what she wanted me to bring home for dinner."

By the time Judith would return to the apartment, Edie would be waiting at the door for her. "She always had something to tell me right away, either something awful Trump had said or a question about something she was writing. I'd have to ask her to give me a minute to take off my coat and use the bathroom! I'd run to the next room to change out of my work clothes, and she'd wait in her favorite blue chair in the living room for me, ready to start talking. For the rest of the night, she'd have my undivided attention."

They loved their nights in, but Edie's schedule was still as hectic as ever. She was in constant demand as a speaker, as an honoree, and a very willing lure for fund-raisers. Lunch with her once auctioned for $30,000, and since the bidding was so high, she impulsively offered up a second, and the organization earned over $60,000 that night. An appropriate price tag, considering how much Edie hated going to lunch. (Judith had been in the audience that night and remembers sighing to her friends and saying, "I'll never get to go out with her.")

When Edie had an event to attend, Judith served as not just her date but her official escort, bodyguard, and social director. "It could become quite the ordeal," she says. "Not in a bad way, it's just that Edie loved meeting anyone who wanted to meet her. And if someone came up to me and asked, 'Is that Edie Windsor?' I'd say yes and ask if they wanted to say hi, as long as I knew Edie was still up for it. The second she got tired, we had a signal, and I'd help her pack up to leave. We'd then have to walk with our heads down, because if she made eye contact with anyone else along the way who wanted to meet her, she knew she wouldn't be able to stop herself from greeting them or stopping for a photo no matter how exhausted she was. We'd make a beeline to the nearest exit so I could get her home."

Another gift Judith brought to Edie's life was the opportunity to fill her in on all the lovely things being said about her at the events they went to. Edie's hearing continued to decline, and even with the help of a hearing aid, the bustle and noise at parties, dinners, and fund-raisers often proved to be too much, and everything would become a dull roar. So Judith would lean over and tell Edie, when, for example, Chelsea Clinton once spoke at a GMHC event and began her speech by saying how humbled she was to be in the same room as Edie.

They traveled often for events and pride marches. Judith traded in her lifelong commitment to convertibles for a large Mercedes SUV that Edie would not only be comfortable in but also contained enough room to transport the giant racks of clothes Edie liked to bring along whenever they went to the Hamptons or to out-of-town engagements. "I'd always lovingly tease her, calling it 'the Windsor Wardrobe,'" Judith says.

Judith also took extra care whenever driving with Edie in the car: "Edie would ask me why I was driving so slow, and I'd tell her, 'Are you kidding? If something happened to you when I was behind the wheel, I'd have to move to another country.' Besides, Edie herself drove like a maniac—she took me to the grocery store once and I was holding on for dear life as she tore through intersections. She told me that stop signs were just a suggestion!"

With Judith in her life, Edie was now thrilled to wake up and face each new day, with a joie de vivre unmatched by anyone Judith had ever met. In fact, Edie's morning alarm on her cell phone was the song "Seventy-Six Trombones" from *The Music Man*.

"Not a Muzak version, and not even just the chorus," Judith says. "The entire song, from beginning to end. It would start blasting and wake me up, then she'd pop right out of bed and march through the apartment, waving a fake baton and playing air trombone."

When Judith told this story, she played the track on Edie's phone and cried while laughing and shaking her head. "This damn song drove me crazy. I'd groan and put a pillow over my head. But I'd do anything to have a video of her marching around to this in her pajamas. That, and anytime she sang Judy Garland songs to me, or 'You're the Top,' by Cole Porter. She loved that one, and she had this whole sad-person shoulder-shrug move that she'd do with her arms outstretched when she got to the line, 'I'm a worthless check, a total wreck, a *flop!*' I'd laugh so hard every single time. God, she cracked me up."

In September of 2016, Edie proposed to Judith after getting suddenly and violently ill from a flu shot. It was during one of her Tuesday dinners with Karen, and Judith was at her apartment. Carla rushed over to help Karen take care of Edie, and the next morning, when Judith learned what had happened, she arrived at Edie's with her laptop so she could work from the apartment and help her recover.

She was in Edie's office when Edie knocked on the door and poked her head in. "You busy?"

Judith was on her cell phone and cupped her hand over the microphone. "A little, but tell me what you need; that's why I'm here!"

"Oh, no, never mind."

Judith worked from Edie's apartment again the following day, and the same thing happened; a knock on the door and Edie stuck her head in. "You busy?"

"Nope, what's up?"

"You on the phone?"

"No."

"Do you want to get married?"

Judith didn't miss a beat. "Anytime, anyplace, anywhere."

"How do we even do it?" Edie asked. "Let's go look at the computer and find out."

Judith felt dazed as they went to Edie's desk, not sure if Edie was being serious, since she'd joked about it before. Edie had often asked Judith why she'd never gotten married, since she knew that Judith had had a lot of girlfriends in the past. Judith told her the truth, that she'd never taken marriage seriously. She'd been proposed to twice back when she still dated men, and like many gay people of her generation, the whole idea of marrying a woman was still so new that it was almost difficult to process as a right that applied to her, no matter how happy she was that it was now possible. But Edie was different. She knew this was a woman she could truly commit to.

As they looked up how to do it online, they both laughed at the fact that the mother of marriage equality wasn't quite sure how the actual process worked, even while Judith remained unclear if this were a passing whim, sweet talk, or reality. Edie was 100 percent serious, and the following

Monday morning, they walked into the city clerk's office in Manhattan, both wearing black suits, to make it official.

Danielle happened to be visiting from France, and they asked her to serve as their witness. "I think I was as shocked as anybody," she says. "Dating Edie was one thing, but marriage was a whole other level. But almost immediately, it just made so much sense. Age had never been a thing for Judith. And she'd met her match in Edie. From Judith's toughness to her vulnerability, from her sharp words to her kindness, they were alike in so many ways."

Judith's friend Holly Buchanan felt the same way. "There was a level of intimacy and trust between them that was just amazing to watch. Edie was such a force, and I remember thinking Judith had found someone who is really going to challenge her."

While Edie and Judith filled out the paperwork, Danielle was the one who suggested that Judith hyphenate her last name, something that hadn't even occurred to her. When Edie promptly said she'd do the same thing, Judith was horrified by the idea. "I told her, 'Absolutely not! You are *United States v. Windsor.* You can't change your name at this point!'"

"Oh, yeah, I guess you're right," Edie replied, but it was more than enough for her that Judith took hers. Edie was finally able to exercise her right to marry in America, something she'd once never believed would happen in her lifetime.

Shortly after the wedding, Edie visited Judith's office, where she pulled a copy of *The New York Times* out from under her desk, one she'd held on to since 2013, announcing Edie's Supreme Court victory. "I saved it," she told Edie. "Never in a million years did I dream that one day I'd be married to you."

Over the previous months Edie had been telling a few select people that she wanted to wed Judith, including Karen, Lewis, and her hairdresser. They were all supportive and happy for her, but the marriage came as a huge surprise to many others, especially because Edie wanted to keep it a secret until Judith had told her own family first. "I'd been having trouble getting them on the phone," she says. She still hadn't reached them the night after the wedding when they went to an event for New York State assembly member Rebecca Seawright with their friends Blanche Wiesen Cook, the author of a three-volume biography on Eleanor Roosevelt, and her partner, Clare Coss. "Clare emailed photos of us the next day and wrote, 'Look at these lovebirds!' and they hadn't known we were already married! It was obvious how we felt about each other."

For the next nine months, Edie lived her maxim of "Don't postpone joy" to the fullest. The couple traveled extensively, took an Olivia cruise, and attended numerous LGBTQ fund-raising events. Judith helped Edie with her many speeches and surprised her with tickets to concerts (including a performance by Lorna Luft, daughter of Edie's idol Judy Garland). As social as they were, they enjoyed their downtime and nights in together the most.

June of 2017 was as busy as ever for Edie, packed with events for Pride Month. She and Judith were looking forward to some much-needed relaxation in Southampton during July and August. They kept things low-key, intimate dinners with friends and receiving house calls.

Many of Edie's friends, and Judith herself, noticed that Edie began to seem somewhat more subdued than usual. Edie even went as far to tell some of her friends that she didn't think she was going to be alive much longer. She didn't say this to Judith, though, not wanting to upset her.

Edie and Judith's friend Tom Kirdahy, a producer and the husband of playwright Terrence McNally, had been close with Edie and Thea since the early 1990s, when he took over the East End Gay Organization and asked for their help reconnecting it to its philanthropic roots, as it had begun to evolve into more of a social scene. "There had been so many advances in the community that a local organization felt less necessary to some people," Tom says, but he strongly disagreed and was advised that he should get Edie and Thea on board to help him out. He remembers being nervous about meeting them, but they welcomed him into their home and were more than happy to assist him in his mission. Years later, when Judith came along, they all bonded over the age differences in their relationships, as Tom is just over twenty years younger than Terrence.

"I met him in June 2001, and that December, he was diagnosed with lung cancer," Tom says. "We talked a lot about it, and to me, the thought of not having our experiences we've shared because it might have been easier to walk away is devastating. Edie was well aware, even before Judith, that if she got involved with someone, the person would be signing up for a limited relationship. Then love presented itself to Edie, and she did worry, but she really wanted to experience love again."

Judith also understood what she was getting into by marrying Edie, who had turned eighty-eight at the start of the summer. But she was so full of life that Judith imagined she'd live well into her nineties, and had even begun secretly planning a ninetieth birthday party.

Toward the end of the summer, Edie became ill and needed to be hospitalized. She hated the idea of Lewis and his family missing their annual vacation, so she and Judith gave them the keys to the house, both heartbroken about having to skip out on the fun.

Once she started to stabilize, Edie quickly grew antsy to become active again. She was upset to have to miss out on events like a Lesbians Who Tech conference where she was scheduled to speak. Judith helped her call in to talk to the crowd on speakerphone, and later, Leanne sent her a video of all the women in attendance chanting Edie's name and their declarations of love and thanks.

Two days before Edie's discharge date, Robbie Kaplan arranged for President Barack Obama to call her with get-well-soon wishes. Once Edie learned the call was going to happen, she was absolutely giddy, and the entire hospital knew not to disturb her room at noon, when he was scheduled to dial in. Since Edie hadn't been to the salon for two weeks, she wasn't sporting her signature coif, but a nurse helped gather her hair up in a 1950s-style bouffant—hardly her usual look (even during the '50s), but she wore it well. She applied a fresh coat of pink lipstick and waited for the call.

Judith captured it on video, and during Edie's talk with Obama, her eyes were wide and bright, her smile lighting up the room. She told him, "It's very hard to know you and not do the right thing." He told her that he and Michelle hoped that she'd be up on her feet again soon, that there was a lot of work to do ahead.

Judith had been staying at the hospital most nights, but Edie insisted she go home since she was being discharged the next day and Judith had to go to work in the morning. "She was all about work ethic and getting things done, until the very end," she says.

Judith stayed a while that night, playing "Over the Rainbow" quietly on her phone, and Edie mouthed the lyrics as she fell asleep. She sat and held on to Edie's hand a while longer before finally going back to the apartment, where their bed felt far too empty to sleep in. She moved over to the guest bedroom but still tossed and turned.

They spoke on the phone the next morning, and Edie thanked her for playing the song the night before. Judith reminded her of their plan to perform at the next Night of a Thousand Judys event, an annual fund-raiser for the Ali Forney Center, which provides housing for homeless LGBTQ youth.

"She always joked that we'd do 'A Couple of Swells,' Judy's duet with Fred Astaire from *Easter Parade*," Judith says. "We sang a few lines together over the phone, and I told her we'd practice once she got home and was feeling better."

An hour later, Edie died peacefully while reading the newspaper.

Twenty-six

Karen accompanied Judith to the funeral home to select an urn, just like she'd done with Edie for Thea. They wanted to find the same one as Thea's, but the place no longer carried that model, so they chose one that they both knew would complement it. Edie and Thea's ashes now rest side by side.

Edie's memorial service was held at the grand Temple Emanu-El on the Upper East Side to accommodate the massive crowds who came to pay their respects. Judith placed Edie's signature pink straw hat on a small table on the stage. Draped around it was Edie's favorite pink-and-orange scarf, the one she'd worn on the steps of the Supreme Court after Robbie argued her case. Both accessories had appeared in thousands of photographs, and their cheery presence center stage in the solemn space made it easy to imagine Edie was right there, beaming, as one person after the other, including Judith, Sunnie and Lewis, Karen, Rose and her partner Marjorie Sherwin, Michael Adams (CEO of SAGE and speaking on behalf of the city's LGBTQ+ organizations), Robbie Kaplan, and Hillary Clinton, all spoke about how much Edie had accomplished and what she'd meant to them.

Hillary talked of how Edie refused to give up on the promise of America and how loss and grief had only made her "more generous, more open-hearted, and more fearless in her fight." She reminded everyone that it is up to all of us to pick up where Edie left off, that we owe it to her to ensure that gay rights are human rights and human rights are gay rights. "She pushed us all to be better, to stand taller, to dream bigger," she said. "She embodied the words of Mary Oliver: 'There is nothing more pathetic than caution when headlong might save a life, even, possibly, your own.'"

She spoke for everyone in the room by thanking her "for being a beacon of hope. For proving that love is more powerful than hate, for filling us with a sense of possibility and promise as we answer the question posed by Mary Oliver, 'Tell me, what it is you plan to do with your own one wild and precious life?' Let us continue to be inspired by Edie's wild and precious life, and let us make her proud every day of how we answer that question for ourselves."

For Judith, part of that answer is working tirelessly to preserve Edie's legacy. "I call it my labor of love," she says. "In the truest sense of the words." In the first year alone after Edie died, Judith worked with SAGE to get their drop-in center named after her (complete with a life-size, arms-outstretched photo of Edie on the wall waiting to greet people as they enter). She rallied New York's Historic Landmark Preservation Center to bestow a cultural medallion on Edie's building in her honor. She got the city of Philadelphia to name a street Edie Windsor Way, and the Stony Brook Southampton hospital not only renamed their HIV and AIDS center after her, but they're expanding it to two more locations on Long Island that will also provide services related to women's health and LGBTQ+ elders and youth. All this is only the beginning; there's so much more to come.

"She fought for equal protection for all, and I'm so grateful that I was and am still able to protect *her*," Judith says. "Loving her was the easiest thing I've ever done. I listen to the song "Best Thing That Ever Happened to Me" by Gladys Knight & the Pips often, because that's how I feel. When

Edie would tell me that she loved me, I'd say, 'I love you too.' Then she'd answer, 'Maybe as much as I do, but not more.' Losing her feels like my heart has been split open. I think about her every second of every day. She was the love of my life. I still try to grasp that she's never coming home, that I'll never hold her hand."

Knowing that Edie didn't die with a broken heart is a strong source of solace for her. "She left us knowing that she was loved in every sense of the word, from the adoring crowds down to me making sure she had fresh coffee every morning. I also listen to the Bill Withers song 'Ain't No Sunshine' a lot, but I call Edie the rainbow in my clouds."

During Edie's long dinners with David Mixner, the two of them had many good-natured debates over the existence of god. "She defined herself as an atheist," he says. "She didn't believe in any god. She'd wave her arm around and say, 'Where is he? Is he coming to dinner?'"

David, a reformed Catholic, has developed his own personal form of spirituality and believes that Edie had one as well even if she didn't realize it. "I think her spirituality was universal love," he says. "She loved everybody. I used to joke with her that I'm going to expect an apology when we meet up somewhere outrageous."

Edie smiled wickedly and told him, "You might expect it, but you aren't getting it."

Edie had nothing to apologize for, and realizing that set her life on a course that changed everything for gays in America. As a young woman, she had no one to confide in about her sexuality, no one on the public stage to turn to for leadership examples. So she became a leader herself, the very definition of self-made. She was a witness to so many defining moments of the twentieth and twenty-first centuries and believed strongly in the next generation to continue the successes she'd fought for.

"We both believed passionately that the whole concept of young people not doing anything was total bullshit," David says. "It's the old ones trying to make them fit into a box that no longer applies in the twenty-first century. Everyone thinks we have to do it the way it was done when we were young, and that's not true."

Edie had been frustrated at the thought of fading into a figurehead. As much as she loved the role of getting dressed up and posing for photos on a step-and-repeat backdrop, it was far more important to her to be thought of as someone who still had a sharp mind to offer, one informed by her constant thirst to stay up to date on everything from pop culture to technology to politics.

She'd had no intention of slowing down and wanted to be asked to board meetings to contribute her thoughts and expertise. When accepting any sort of honor, instead of a standard thank-you speech at the podium, she'd deliver very specific advice about topics, like pushing legislation that advocated for more data collection on LGBTQ communities so that it might provide insight to problems like suicide and drug use, and she'd urge the audience to contact their local representatives. She had an even larger vision for all the prominent LGBTQ organizations to connect, to work and support each other. She'd already begun work on a coalition made up of many of the leaders to try to do just that.

From her own closeted youth, she knew how important it was to stand as a positive queer role model for the next generation and to ensure that they understand everything that came before them so they have a sense of history. She wanted the youth to know they'd come from a long line of people like them, to help prove to them that they *belong*.

Michael Adams, the CEO from SAGE, knew Edie's value when he rang her up earlier that summer and asked her to be the honorary chair of their fortieth anniversary in 2018. He wanted fresh input about their events and plans about getting the word out. She told him that the offer was so important and meant so much to her that she must come talk to him in person.

"So she did," he says, "and she had all of these incredible plans about things we could do, many of which we ended up putting into place."

· · ·

President Barack Obama gave Edie an extraordinary gift at the very end of her life: not only calling her (an incredibly kind gesture to begin with) but also urging her to get well because there was work to be done. It was exactly what she needed and wanted to hear most—a global leader who she loved and respected telling her that her work mattered and that she was still valued as an inspiration and a leader of the community.

No doubt she was coming up with new ideas as she combed through the morning paper days after the call and closed her eyes for the last time.

That a person could experience and accomplish so much in one lifetime is nothing short of astounding. The legacy of Edie Windsor will continue, her name forever evoked not just when bonds of love are affirmed and legally protected but whenever bravery and strength are called for.

Acknowledgments

When Edie hired me to work on this book, I never imagined she wouldn't be here to share in what's normally the really fun part—thanking the many people who helped along the way. I know there are names she would have likely included that I have not, simply because she didn't have the chance to tell me. If you feel you're one of these people, please take comfort in knowing you were in Edie's heart, and that's a much better place to be than on a page.

This book would not have been possible without the unwavering support of Judith Kasen-Windsor. Judith, I'm honored to call you my friend and I'll never forget our many late nights of crying, laughing, and watching videos of Edie on your phone. You gave her what she wanted and needed most—a second great love—and her legacy could not be in safer hands.

The deep knowledge about Edie and Thea's past that Karen Sauvigné shared with me was invaluable. Karen, I felt their trust in you and your love for them in all of our conversations. Thank you for your constant wisdom and insight.

Edie liked to say that one of her talents was finding talent, and that's proven by the collective brilliance of her entire book team—starting with our fearless editor, Anna deVries, who initially acquired the title with Stephen Morrison at Picador before taking us with her to St. Martin's Press. Edie's agent, Susanna Einstein at Einstein Literary Management, and my own, Erin Hosier of Dunow, Carlson, & Lerner, provided wise and loving guidance every step of the way for both Judith and me during what was at times a grief-heavy process. Also at St. Martin's, many thanks go to Alex Brown, Laura Clark, Sylvan Creekmore, Lisa Davis, Jennifer Enderlin, Paul Hochman, John Karle, Karen Lumley, Michelle McMillian, Martin Quinn, Michael Storrings, and George Witte. Rounding out the group are Stephanie Furgang Adwar, Devereux Chatillon, Sara and Chris Ensey of ScriptAcuity Studio, and Nancy Tate.

For contributions technical or emotional, and oftentimes both, Judith and I would both like to convey our gratitude to Donna Aceto, Michael Adams, Daniel Albanese, Eric Scott Baker, Cub Barrett, Ilene Borden, Holly Buchanan, Carine Cachorro, Clare Coss, Frederick T. Courtright and the Edna St. Vincent Millay Society, Judy Daniels, Beva Eastman, Carter Edwards, James Esseks, Erin Flaherty, Lewis Freeman, Sunnie Freeman, Gabriella Gershenson, Judy Gold, Debbie Goldfarb, Ben Goldfarb Freeman, Maya Goldfarb Freeman, Lee Goldsmith, Darra Gordon, Carla Grande, Geri Grossman, Jeff Haller, Elysa Halpern, Elise Harris, Stan Herman, Shirlee Hirschberg, William Kapfer, Tom Kirdahy, Beatrice (Teddy) Laurel, James Lecesne, Frederica Lesser, Donna Lieberman, Abigail Lofberg, Melora Love, Erica Lyon, Nyssa Lyon, Jimmy Mac, Cathy Marino-Thomas, Sheila Marino-Thomas, Patricia Martone, Terrence McNally, Marilyn Mercogliano, David Mixner, Brian Mott, Susan Muska, Alana Newhouse, Shelly Nudell, Jim Obergefell, Gréta Ólafsdottir, Ronald Patkus, Matthew Philip, Leanne Pittsford, Mel Plaut, Billy Porter, Angela Rodriguez, Barbara Rosen, Danielle Reda, Daniel Reed, Rem Rieder, Donnie Roberts, Dean Rogers, Sarita Rosa, Rena Rosenfeld, Karen Schlain and family, Rebecca Seawright, Mary Shea, Marjorie Sherwin, Gwen Shockey, Bryant Simon, Ginny Spyer, Patsy Spyer, Martha Stark, Wendy Stark, Mary Steyer, Glennda Testone, Doris Theiler, Stephanie Trong, Orie Urami, Rose Walton, Joyce Whitby, Muriel Wiener, Blanche Wiesen Cook, and Robert Woodworth.

And finally, Edie Windsor, thank you for choosing me and changing my life. Like David Mixner, I, too, hope we meet again someday. I'll be expecting your notes.

—Joshua Lyon

Index